Leslie,

Wishes

enjoyable reading, and
even more hours of applied
research!

Best wishes,

Graham.

28 ⅹⅰ 1984.

The Compleat
WINETASTER
—— and ——
CELLARMAN
— Michael Broadbent —

The Compleat
WINETASTER
and
CELLARMAN
— Michael Broadbent —

Mitchell Beazley
in association with
Christie's Wine Publications

Acknowledgements

The following brief list names some of the people, firms and organizations who have on one or many more occasions over the past thirty years, provided me with unusually interesting tasting opportunities. To them, and to the many others, I am greatly indebted.

Dr. Robert A. Adamson, Roger Aldridge, David Allan, Sir Anthony Alment, *Les Amis du Vin*, Antinori, *Aquitaine Society*, *Avery's*, *Barolet*, Joseph Berkmann, *Bischöfliches Konvikt*, *The Bordeaux Club*, Jean-Eugène Borie, *Bouchard Père et Fils*, K.C. Bourke, *Brooks's*, *Brown Bros*, Milawa, *von Buhl*, *Cambridge University Wine & Food Society*, Ch. Canon, *Castle Hotel Taunton*, *Champagne Academy*, Chapoutier, *Consumers' Association*, *Coq Hardi*, Cordier, *Corney & Barrow*, *Cossart Gordon*, Lord Crawshaw, *Cruse et Fils*, Jean Darroze, John Davy, *Decanter Magazine*, *Deinhard's*, *Delor*, Dr. Willis Dickens, *Dolamore's*, Heinz ten Doornkatt, Robin Don, *Doudet-Naudin*, *Dow*, Robert Drouhin, Maj. General Dyer, Richard Edmunds/Boodle's, Douglas Erickson, *E.V.A.*, Len Evans, *Exeter University Wine Society*, *Ferreira's*, Lloyd Flatt, Denis Foley, *Percy Fox and Co.*, Konstantin Franck, *Freemark Abbey*, *French Wine Farmers*, Frescobaldi, *Gault-Millau*, Victor Gibson, *Gidleigh Park*, *Goedhuis & Co.*, Ernst Gorge, *Gramps*, *Grant's of St. James's*, Edward Hale, Arthur Hallé, *Hallgarten's*, *Hardy's*, *Harvey's of Bristol*, Ch. Haut-Brion, *Hedges & Butler*, Charles Heidsieck, Joe Heitz, *Hellmer's*, *Heublein's*, Jack Hill, *Houston House*, *Hugel et Fils*, *Paul Jaboulet Aîné*, Hugh Johnson, *Nathl. Johnston*, Col. N. Johnstone, Lenoir Josey, *Justerini & Brooks*, Hans-Walter Kenderman, *Reichgraf v. Kesselstatt*, Tawfig Khoury, *Krug*, Ch. *Lafite*, Max Lake, Lalou Bize-Leroy, Mills B. Lane, Ch. *Lascombes*, Ch. *Latour*, Louis Latour, *Lawler's*, Hugues Lawton, T.A. Layton, *Layton's*, *Lebègue*, Alexis Lichine, A. Ling, *Lindeman's*, *Loebs & Co.*, de Luze, Ch. *Lynch-Bages*, Graham Lyons, *Madeira Wine Co.*, Ch. *Margaux*, Louis Martini, Melvyn Masters, Graf Matouschka-Greiffenclau, Fred May, *Mayacamas*, *Mentzendorff's*, Jean Miailhe, Tim Miller, David Milligan, *La Mission Haut-Brion*, Robert Mondavi, R. Montgomery-Scott, Denman Moody Jr., *Morris's Rutherglen*, J-P. Moueix, Ch. *Mouton-Rothschild*, *Moillard*, Ch. *Musar*, B.R. Nash, *Northern Wine Society*, *Quinta do Noval*, Marvin Overton, *Oxford University Wine Society*, Peter Palumbo, *Parrot and Co.*, Ch. *Pavie*, Kerry Payne, *Penfold's*, David Peppercorn, Sir John Plumb, Sam Pray, Freddie Price, *Prunier's*, *Redman's*, Hanspeter Reichmuth, Willi J.Reitz, Peter Reynier, Dr. Bernard L. Rhodes, Count Riccardo Riccardi, Geoffrey Roberts, *Dom. de la Romanée-Conti*, Baron Philippe de Rothschild, Eric de Rothschild, E. Penning-Rowsell, David Rutherford, *The Saintsbury Club*, Robert Sakowitz, *Sandeman's*, *von Schorlemer*, Berek Segan, Hermann Segnitz, Jacques Seysses, Peter A. Sichel, Dr. Louis Skinner Jr., David Somerset (Duke of Beaufort), Steven Spurrier, *Stag's Leap*, Ch. *Suduiraut*, Dr. John Taams, Ch. *Tahbilk*, Christopher Tatham, *Taylor's*, *Third Form Club*, *Thoman's*, *Thorman Hunt*, Trimbach, *Tyrrell's*, *Clos du Val*, de Villamont, *Vintner's Club San Francisco*, Harry Waugh, *Whitwham's*, *International Wine and Food Society*, Parry de Winton, *Wynns*, *Yalumba*, Robin Yapp, Harry Yoxall, Ch. *d'Yquem*.

Revised and expanded from the book originally published in 1968 as *Wine Tasting* and in 1982 as *Michael Broadbent's pocket guide to Wine Tasting*.

The Compleat Winetaster and Cellarman © Mitchell Beazley Publishers 1982 and 1984. Text © Michael Broadbent 1982 and 1984. Edited and designed by Mitchell Beazley International Limited 14–15 Manette Street, London W1V 5LB

ISBN 0 85533 505 X

Illustrations by Sue Sharples
Phototypeset by Tradespools Ltd, Frome, Somerset
Printed and bound by New Inter Litho SPA, Milan

CONTENTS

Preface   7

Introduction   8

The Approach to Tasting   11

Why Taste?   13

When to Taste: Some Basic Points   16

The Senses of Sight, Smell and Taste   20

Elements of Taste   24

Origin of Taste Characteristics   38

Colour Variations in Selected Wines   49

Main Regional Characteristics   65

On Tasting Expertise   82

Appreciation, Recognition and Deduction   86

How to Organize a Tasting   93

The Use of Words   106

Full Glossary of Tasting Terms   114

How to Record Tasting Notes   135

Tasting Notes   149

From Cellar to Table   186

Cellar Notes   199

Buyer's Guide   235

The Character of Wine   248

Bibliography   250

Personal Index   259

Index   266

PREFACE

By Alexis Lichine

It is not easy, at this point, to write an introduction to the work of Michael Broadbent. His talents and accomplishments are acclaimed on the book jacket, and his reputation as a guide to wine-tasting and a stimulating writer on his subject is already international. I don't know how many budding amateurs have been told that they would find his Pocket Guide as valuable as many a course in wine appreciation, but those who followed the advice have shown good sense.

I have enjoyed some fine vintages and good conversations with Michael, and I wish I had space to expatiate on his thorough and lucid essays on the whys and wherefores of tasting, on his methods of educating the palate, sensitizing the sense of smell and recognizing the taste of each outstanding grape, and last but not least on his unrivalled knowledge of old vintages of great wines. I like his succinct and sensible way with the wine writer's vocabulary (nothing fey or pretentious here); and I would stress, as he does, the importance of memory training, and of complete concentration on a tasting. If you come to it tired, or allow your interest to flag, you will make mistakes. Also, I heartily endorse his reflections on blind tasting and those dinner guests who tease the one professional present to get back to work and show off like a performing dolphin at what should be a party of pleasure.

Michael Broadbent, trained as a wine merchant, approaches his subject, he says, as a consumer rather than an oenologist. His up-to-date knowledge of the world markets and the sometimes variable quality of individual vineyards will be enormously helpful in the 'Buyers' Guide', as will his simple sheet in the pages for 'Cellar Notes' incorporated in this revised, extended and welcome version of his classic book.

Alexis Lichine

Château Prieuré – Lichine

Margaux

INTRODUCTION

'What makes the reputation of a taster is, for a large part, his manner of speaking of wine, the clarity, justice and nuance of his comments.' **Emile Peynaud.**

What, not another edition of *Wine Tasting* in yet another guise? The answer is yes and no. All the basic information about tasting – the purpose, the senses, how to taste, etc, is included and I make no apologies for this. For although I have continually added to and qualified the tasting sections in the light of further, mainly teaching, experience, I have not changed the approach. However, as the title of this handbook suggests, the scope has been greatly expanded to include a chapter on what wines to choose and where to find them, with detailed advice on storing and serving wine.

Some readers might wonder if anything new can be said about decanting and whether tips on drawing corks, a crucial and sometimes tricky operation, might smack of condescension on my part. Let me tell those readers right away that these are the very questions I am endlessly asked, and having witnessed the scion of a distinguished Burgundy house give, unwittingly, an almost perfect demonstration, in front of a $200 a head 'black tie tasting' in New Orleans, of how *not* to decant, and, to be honest, having made a mess of things myself from time to time, I feel that a gentle guiding hand might not come amiss.

As implied by 'Cellarman', a chapter about storage, also based on practical experience has been included. One of the first things I try and find out, as an auctioneer of fine and rare wines, is how the bottles being sent to Christie's for sale have been stored, for their ultimate condition, saleability and drinkability, depends on good cellarage. When to bring wines up from the cellar, or out of the air-conditioned store, also requires a bit of thought. Sensible handling will not actually improve a wine but careless handling can certainly spoil it.

So, this handbook is intended to be practical and useful.

The subject of choosing wine is immense. Even if we had space for a complete gazetteer, listing all the names, qualities and tastes, it would be mightily confusing and, in practice, would soon become out of date and irrelevant. So what I have tried to do in this quite extensive section is to lead the reader in positive directions, always bearing in mind the context in which a wine will be bought and drunk. Again, this is based on practical experience. Without going so far as to state precisely what particular wine is available from what shop at what price (after all it would be out of stock, even without a rush of readers, by the time the book came out) I am not shy about stating my own preferences or, as I am frequently asked, what I actually drink at home with my family. In the buyer's guide chapter I also dwell on the number and type of outlets open to the customer. Thinking about the whole of this subject, as I have done, I am left firmly with this impression that the lover of wine has never in the course of history had such an enormous range of types, styles and qualities from so many wine-producing districts, worldwide, to choose from. If this is not necessarily, as some distinguished oenologists aver, the golden age of wine making, it is without a doubt the golden age of wine distribution and availability.

If I might revert to the seed from which this work has flowered, or perhaps I should say from original graft – mostly hard graft – I would just like to mention that the nucleus of this work was a pamphlet I dashed off in 1962 called *Notes on the Techniques of Tasting* printed by Harveys of Bristol for staff training. Shortly afterwards it was published, in serial form, by a wine trade monthly and then as a little book, simply called *Wine Tasting* in 1968. Strangely enough, despite the essential nature of the subject matter, it was the first book to be published on tasting in the English language. To cut a long story short, *Wine Tasting* has run through 18 editions, 11 of them being in foreign languages. Each edition has been revised and I confess to learning quite a bit from the pertinent questions that various translators have asked, but even more from the questions asked and the lessons learned from 25 years of lecturing to wine trade students and keen amateurs. The old saying is 'those who can't, teach', to which I would add, 'those who teach, learn'.

It is customary, indeed polite, to acknowledge the debt of gratitude owed to those who have helped with the book, and, in my case, with my career. Starting with the latter. I was a late starter, entering the wine trade at the age of 25, with no previous experience and no connections – which should encourage others – so I had to learn fast. In this I was enormously fortunate in my mentors and immediate bosses: Tommy Layton who taught me a lot in my first year as a trainee, and made me jump; Sir Guy Fison, Saccone and Speed's wine buyer and, latterly, a colleague on wine trade educational committees; and at Harveys, Harry Waugh, now a sprightly octogenarian – what a splendid advertisment for good wine! I also have to thank those, particularly firms in the wine trade, who over the years have invited me to their tastings. Perhaps even more so, the larger than life characters, most of them American, who have over the past 10 years staged tastings of unprecedented quality and range, at which, I must confess, I have usually 'sung for my supper' by presiding over or conducting the tastings. Their names are listed on page 4.

But, as hinted at in the last paragraph, I have learned so much from those I have taught and still continue to teach. For me, every tasting is a revelation. With an audience I always explain that it is the wine doing the talking, I am merely the translator.

I hope that this book will enable the beginner to approach wine with confidence, to know how to handle it, how to approach it and what to look for; and to suggest to the more experienced amateur and professional some new ways of looking at wine and, in particular, some further thoughts on the use of words.

Regarding the book itself, it was Kathleen Bourke, the almost legendary editor/owner of *Wine* magazine, who originally prodded me into print. I then became my own publisher, then sensibly put myself in the hands of the professionals. At Mitchell Beazley I have to thank the editor, Chris Foulkes, who lost weight and a lot of hair because of my cavalier approach to crucial deadlines.

Whose idea it was to incorporate cellarbook and tasting note sheets I do not know. The former are straightforward and practical, the latter might have the additional benefit of stimulating thought on the subject, sending the reader back to the text to brush up the vocabulary, even to the basic tasting steps. Why, they might even tempt you into reading the text from start to finish. I hope so.

Michael Broadbent
Autumn 1984

I
THE APPROACH
TO TASTING

I was convinced forty years ago – and the conviction remains to this day – that in wine tasting and wine-talk there is an enormous amount of humbug. **T. G. Shaw,** Wine, the Vine and the Cellar, 1863

Basic approach

It is not necessary to know all about the internal combustion engine in order to drive a car. It is, however, generally agreed that driving lessons are essential and, in the final analysis, practice makes perfect. In the same way, a detailed knowledge of viniculture and viticulture is not a prerequisite for the enjoyment of wine, though an understanding of basic principles, some experience and a fairly discerning palate are essential if wine is to be appreciated as something more than an ordinary drink.

Ability to taste

If one can taste food, one can taste wine. Generally speaking what *is* good smells and tastes good; what smells 'off' and has a nasty taste is bad. I believe this is the reason for most people being able, correctly, to place one wine better than another simply on the basis that it tastes or smells nicer: that elementary 'hedonistic' judgment will fairly accurately pin down the relative quality of the wines in question. Saying *why* one is better than another is a different matter. There are, however, exceptions to the above rule: an over-mature wine, like an over-ripe cheese or well-hung game bird, sometimes has a putrid overtone to the smell and taste which can be unattractive, even repellent, to the uninitiated, though appreciated, sometimes sought after, by a connoisseur. It is all a matter of taste, *and* experience. Experience, as always, takes time; it cannot be bought or 'swotted up'.

First principles

But what about the first principles? Of all the books, articles and spoken words on the subject of wine, what number describe what the wine actually tastes like or indeed how to set about tasting it? In the course of some pretty voracious reading, up to the time I originally wrote this work, I had come across not a book, hardly a chapter, which dealt with what I considered a fairly basic subject: taste. This is not to say that background information about districts, soil, grape varieties, wine making and wine makers is not interesting or valuable; indeed, later chapters deal with the influence of such elements on taste. The history of wine, of firms and people, add to one's awareness, but such vital fringe activities are apt to obscure the main object of the exercise, which is the appreciation of wine: its colour, bouquet and flavour. Over the past few years there has been a positive spate of attempts, more and less successful, to deal with the subject. The French, in particular, seem to be making up for lost time (as witnessed by the number of books in the Bibliography).

There are, of course, difficulties in getting down to brass tacks. Tasting is subjective, and the language needed for describing wine smells and flavours is still singularly ill-defined and anything but universally accepted. What perhaps is needed is something approaching musical notation, for in many ways the problems are similar. Both music and wine appeal to the senses, one of hearing and the other of taste and smell; both are fleeting, in the sense that actual sounds and flavours cannot be retained by the receptive ear or palate; both, on the other hand, can be appreciated, even greatly loved, by people who lack technical knowledge or who are without a deep interest. But to reach the heights of full understanding and to convey this to someone else rather more is required.

The first stage is an awareness of first principles; the second is a detailed understanding of what lies behind the colour, smell and taste of any wine; and the third is plenty of practice.

Practice and memory

Although wine can be consumed with enjoyment without a lot of fuss and nonsense, reasoned judgment of the finer wines must be based on knowledge, and this can only be acquired by the sort of practice in tasting that will help a vinous memory – a memory that will hold in store the great touchstones, the standard norms and the exceptions to the rules.

There is no doubt that some people are endowed with a more delicate and sensitive palate than others, but this alone is less useful than a normal but well-trained and experienced palate. Mind you, a refined palate *and* an excellent memory will give a relatively new taster a head start. The greatest tasters will surely be those with all the physical attributes, wide experience and a flawless memory. In the end it is almost always memory which lets one down, which is why it is advisable to make notes.

Perspective and common sense

The main thing is to keep tasting in perspective: spend time and effort only on those wines that are worthy of attention, and talk intensely about wine only to those who are of like mind. In short, don't get carried away; use a little common sense.

Above all, be true to yourself.

══════ II ══════
WHY TASTE?

Taste cannot be controlled by law. **Thomas Jefferson** on Wine, Vinifera Journal, 1973

Wine is a beverage of enormous agricultural and commercial importance. Every drop of the millions of gallons made annually has one final objective: to be consumed. And, in passing the lips, crossing the tongue and descending the throat, wine is 'tasted', whether or not a conscious comment or judgment is made. However, the word 'tasting' in relation to wine refers to a deliberate, conscious and subjective act, the aim of which is to assess the qualities of the wine under review. Incidentally, the word 'tasting' is used here (as the French use *dégustation*) in the broader conventional sense, which I prefer to the more pedantic and academic terms 'sensory' and 'organoleptic' examinations.

Need to taste?

Does *all* wine need to be tasted in this sense? The answer is no. For of the millions of gallons produced and marketed, by far the largest proportion is the plainest of ordinary beverage wine, made to be consumed as an adequate accompaniment to a meal or merely as a refreshing and restorative drink. This sort of wine is *not* made to be sipped reverently; nor is it meant to provide the basis of intellectual discussion. (It is immaterial that one of the end-products of its consumption may be the mellowing of the drinkers and loosening of their tongues to discuss *other* subjects with new enlightenment. Ordinary wine is for talking over, not talking about.)

Before finally dismissing plain, honest to-goodness (one hopes) *vin de table*, a word about mass-produced wines may not come amiss.

Oenology, commerce and mediocrity

We are living in a world where, whether we like it or not, standards are concertina-ing. Thanks to new pesticides, new methods of controlling fermentation and other new techniques, less is now left to chance. Although fine vintages cannot be created artificially, certainly poor vintages are less disastrous than they used to be. This is a mixed blessing. If oenologists can rightly take credit for much of the improvement in the overall standard of wine making, they are also answerable for some of the decrease in character and individuality of 'fine wines' in certain classic areas. If more sound wine is made, then more is to be marketed; and the production of wine is as subject to the law of supply and demand as any other commodity. Wine to be sold on a large scale has to be blended and, to be universally acceptable, has to be innocuous – which is a fortunate situation for the marketing man.

It is no coincidence that we live in the era of the 'light' and 'mild', subjected to a relatively new set of standards which applies to nearly all consumer products from 'mild-flavoured' cornflakes to 'light' whiskies. Unhappily, commercial necessity forces this pace, taking character and stuffing out of the raw material, reducing the awareness of the consumer to any elements of positive taste. What is not sufficiently realized is that mixing individual flavours can have a similar effect to mixing colours: the more they are mixed, the greyer the result. Mass-marketed wines must be blended. Blended wines, of necessity and by design, lose much of their individuality and character and a 'grey' neutral wine often results. Neutral wines are inoffensive and therefore will not displease the majority. Which, unfortunately, is just one more example of how commercial necessity can become a marketing virtue.

Vital critical standards

It is in the context of maintaining interest and positive standards that critical tasting must be kept alive. It would be a pity to allow man's finer perceptions of tasting experience (and resultant range of pleasures) to atrophy. Moreover, I do not think we should feel obliged to 're-evaluate', i.e. lower, our standards in the light of technical 'improvements'.

The difference in a trial of wine by the consumer and the expert is that the former seeks for something agreeable, something to praise; whilst the latter seeks for a fault, a blemish, or something to condemn. **Arpad Haraszthy,** Wines and Vines of California, 1889

Reasons for tasting

What, then, are the main reasons for tasting? The important thing to realize is that wine will be tasted throughout its life in different places, by different people and for a variety of practical reasons. Here are some of them:
- In the *chai* (*keller, cantina*, whatever local name is given to the producer's cellar), the *maître de chai* or the proprietor will be acting as nurse and midwife. He will taste from the moment the grape juice is fermented into wine, watching its condition, balance and development, until it is sold or bottled.
- The broker and the merchant prior to making a purchase will also taste from the producer's cask during this period. For the lay amateur, tasting young wine from a cask in a *chai* – such a romantic-sounding occupation – may be sadly disappointing. Few things can be so starkly raw and scouring as a mouthful of purple new wine. Much better to leave it at this stage to the professionals!
- Samples may have to be submitted by the producer to an official body for a seal of approval. For example new regulations issued in 1974 by the French Government introduced analysis *and tasting* for all *appellation contrôlée* wines.* The finer German wines are also tasted by a panel before they are awarded a quality seal.

*The main provisions of the new Decree 74-871 are as follows:
ARTICLE 1: the wines for which an AOC is claimed cannot be put into circulation without a 'certificate of agreement' issued by the *Institut National des Appellations d'Origine des Vins et Eaux-de-Vie* (INAO) after an examination conforming to the terms of Article II of EEC regulation No. 817/70 of the Council of 28 April 1970.
ARTICLE 2: the examination, organized by INAO or local wine-growing *syndicats* consists of an analysis and tasting, the latter carried out by a Commission, following officially laid-down procedures.

14

- In the cellars of the local merchant, *négociant* or shipper, the selected wine may be nursed a little further up to the stage of shipment in cask or bottling. During this period, it is tasted by professional buyers with a keen eye on price, style and potential development.
- Competitive tastings at wine fairs and conventions. These are fairly common in wine-producing countries, particularly in California, Australia and eastern Europe.
- After shipment in cask★ it will rest in the cellar of the shipper or merchant until it is ready for bottling. The firm's tasters – and the analyst, if there is a laboratory – will examine its condition prior to bottling. Thereafter, from time to time, quality-control personnel will monitor the behaviour and development of the wine in bottle.
- The next category of tasting is the trade tasting, where the merchant, wholesaler or institutional buyer selects wine for re-sale. This sort of function may be of the headline-hitting variety in a vast candle-lit cellar, or may take the form of a quiet, down-to-earth tasting in a rather clinical-looking tasting room. In either case, the buyer is looking for wines either to lay down or to offer for laying down or, of course, for immediate consumption.
- Further tasting may occur during subject tastings and tutorials organized by wine societies and tasting clubs.
- Lastly, the keen amateur, with a good cellar, will taste his own wines to see how they are progressing and to choose wines suitable for a particular occasion, guest or type of food. He also will taste them, before serving, to make sure that the condition and temperature are right.

Tasting contexts

In all the above instances, it will be seen that each taster will be examining a wine in a different context and with a particular point of view: the wine maker with a paternal eye, the buyer with price and market uppermost, the quality-control taster or chemist for condition and stability, the salesman for attractive qualities of price and style, the club member for education and amusement, and the ultimate consumer with his palate, pocket and future entertaining plans in mind.

From the second stage to the penultimate, the value of the tasting to the participants will increase roughly proportionately to the range of wines on show. Even at a dinner party, the qualities of a really fine wine will be more fully revealed if paired off with, or preceded by, a lesser but comparable wine.

It follows, however, that as each category of taster is apt to concern himself with a limited aspect of wines, his general perspective will narrow, and it is only too easy for the professional and the amateur to adopt, out of habit, a 'blinkered', one-sided approach. The professional taster, with limited time at his disposal and a narrow objective, cannot be expected to probe and analyse the hidden depths of 60 young wines at 10 o'clock in the morning. Nevertheless, he should be conscious of the dangers of slipping into a rut. Equally, the amateur will enrich his experience by taking more than a superficial glimpse at the wonderful liquids that nature, with man's aid, has contrived for his pleasure.

★To the UK or elsewhere in Europe. The volume of quality wine being bottled at source is increasing and in many districts this is now mandatory. Importation in cask is not permitted in the USA.

III

WHEN TO TASTE:
SOME BASIC POINTS

The only way to appreciate wine is when a few men who understand and enjoy it meet together, feeling free to luxuriate in the delight imparted. . . . **T. G. Shaw,** Wine, the Vine and the Cellar, 1863

Morning freshness

The best time for doing anything constructive and creative is when the mental and physical states are freshest. This, for most people (whether they appreciate it or not) is in the morning. It is said, incidentally, that the palate is sharpened by hunger, which would indicate the benefits of pre-luncheon tasting sessions.

In point of fact, the majority of trade tastings *are* held in the morning. The most quiet and business-like tastings may be held around 10 o'clock, possibly at noon. Tastings to which trade or private customers are invited usually begin about 11.30 and may end with a buffet or light luncheon, during the course of which selected wines are shown off against appropriate food. (It is not without significance that the simpler and more wholesome the repast, the better the wines show; there are fewer distractions of flavour. For example, simple cold roast beef and mild English cheeses provide the most perfect foil for good French reds.)

Evening sessions

Early evening tastings are also popular. They are generally held by the trade between 6 and 8 o'clock to attract customers who would otherwise find it difficult to attend during their working day. These evening tastings tend to be less serious – people are tired after a day's work and feel more in need of a reviver than the concentration needed to taste in earnest. Or they have had time to go home and change, and may treat the whole affair as a rather jolly social occasion. The wine-merchant host dispensing his stock-in-trade may not really mind, so long as the party-goer leaves in a sober enough state to remember the name of his firm!

Wine society tastings are also held mainly in the early evening, for similar reasons, though the degree of serious attention is often noticeably higher, perhaps because the members have paid to attend!

General points to observe

Before getting down to the serious business of tasting, there are quite a number of general points to watch out for. Not all are appropriate for professionals and amateurs alike. Some are quite basic, some merely minor details and some may even appear trivial. Not necessarily in order of importance, they are as follows:

No smoking Smoking in a tasting room is not only considered inconsiderate and offensive, it will seriously reduce the effectiveness of other tasters, particularly if they are non-smokers. It is difficult enough as it is to detect subtleties of bouquet without a nullifying smoke-screen attacking one's nostrils at the same time. For those who doubt this, try puffing smoke into a glass of wine, then sniffing it.

It should be said immediately that the rule of 'no smoking' in the tasting room does not mean that a taster should not smoke at all. In point of fact, there seems little evidence that a smoker's tasting abilities are less than a non-smoker's. The palate appears to compensate for this regular coating of tobacco smoke and nicotine, and there are numerous examples in the trade of fairly heavy smokers being good tasters. Some are even reputed to have a 'drag' at a strong French cigarette between tasting sessions.

Make notes Remembering the taste of a wine, but forgetting its name, and vice versa, is very tiresome. It is astonishing how easy it is to forget the name of even an outstanding wine only an hour or so after tasting. These blank spots occur to the professional, whose memory is cluttered with multitudinous examples, as well as to the novice. It is particularly frustrating for a merchant to recommend a range of wines to a customer and for the latter to say that he thought one of them outstanding – only to forget its name.

The answer is, make a note. At least scribble on a piece of paper or in your diary the name of the wine and vintage, and whether it was agreeable or not.

Note making can turn into a fetish; it can become a hobby like collecting stamps. The moderate use of intelligible notes will, however, be invaluable, and even a good memory is better served by the briefest record of name, description and opinion. Various methods of note making are dealt with on page 135.

Good company An exchange of views helps to shape and strengthen a hazy impression, revealing aspects of a wine that might not otherwise have been noticed. It goes without saying that the company in question must be equally interested – a large party of casual observers or hard drinkers is merely off-putting.

An organized tasting group is often the best solution, not the least of its virtues being the increased purchasing power of pooled resources which make it possible to accumulate a wider range of better-class wines.

The main snag about a free-for-all tasting is the distraction of chatterboxes. It is difficult enough as it is without being interrupted between sniffing and note making.

Quite the best advice one can give the newcomer is to taste in the company of an expert, or at least with a taster of some experience.

Related wines It is perfectly possible to judge a fine wine on its own, but its true qualities will be thrown into much sharper perspective when it is tasted alongside another wine, even if dissimilar in style. By far the most revealing type of tasting is one where comparisons can be made between wines of the same vintage but from different districts, or from the same vineyard but of different vintages (see p. 94).

Appropriate order of tasting Dry before sweet; young before old; modest before fine. Whether red wines are tasted before white depends on the relative 'weights'. Light dry whites are better before fuller-bodied reds, but light young red wine is better tasted before full-bodied sweet white wine with heavy 'extract' and residual sugar.

It is perfectly possible for a professional taster to assess the relative qualities of a large range of related wines, say 30 to

60, in a session. It is doubtful, however, whether more than an essential facet or two can be obtained by tasting on this scale, and certainly for the beginner, six to ten wines are usually as many as he can effectively cope with. Over this number the taste buds can become tired, the mind confused.

Try to relate the time spent per wine to the total available and, if necessary, be selective: concentrate on those you particularly wish to taste. Nothing is more frustrating than to find that you have spent nearly all the tasting session on a handful of wines at the beginning, invariably the least interesting, leaving yourself neither time nor energy for the best at the end.

Temperature and presentation Present the wines appropriately: red wines at room temperature, white wines (rosé, champagne, sherry) at cellar temperature (see p. 187). Do not draw the corks too far in advance: up to one hour before the tasting is a reasonable average. Decant old and mature wines, as the sediment will well up in the bottle after a couple of handlings.

Taste 'blind' 'A sight of the label is worth fifty years' experience' – a cynical truism: for what an impressionable lot we are! Even the most sternly disciplined taster is biased by the merest glimpse of the label, even by the shape of the bottle. One can also be swayed by the appreciative – or otherwise – noises and looks of other tasters.

For a completely objective assessment, arrange the wines to be tasted in numbered glasses (use a wax pencil or stick self-adhesive labels to the upper side of the base), the numbers being related to the bottles which are, of course, out of sight. Alternatively, cover up the bottles, standing the glasses in front. Failing this, turn the bottles round so that the labels cannot be seen.

Don't drink, spit It is nothing short of ridiculous to *drink* one's way through a tasting. How can the last few wines yield more than a hazy impression? This is particularly important when tasting fortified wines.

To taste critically is one thing, to enjoy wines with a meal is another. So when tasting, spit out the wine, don't swallow it. The performance is not considered rude, nor need it be undignified: purse the lips, draw in the cheeks and expel the wine with enough force to project it into the spittoon. It is considered a normal thing to do.

In a *chai* or cellar it is considered perfectly acceptable to spit on the floor, which anyway is often of earth, or, if of concrete, perhaps strewn with sand or sawdust. All proper tasting rooms are furnished with sink spittoons, usually with running water. If a tasting is held in a public building, or in a private room, spittoons should be provided. A wooden wine box containing sawdust is simple to prepare and has the advantage of dimensions generous enough to accommodate all but the very worst shots. It is advisable not to spit on your host's carpet!

Taste the best Ordinary wines are for drinking, not for deliberating over. Moderate-quality wines afford good practice and can be interesting, but they are often indefinable and rarely clear-cut in character. The most vivid characteristics of a district or a vintage are best exemplified by wines of high quality. In any case, an assessment of lesser wines must inevitably be made in relation to an exemplar or touchstone. Don't be an inverted snob; occasionally buy a great wine and try to see what extra dimensions it has to offer.

Physical hazards Don't waste time trying to taste if you have a streaming cold. Catarrh doesn't help either. Clear your nostrils.

Don't try to taste with traces of alien matter in the mouth. Alkaline toothpaste interacts with the acidity of wine. Fruit, with its high acid content, will affect the taste too; so will highly spiced breakfast sausages. Fish and crabmeat stuck in the teeth can be a hazard.

Order and discipline Taste in a regular sequence; examine the appearance of the wine first, its bouquet next and finally its taste. And within those three main sub-divisions, look out for definite salient features.

A prepared tasting sheet or notebook can be a great help in this respect, and moreover guards against the temptation to leapfrog from wine to wine in a haphazard fashion. This does not mean, in fact, that one should never dodge back and forth. Indeed, when tasting wines in ascending order of quality or descending order of age, the earlier wines can be seen in sharper perspective if one re-tastes them after completing the range.

Awareness of context This is highly important and usually under-rated. There are several relevant aspects.

The climate as well as the food has to be considered. For example, a charming light wine with a refreshingly high acidity drunk with fresh trout on the banks of the Loire in midsummer, or a vinho verde enjoyed with rich pork in the Minho can taste entirely different on a cold and misty autumn evening with Arbroath 'smokies' in Scotland. Quite apart from the need to match wine with food, the temperature, humidity and time of year have a bearing. The colder the climate, the more full-bodied the wine needs to be, or can be tolerated, and vice versa.

Wine and food

The inter-relationship of wine and food is too well known to be re-stated here. Certainly, endless books deal with the subject. Suffice it to say that a good wine can be wasted in a wrong food context. It may seem unenterprising, but it is usually safer and more sensible to follow the conventional rules.

What is less well appreciated is that those who are used to tasting mainly fortified wines (sherry; port in particular) may find some difficulty in adjusting their palates to very light table wines. Also, those who are fortunate enough to afford, and to restrict their interest to, only the finest wines will tend to undervalue the quality of much lesser wines. The opposite does not, however, obtain. A regular drinker of ordinary table wine does not tend to overvalue a fine wine when it is put before him; if anything, he is more likely to be unappreciative of its subtleties and to wonder why anyone would be crazy enough to pay, for one bottle, a sum that might cover his daily fare for a month.

IV

THE SENSES OF SIGHT, SMELL AND TASTE

Tasting is the introduction of wine to our senses: sight, smell and taste. **Emile Peynaud**

Those fortunate to have eyesight employ this sense every minute of their waking day. Our eyes have plenty of practice. Even colour awareness, for example, which may not be as fully developed as an artist's, is normally at a high level, mainly because of constant usage. The enormous advantage that colour has over smell and taste is that it can be so much more easily described, recorded or matched and conveyed from one person to another.* In the last resort it can be accurately reproduced.

On the other hand, the senses of smell and taste are rarely so highly or so continuously employed. Indeed, the level of awareness can be abysmally low. This is partly owing to the fact that the sense of smell is easily fatigued (after only a short time a worker in a chocolate factory or a tannery does not notice the smell) and partly because it is less frequently exercised.

I am tempted to believe that smell and taste are in fact but a single composite sense, whose laboratory is the mouth and its chimney the nose. **Brillat-Savarin,** The Physiology of Taste, 1825

Flavour is a compound of taste and smell, yet although the sensitivity and selectivity of the latter sense is infinitely higher it is the least consciously applied. In relation to wine, most people 'taste' – in a superficially literal sense – but very few deliberately and consciously smell the wine first, let alone derive any positive information or pleasure from that act. What is far too little known is that a great deal of what one wants, or needs, to know about wine can be detected from its appearance and bouquet alone. The actual taste on the palate basically confirms the impressions that sight and smell have previously conveyed and adds to the sum total.

Sense of smell

Smell is perhaps the most basic and most primitive of all the senses; more than any other it invokes memory in a particularly direct manner. The 'smell-brain', with its direct contact with the memory areas, can act as an immediate catalyst of recognition and identification. This accounts for the value of the 'first impression' that, justifiably, can be relied upon by experienced tasters.

---

*A complete and universally accepted scientific analysis, classification and description of smells and tastes, despite multi-disciplinary research and enquiries, appears to defy solution. Perhaps, slightly out of context, I can quote the last sentence of the epilogue of Dr Roland Harper's *Odour Description and Odour Classification*: 'Perhaps at present this remains more of an art than a science.'

Let me deal now in some detail with the mechanics of smell. Physically, this is what happens: the stimulus that excites the sense of smell results from certain substances, in solution, coming into contact with myriads of highly complex cells in the nose. Such substances usually enter the nose in the form of vapour. In the case of wine they are conveyed by volatile esters and aldehydes. At this stage they are taken over by the olfactory system. The first pair of cranial nerves are called olfactory nerves. They begin as specialized olfactory cells in the lining of the upper part of the nose. Fibrils from these cells pass up into the olfactory bulbs, lying in the base of the skull. From the bulbs the olfactory tracts – thick bands of white brain matter – pass backwards to enter the brain, and the fibres contained in the tracts are brought into relationship with nerve cells in certain parts of the brain. The original stimulus at the nerve endings is, in effect, converted into a sensation for the brain to interpret.

An interesting fact is that over-prolonged exposure to one smell may reduce the effectiveness of that smell, but that other smells may be readily detected. From a practical point of view this means that it is pointless to sniff too long or too frequently at one wine. If the first impression is lost, it is probably better to move on to the next wine. Then move back to the original or tackle it again after a rest (see also p. 145).

In my experience, passing one's nose over the glass and lightly inhaling will often yield virtually all the bouquet has to offer. Nevertheless, it is sensible to swirl the wine gently and smell it again more carefully. Sometimes it is necessary to sniff vigorously and inhale deeply either to determine whether there is fruit under the unyielding exterior or, perhaps, to isolate a fault in a poor wine.

Claret and Burgundy should be drank [sic] *moderately warm. A gentle warmth brings out an appreciation of body, diminishes the astringency, and develops all the finer qualities prominently including that of bouquet.* **Arpad Haraszthy,** Wines and Vines of California, 1889

Chambré-ing red wines or cupping the glass in one's hands has a good practical reason. There is evidence that whatever the state of the substance having smell, its appreciation depends on that substance passing into the solution with which the olfactory cells are normally bathed. But the higher the molecular weight of the wine, the greater the need to encourage the process of vaporization. This is accomplished by gently raising its temperature. When wine is warmed, convectional currents arise, moving the wine and releasing its bouquet.

A 'cold start' accounts for the 'dumbness' of a massively constituted red wine, even if mature. It also accounts for the remarkable aftertaste and 'lingering farewell' that arises from the naso-pharynx as the mouth-warmed wine passes down the throat and the released volatile esters rise through the back nasal passages.

Conversely, light wines, with low extract and weight, do not need to be warmed. Those which are light but relatively high-toned (such as a Mosel of a moderate year) will release bouquet with an impact that is immediate but which lacks depth. They rely not on an aftertaste but on a high degree of natural acidity to give the wine a 'finish' – to which chilling adds crispness.

Some pungent substances have a more physical impact, stimulating the nerve endings in a tactile sense. For example, sulphur dioxide can be detected by a prickle in the nose even though its presence in the wine may not be strong enough to affect the olfactory system. Certain of the higher alcohols can also have a similar effect, producing a feeling rather than a smell. Acetic acid can be both felt and smelled.

Sense of taste

Next, I shall examine the physical nature of taste. The sense of taste depends on the stimulation of organs known as taste buds. These are mainly situated in the tongue, though a few are found in the soft palate, and their sensitivity varies. The nerves connected with the taste buds carry impulses to the nerve centre in the medulla (which is the name for the marrow at the top of the spinal cord), whence they are carried to the parts of the brain towards the tip and inner sides of the temporal lobe – in close relation to the area of the brain concerned with the sense of smell.

To cause the necessary stimulus, a substance must be in solution and the sensation it evokes relates to one, or a combination, of the four so-called primary elements of taste: sweetness (best appreciated at the tip of the tongue), sourness* (upper edges of the tongue), bitterness (at the back) and saltiness (at the sides).

There is relatively little evidence to support the concept of primary tastes. **Dr Roland Harper,** The Human Senses in Action, 1972

If one has this understanding of which parts of the palate detect which basic tastes, it will be quite apparent that to 'peck' at wine, i.e. to take a very small sip or leave only the tip of the tongue in contact, will not enable the taster to appreciate more than a fraction of the wine's physical characteristics. A reasonable mouthful must be taken and it must be swirled round the mouth so that all the taste buds can get to work on it. Some experienced tasters take a large mouthful and draw air across their palate, sometimes with rather an off-putting guzzling noise. This distributes the wine across the whole of the palate and allows the volatile scents to ascend the back of the nose for the olfactory nerves to play their part.

A word of warning about a common problem which is rarely discussed by other tasters and yet one to which, I must confess, I am frequently susceptible. Beware of scalding the mouth with hot liquids: the wine will taste abnormally sharp due to the acidity 'biting' the raw tongue.

Sense of touch

Tactile impressions, implying the use of fingers and hands, do not, strictly speaking, apply to the tasting process. Nevertheless, wine produces reactions which have certainly nothing to do with sight, smell or taste, and are as equally certainly tactile [for example, the weight (body) of wine in the mouth, the evaluation of certain extracts which are detected physically in the mouth, and the prickle of carbon dioxide (*spritzig*)

---

*Sourness, in a wine context, has a derogatory connotation. Acidity, an essential component, is the word English wine tasters use (see Full Glossary of Tasting Terms, p. 114).

in the lightly sparkling or fully sparkling state]. Also certain chemical reactions in the mouth and nose affect the tactile sense more than the sense of smell. Sulphur dioxide, already mentioned, is an example.

Sense of hearing

The sense of hearing does not seriously enter into wine tasting. There is nothing like the delightful crunchiness of a crisp biscuit – unless it be the anticipatory pop of a cork, the sound of pouring and tinkling of glasses, the fizz of champagne or the ministering sizzle of Alka-Seltzer the following morning! As for those audible signs of approval, considered good manners at the Chinese dinner table, they have no part, whether involuntary or voluntary, in polite western society.

Gastric stimulation

Before leaving the physical element of wine tasting, it is perhaps worth mentioning an important by-product; in some instances this might be considered the be-all-and-end-all of wine drinking, namely the stimulation of the gastric juices. Quite apart from its health-giving natural properties, wine is a superlative aid to digestion. The appetite is whetted by the smell and taste of a refreshingly youthful white wine, and by the tingling dryness, the acidity and even the slight bitterness of many reds. The nerves of taste and smell are stimulated, which, in turn, increase the activity of the salivary glands. Also, through a reflex nervous action, the wine markedly increases the amount of digestive juice secreted in the walls of the stomach; it flows more rapidly, and the movements of the stomach are speeded up. This stimulation of the muscular wall of the stomach extends to that of the bowel, greatly aiding the digestion of the accompanying food.

But let us turn to the act of tasting. . . .

V
ELEMENTS OF TASTE

Your true amateur sips his wine; as he lingers over each separate mouthful, he obtains from each the sum total of pleasure which he would have experienced had he emptied his glass at a single draught. **Brillat-Savarin,** The Physiology of Taste, 1825

Tasting sequence

The order in which one tastes a wine is based on the natural physical movement of the glass from table to mouth. First of all, the glass is picked up and the wine examined. This is stage one. As it is raised towards the mouth the nose catches the bouquet – stage two. Then the lips meet the rim of the glass, and the literal tasting, stage three, commences.

But, over and above this, there is a correlation: what one sees is 'taken up' by the nose; what one tastes tends to confirm visual and nasal impressions. The logical conclusion is stage four, the summary of overall impressions, and the final verdict.

Before starting, make sure that the glasses are suitable and the lighting adequate.

Glasses

If you do not possess an ideal tasting glass just use a conventional, tulip-shaped, crystal-clear wine glass, *not* a fancy or coloured one. An ideal tasting glass is one which conforms to a specific design laid down by an international panel for official standards organizations. Such a glass is illustrated opposite. There are several acceptable variations on this theme, but this is the glass which has been adopted by all the major European bodies for use in recognized tasting competitions.

If tasting a range of wines, use matching glasses of a generous size and rinse them out with wine if they are at all musty or unclean or if they have been previously washed with detergent. Pour an equal measure in each so that the relative depth of hue can be seen at a glance. Do not fill the glass more than half-full, as it will be easier to tilt above a white table top, an essential manoeuvre if the informative colour at the rim of the wine is to be seen clearly. It will also enable the wine to be swirled around in the glass without spilling, collecting the volatile substances prior to nosing.

Pick up the glass by its stem or foot, not by the bowl. This makes it easier to examine the wine, particularly if held in front of a lighted candle. It also avoids the influence of body warmth and has the minor virtue of avoiding finger marks on the sides of the glass. (Handling old bottles can be a dirty business; wine itself tends to be sticky if dripping or spilt.)

Lighting

Daylight is best, preferably a good north light, as artificial lighting can affect both hue and tone. In particular, avoid fluorescent lighting; it makes red wine look unhealthily brown, even blue-tinged. Candle light is glamorous; it enhances the appearance of both wine and lady guest! But for

THE IDEAL TASTING GLASS

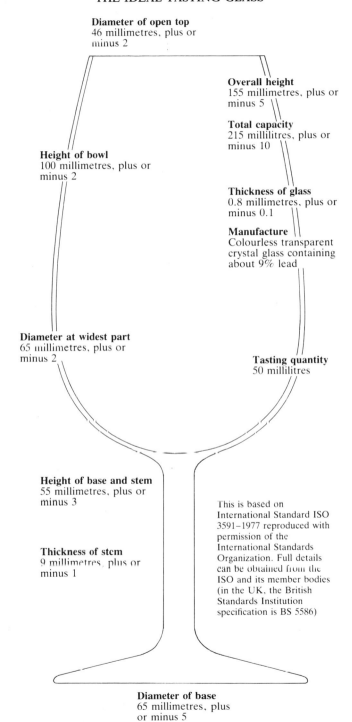

Diameter of open top
46 millimetres, plus or
minus 2

Overall height
155 millimetres, plus or
minus 5

Total capacity
215 millilitres, plus or
minus 10

Thickness of glass
0.8 millimetres, plus or
minus 0.1

Manufacture
Colourless transparent
crystal glass containing
about 9% lead

Height of bowl
100 millimetres, plus or
minus 2

Diameter at widest part
65 millimetres, plus or
minus 2

Tasting quantity
50 millilitres

Height of base and stem
55 millimetres, plus or
minus 3

Thickness of stem
9 millimetres, plus or
minus 1

This is based on
International Standard ISO
3591–1977 reproduced with
permission of the
International Standards
Organization. Full details
can be obtained from the
ISO and its member bodies
(in the UK, the British
Standards Institution
specification is BS 5586)

Diameter of base
65 millimetres, plus
or minus 5

a serious tasting the only benefit of a candle is to reveal the true degree of clarity of the wine. Thus it is useful in a cellar when young wine is drawn from the cask, or when decanting a bottle before dinner.

Temperature

Make sure the temperature of the wine is correct: room temperature* for reds (including port), cool for rosé (say 50–55°F or 10–13°C) and cold for white (around 48–50°F or 9–10°C). The actual room temperature will naturally vary from place to place and with the time of year – but will be a pleasant natural temperature. The range could well be anywhere between 60 and 65°F, 16 to 18°C. Make sure the glasses for red wine are at the same temperature and not brought out of a cold cupboard at the last minute.

It is worth noting that dry white wines cool more quickly than sweet: sauternes needs more time in an ice-bucket, and sprinkling sea salt on the ice can be a very effective aid to cooling. But best of all, in my experience, is to have an ice-box or refrigerator at the right temperature and then transfer the wine to an open vacuum flask. There is an excellent one on the market called Vinicool®.

Stage 1
APPEARANCE

Under the heading of appearance,† the taster looks at three facets: colour, depth and clarity. As each of these facets is examined, the reader is advised to refer to the illustrated examples on pp. 49–64.

Colour or hue

Most table wines fall into one of three basic categories: red, white or rosé. Fortified wines vary: sherry is technically a white wine and ranges from pale straw-yellow to deep brown; port may be red or white, the former ranging from deep purple, ruby to pale tawny. Perhaps the main thing to bear in mind is that the colour should be appropriate for the type and age of wine.

Red Wines

What we call a *red* wine will, in fact, vary in hue from deep purple through various shades of red to mahogany or even amber, depending mainly on its state of maturity, the vintage and the district. The length of fermentation and the time the grape juice is kept on the skins have a major influence, as does the time kept in cask. (The red colour comes from a group of pigments called anthocyanins extracted from the grape skins by the action of alcohol. Different grape species have varying types of anthocyanins. These 'free' anthocyanins provide most of the (purple) colour of young wine but, in effect, they fade or merge into larger tannin molecules which take on the brick red to red-brown colours as the wine ages. Oxidation speeds up this process. Dead colouring matter is precipitated and forms part of the sediment of an old wine.)

*Professor Peynaud's ideal tasting room is 65°F or 18°C with 60% humidity.

†I use the term in its broadest sense: that which is perceived by the eye, and not in a limited sense like 'clarity'.

Purple Indicates extreme youth and/or immaturity. Almost all young red wine in cask will have this colour. The time taken in bottle to lose its strong purple tinge depends on the initial depth of colour.

Ruby Self-descriptive. The colour of a young port or a deepish claret or burgundy, having lost its pristine flush of purple.

Red In vinous terms red is the colour approximating to 'claret'. It indicates the transitional period between youth and the acquisition of maturity and bottle-age. The lower the pH the greater the amount of active pigments and the higher the intensity of colour. A particularly intense red is therefore often indication of high acid content.

Red-brown In a table wine this hue indicates maturity (for example, claret with 5 years or more in bottle, burgundy 3 years or more – depending on the weight and quality of the vintage). A brown tinge can also result from baked vines after a hot summer, also from artificially heated and 'cooked' wine (i.e. during fermentation), or from oxidation owing to over-exposure to air in cask.

Mahogany A more mellow, subtle red-brown indicating maturity (claret with 10–20 years' bottle-age, burgundy of a moderate vintage with over 10 years' bottle-age).

Tawny A term, like ruby, usually associated with port. It describes a hue that has been attained through loss of colour over a period of years in cask, a natural but expensive maturing process. Cheap commercial 'tawnies' are made by blending white wines with red.

Amber-brown Indicates either a wine of very considerable age or one which is prematurely old and/or oxidized. Once the remaining healthy ruddy glow fades the wine is usually dead.

White Wines

White wines range from virtual colourlessness through the palest yellow-green and deeper shades of yellow, to gold and to deep amber-brown.

Dry white wines usually start off life pale in colour, and, unlike red wines, slowly gain colour with age. Sweet wines generally start off a deeper shade of yellow, turn to gold and then take on an amber-brown tinge with age. Phenolic compounds provide the yellow pigment of young white wines and these vary according to the grape used (for example, low in Rieslings) and wine making methods. Higher phenolics can be produced by grape ripeness (by skins affected with *botrytis* producing the yellow-gold of young sauternes and TBA's) by the length of time the young wine spends in wooden casks, and according to the types of wood used.

Young natural sherry is basically a pale straw-yellow, the deeper shades being the result of ageing and/or blending. Practically all the dark oloroso and brown sherries gain their colour from added *color* wine of one sort or another.

Pale yellow-green A distinct green tinge is quite common in youthful white wines, due to residual chlorophyll, and is a particular, if not essential, characteristic of a Chablis or a young Mosel. It is rarely seen in wines made in hot climates.

Straw-yellow A pleasant lively colour common to the majority of white wines, particularly the drier ones. In Burgundy, Meursault tends to be more yellow than Montrachet, and in Alsace, *traminer* more yellow than *riesling*, though this cannot be relied on.

Yellow-gold An abnormal colour for a young dry white wine but most frequently seen in the sweeter varieties such as sauternes and high-quality German dessert wines of *beerenauslese* and *trockenbeerenauslese* quality.

Gold Generally indicates either a lusciously sweet wine, or one with considerable bottle-age (for example, a white burgundy, usually pale straw when young, will develop a slight golden sheen after about 6 years in bottle).

Yellow-brown or old gold The colour of many dessert wines, fortified ones in particular. However, a brown or orange tinge in a white table wine indicates considerable bottle-age, over-maturity or even oxidation. Many white burgundies will take on an unhealthy brown tinge after about 12 years in bottle; yet a fine sauternes may not develop it for 30 years or more.

Maderised This word is used to describe the appearance and condition of over-maturity and some degree of oxidation. A maderised white wine presents a dull, drab appearance, with a pallid yellow-brown colour.

Brown Probably well past drinking (unless it is a sherry of that name or the tawny-brown of a very old port).

Rosé Wines

Wines described as rosé can vary considerably in colour and depth. Each district has its own style, depending on the type of grape used and on the method of making. The better rosés are made from black grapes, the skins being left in contact with the fermenting grape juice just long enough for red pigment to be extracted. Cheap rosés are sometimes a blend of red and white wines. Some commercial blends of pink champagne are made by adding red wine from the Montagnes de Reims.

The colour of a rosé is half its charm. A rosé wine is usually drunk young, for if allowed to age it would lose its freshness of colour and taste. Some rosés begin life the colour of onion skin, a characteristic of those wines appropriately termed *pélure d'oignon* and *vin gris*.

Rosé The perfect rosé should not look like a watered-down red wine, nor should it support an excess of orange or purple. It should be positive, bright and appealing.

Orange Some grape varieties produce a distinct orange tint. Pure orange is not a desirable hue although a pleasant orange-pink is quite normal and characteristic of many rosés from the Loire. Orange is often more marked in Provence and the hot south.

Pink A self-descriptive hue, suggestive of artificiality. Any suspicion of a blue tinge indicates unhealthiness, probably from bad fining or metallic contamination.

Depth of colour

Although the basic fullness or paleness of a wine depends to a certain extent on its origin, the relative depth of colour will give a good indication of its physical content.

Red Wines

Depth, in association with the actual colour or hue, will also give an indication of the age and maturity of the wine. For example, a very deep, nearly opaque, red-purple wine will almost certainly have more than its fair share of tannin and other natural components. A colour like this will only be seen in a well-made wine of a fine vintage, its properties being derived from rich, fully ripe grapes with sun-thickened skins. The converse applies equally: a pale red wine results from too high a yield per hectare, from hasty vinification, or a poor year in which the grapes have failed to mature and whose skins are thin and deficient in pigment.

White Wines

In regard to young dry white wines, depth of colour is relatively unimportant. The variations are comparatively small and the connotations usually inconclusive. A very pale Mosel, for example, is likely to be neither better nor worse than one which is medium-pale. White wines tend to deepen with bottle-age. This is due to phenolic molecules joining together, the larger molecules having deeper amber-gold and brown colours. Oxidation speeds up the process.

The depth of colour of sweet white wines is more meaningful. Care must be taken not to confuse the deep gold of an old sauternes of a great vintage with 'maderisation'. Château d'Yquem of the 1921 and 1929 vintages is very deep – deep gold, not deep brown – indicative of the extraordinarily high initial sugar content and extract. The point is that these vintages were deep in colour when young. Beware also of drawing a wrong conclusion from a *pale* old sauternes. This is indicative of either a lesser vintage, the use of steel vats rather than wood and/or over-sulphuring prior to bottling. The latter acts as a preservative, inhibiting development and colour change.

It is sometimes difficult to judge the comparative depth of colour of two wines. One method is to fill each of the glasses to the same height, place them side by side and look at each from a position vertically above; alternatively arrange a light behind the glasses and compare the relative depth of colour of the shadow cast by each wine on a white table top, a little-known but very effective way for all colours of wine.

Clarity

This is of prime importance in the various stages of development of all wines from the time of fermentation, during cask life, through to the time of bottling. Thereafter, white wines should be star-bright and trouble-free. Red wines are normally expected to throw a sediment in bottle. Fine wines often have extra lustre and luminosity. The clarity of a wine is best judged by holding the glass in front of a candle or some other bright light.

Tastevins The rather attractive silver *tastevins* which are sold in Burgundian souvenir shops (and used by tourists as ashtrays) are, in fact, traditional tasting vessels with a peculiar usefulness. The circular indentations in the shallow sides reflect candle light across the metal base to reveal at a glance in an ill-lit cellar the clarity of the new wine drawn from the cask. A *tastevin* is also more portable and less fragile than a glass though it is somewhat pretentious to take one to a normal tasting; a proper tasting glass is more useful. (In the Burgundy and Beaujolais regions the *tastevin* also has symbolic guild connotations.)

Upper surface The upper surface of the wine in the glass is worth inspection. It should of course be bright. If it appears dull, iridescent or bitty, trouble may be indicated. With very old wine, I also look out for the tell-tale bead of persistent small bubbles around the meniscus which generally gives advance warning that the wine is cracking up.

Cloudiness Hold up the glass to the light, or against a candle. A dull cloudiness or obstinate haze of suspended matter in bottled wine is a bad sign; in normal circumstances, the wine should be returned to the supplier. Incidentally, think carefully before condemning a cloudy *red* wine. Was it recently delivered or carried up from the cellar hastily and clumsily? Old vintage port usually has a heavy sediment or 'crust' and even when carefully decanted may still have 'fliers' or 'beeswing' (very descriptive) in it. The latter are normal (and tasteless) and can be ignored.

Cork, not 'corked' Tiny pieces of floating cork are harmless; so are most forms of sediment which settle easily in the bottle. Bits of cork in the wine may be due to a bad corking machine or, more usually, to the careless use of a poor corkscrew. Wine with cork floating on it is *not* 'corked' – an ignorant misunderstanding in restaurants that too often leads to completely fatuous and unnecessary complaints. Just pick the cork out!

Crystals Flakes of tartaric acid crystals are sometimes seen in fortified wine and white table wine. They have usually been caused by a sudden fall in temperature. These flakes or crystals generally settle quickly, are quite harmless and do not impair the flavour of the wine.

Limpidity It is an appropriate phenomenon that a really beautiful limpid colour is often indicative of a really fine wine whereas an ordinary blended wine will often have a dull nondescript lack-lustre appearance.

Grades of clarity shade down from brilliant, star-bright, bright and clear to dull, bitty, hazy and cloudy.

Intensity Last but not least the intensity of colour, by which I mean the strength of colour at the rim, as opposed to the more usual tailing off to a watery edge, is, in relation to red wines and old fortified wines in particular, an indication of quality, strength, extract.

Legs or tears I have never been a 'leg' man myself; indeed, there seems to be some confusion over the term in relation to wine. Full-bodied wines, those with high extract and alcohol content form 'legs' or 'tears' – globules with extended tails – which fall slowly to the surface of the wine after the glass has been swirled. This can, with some justification, be considered to presage richness, but I personally prefer to rely on my palate. Incidentally, carelessly washed and dried glasses can play havoc with the meniscus. 'Legs' can also be created by the 'surface tension pump' which is due to the evaporation of ethyl-alcohol at the meniscus or rim which mysteriously draws up a small quantity of wine.

Level or ullage

Although this relates to the appearance of wine in the bottle rather than in the glass, it is appropriate to refer to it here. A lower level than normal can be due to:

Short fill The result of sloppy bottling and careless inspection; level low neck or around upper shoulder. Usually little to worry about.

Reduction A natural contraction* which can occur in bottle over a period of time. In my experience mature burgundies can show a $4\frac{1}{2}$ to 7 cm ullage without deleterious effect.

Cork failure The commonest cause of ullage is cork failure due to cork weevil or lack of springiness due to old age. Cork weevil is not uncommon, particularly in badly maintained

---

*I understand that if a gallon of water and a gallon of alcohol are mixed, the total measures less than two gallons.

Base of cork

Normal fill

Low neck/top of shoulder
Acceptable level for Bordeaux over 15 years old. If a young wine, it is probably natural reduction *or* short fill. Highly acceptable – 'good level for age' – for any pre-1960 wine.

Upper shoulder Natural reduction level for unrecorked wine over 30 years old

Mid-shoulder If under 25 years old, possible cork failure. Not abnormal, certainly acceptable, for *very* old wine, though there is always an element of risk

Low shoulder Almost certainly an indication of cork failure and leakage. Oxidation/acetification risks high, whatever the age.

Low and under The wine will almost certainly be undrinkable and unacceptable for sale except, if rare and fully labelled, as a curiosity

private cellars. It is about the only thing which will affect the condition of old vintage port, particularly if the protective wax seal has broken or worn away: the weevil will bore holes in the cork and let air in. The wine will become acetic, or at least be tainted with the soiled cork.

Corks, like human bodies, eventually lose their suppleness and firmness with age. After 20 years or so, the elasticity of cork weakens, though high-quality long claret corks can protect wine for a century. Uneven ullages, quite common with very old wine, are almost always due to cork failure.* Recorking – standard practice in the great châteaux and *domaine* cellars – is the answer. Failing this (as with the great Rosebery pre-phylloxera clarets) regular waxing of seals and capsules, whilst otherwise remaining unmoved in a cold slightly damp cellar, will preserve the corks, and wine.

Ullaged bottles *can* turn out surprisingly well. Sometimes the air in the space does not harm the wine. If the cork is not foul, and the colour of the wine deep and good, the wine, even though old and vulnerable, may miraculously survive. But it must be of high quality to begin with.

Old champagne can look ullaged, but if the cork and foil are sound this ullage generally turns out to be carbon dioxide out of solution. No longer bubbly, the champagne will have turned into a calm, golden-sheened wine much beloved of English connoisseurs, to the exasperation of the French.

*I frequently come across ullaged bottles in old cellars. If the ullages, in a bin full of one wine, are fairly uniform, and the corks and caps appear sound, I do not worry overmuch.

Stage 2
NOSE OR BOUQUET

Bouquet is the soul of wine, while an agreeable aroma unfailingly imparts a delicious sensation. **Frona Eunice Wait,** Wines and Vines of California, 1889

The importance and value of nosing a wine are generally under-rated, for a great deal of valuable, nay essential, information about any wine may be gained from the smell alone. The first impression is important. The more mature the wine, the more significant the nose becomes.

The best procedure is to take hold of the stem of the glass lightly and, keeping its base on the table, rotate it briskly. This exposes the maximum surface area of wine, encouraging the release by vaporization of its esters. It also neutralizes the smell of a dirty glass.

Bring the glass to the nose and concentrate on the first fleeting impression. Is it clean and fresh? Are there any very positive characteristics: the grape aroma, high mouth-watering acidity, etc. etc. Next, give the glass another swirl and give a number of short sharp sniffs. This will reveal depths of fruit and other salient features not, perhaps, noticed at first. I do *not* recommend very deep inhalation: this merely deadens the senses.*

The smell of wine can be of two types: that which reminds one of another smell, or one that is, with experience, recognizable as a more-or-less pure chemical substance or compound. In essence, however, the wine taster has to learn to detect and recognize different grape aromas, youthfulness and maturity, pure wine scents and, with more experience, complex overtones.

It is difficult enough to analyse and describe most common-or-garden smells; even more so the subtleties of a refined bouquet. And if it is difficult to pin down the elements of bouquet, it is almost impossible to convey them to another person. Some of the characteristics are obvious and easily describable, some can only be recognized by an experienced 'nose'. The following facets should be examined, preferably in this order:

Cleanliness

Basically what is meant is that the wine should smell like wine, pure and unencumbered. Anything redolent of bad cabbages, old socks, vinegar, almond kernels, pear drops or any clearly extraneous or foreign smells, should be regarded as suspect, to say the least. In practice this is an automatic reflex action.

Sulphur dioxide, quite common on European white wines (it is reminiscent of burnt match sticks or the whiff of a coke oven), is regarded as more of a nuisance than an 'off' smell. Aeration, decanting and swirling in the glass all lessen the

---

*The late Allan Sichel favoured 'short sharp sniffs with his mouth open'. Frankly I find that this does not work for me with wine although I have recently discovered that it is it very effective for smelling brandy which, with nose alone, so often gives a too sharply spirity impression.

effect. If no off-odours are readily apparent one passes on to the more positive wine smells.

Grape variety

The experienced taster will next look out for the first major clue to the origin of the wine: the characteristic grape aroma.* The classic 'noble' vines, *cabernet-sauvignon, pinot, riesling, traminer* and so on, produce their own individual aromas. However, even these are not always easy to detect, and the only way to memorize them is to taste and re-taste first-rate examples until their characteristics are firmly lodged in the mind (see pp. 39–44 and Full Glossary of Tasting Terms, pp. 114–134).

Minor wines Those made from lesser grape varieties and those from minor districts will less frequently produce a distinct and recognizable aroma. More often it will be just vaguely 'varietal', and if totally indistinguishable but pleasant will merely be described as 'winey'.

Youth, age and maturity

The age of a wine can be accurately judged on the nose by an experienced taster. It is not as difficult as it might appear at first and, as always, the comparison of good specimens of different vintages is the best way to learn.

The physical components of young wine tend to be pronounced and raw as they have had little time to settle down and blend together. Acidity in young wine has a mouth-watering effect. A raw cooking apple smell indicates excess malic acid and is frequently found in young, unripe white wines, particularly from poorer vintage years in northerly climes.

As the wine mellows with age, its bouquet* becomes noticeably softer and more harmonious. It also develops what is known as 'bottle-age'. It is almost impossible to describe bottle-age; on most white wines this shows up as a 'honeyed' quality, red wines become richer and deeper with bottle-age. Complex and harmonious are perhaps the operative words. A wine with too much bottle-age will show deterioration by taking on a flat, dull, toffee-like smell (maderised) or what is known as bottle-stink (oxidation, which can produce a smell like bad cabbages). The point is that bottle-age is all part of the maturing process that is revealed to the taster.

Fruit

'Fruit' is a desirable quality, but it should be noted that a wine can be described as fruity without having any trace of grapeyness. A distinctly grapey bouquet is only found in wines that are made from certain unmistakable grape varieties.

Depth and intensity

A bouquet can be described as light or deep, intense, nondescript, superficial, full or rounded, depending on the development of the wine. However, care must be taken not to be misled by the 'full' (i.e. fully developed bouquet of a mature but poor-quality wine) or, conversely, by the 'dumb' or undeveloped bouquet of a very fine but immature wine.

*The expressions 'aroma' and 'bouquet' are used in the senses defined in the Full Glossary of Tasting Terms. However, both are frequently muddled in usage – by me as well as others.

It is hard to define quality. What one is looking for is an unfolding, an exposure, of bouquet that is rich, many-faceted, but soft; forthcoming yet harmonious. And the bouquet of a *great* wine is not only overwhelmingly beautiful but tends to linger in the glass even when it has been drained to the last drop.

There are many conventional terms used to describe the bouquet of wine and the principal ones are defined in the Full Glossary of Tasting Terms.

Stage 3
TASTE

The taste, or gustatory stage, should first and foremost confirm conclusions drawn from the appearance and bouquet. The palate is a fairly basic evaluator. In fact it provides the taster with rather less information than the eye and nose, unless the wine is new in cask. The younger the wine, the more important the palate element becomes. This is not to suggest that taste is unimportant. Far from it. In any case a factor, excess acidity for example, not spotted by the nose may be detected on the palate: a sort of long-stop situation.

As indicated in Chapter 4, there are several points of oral contact which will reveal different taste characteristics. For this reason, one tiny sip is usually inadequate. Do not peck at the wine; take a reasonable mouthful, swirl it round the mouth; then spit it out and repeat the process if necessary.

Elements of taste

It is recommended that the elemental characteristics that are detected on the palate be noted in strict order. It matters less what the order is than that the order is a habitual one. In this way one avoids overlooking vital factors. Here are the basic 'movements' and observations. Read through and then refer to the Glossary.

Dryness and sweetness A basic and easily judged constituent, particularly important in white wines. Do not be misled by thinness or excessive acidity, which tend to make one underestimate the actual sugar content, and vice versa. There is also an apparent sweetness noticeable in hot-country wines and in the wines of particularly good vintages in northern Europe: in each case this derives from fully ripe grapes and from ethyl-alcohol which has a slight sweetening effect.

Acidity Acidity is a major element in the make-up of any wine. It gives a wine purpose, life, zing and finish. I tend to think of acidity as the nervous system of a wine. Extremes of acidity are, however, undesirable. Excess sugar and glycerol, natural or otherwise, tend to mask the true degree of acidity.

Body The weight of wine in the mouth basically is the result of its extract and alcoholic content. This is the 'bone system'. Body is an important factor that varies according to the district, vintage, vinification, etc.

Tannin Although disagreeable on the palate (harsh, dry and mouth-puckering) it is an essential element of any young *red* wine. Tannin is extracted during fermentation from pips and skins, the thickness of the skins of red grapes and length of fermentation having a major bearing. Tannin is also derived from the wood of casks, new oak having the strongest effect. Tannin precipitates proteins and acts as a general preservative. It is essential for long life.

Tactile stimuli Smooth, creamy, velvety qualities can be felt in the mouth; so can astringent factors, and the burning sensation of alcohol.

Flavour This is all-important. Even if it is impossible to describe, at least record whether agreeable. The word 'typical' should be used sparingly. The intensity and length of flavour reflect quality.

Balance This is basically what the wine maker, the merchant and the connoisseur seek. What is meant by balance is that all the components are in harmony, with, for example, no excess of acid or tannin, just at the time when the wine is ready for drinking. The whole point is that individually the components are useless, indeed mainly unpleasant to the taster; it is in combination that they become wine, and, when complete and in perfect balance, *fine* wine. Two things have to be borne in mind: one is that the intrinsic components will vary from district to district, from style to style; and that over a period of time the balance will almost certainly change.

Take a red Bordeaux: when young, its tannin and acidity will be exposed and raw. It takes time, say 5–10 years, for the components of a fine wine to 'simmer down' and marry, becoming a well-knit harmonious drink. (It is the job of the merchant to be able to judge the future development of what seems to the layman a raw young red wine.)

In the case of a fine German wine, the grower strives to achieve, almost from the start, the right balance of acidity, sugar content and alcohol so that it can be early-bottled to capture, for his particular market, the desirable fruity-acidity which, with fragrant aroma and bouquet, are the touchstones of fine hocks and Mosels.

Finish A clean, crisp finish is the mark of a good, well-made wine. Poor-quality wines finish 'short' or tail off to a watery, insubstantial end. Top-quality wines have a long finish, often extending to an aftertaste or lingering 'farewell' – a beautiful flavour that remains in the mouth after the wine has been swallowed.

Quality, finesse, elegance, breed The elements of quality are represented by the completeness and balance of the various components. Quality can be assessed by the length of time the flavour lingers in the mouth, by its richness and subtlety and by its aftertaste. A variety of expressive abstract terms can be used to express degrees of quality. They tend to be subjective and should be chosen with care. See Chapter 12 and Full Glossary of Tasting Terms.

Stage 4
CONCLUSIONS

It should hardly be surprising that there is a relationship between the appearance, bouquet and taste of any one wine. Yet, in my experience, even competent tasters tend to examine each stage in isolation whereas some, myself included, see each stage as a revelation leading naturally to the next, and irrevocably to a logical conclusion.

Context The context is important. One makes allowances for minor wines and is hypercritical of fine wines, just as one should be tolerant of the weaknesses of the ill-educated or the less fortunate and perhaps more critical of the well-endowed, intelligent and beautiful people! In another context, the speedy visit to a dim cellar or a casual dinner party are hardly the places for a prolonged and detailed critique.

Again, in practice, the experienced taster need not note

precisely, in thoughts or words, his reactions to appearance, bouquet and taste; indeed, with our wonderful built-in computers, a look, a sniff and a mouthful can – if we are correctly programmed – give us instant summaries equivalent to 'a magnificent, soft, supple wine of great breed, intensity; fully mature' or 'raw, harsh, immature and poor quality – discard'.

Notes For the student, for the beginner or for the conscientious connoisseur, a detailed tasting note arriving at a considered conclusion is a useful exercise. It gathers the thoughts and ties up the loose ends.

The conclusion therefore should summarize compactly the salient points and add comments regarding the overall quality of the wine, its maturity, possibly its value and certainly its rating in the context of the tasting.

Scoring If you happen to be a judge in a competition, then almost certainly your notes and conclusions will have to be made in a precise form, usually tabulated with numerical values. Scoring is dealt with briefly on p. 137, but for exhaustive details I must refer readers to Amerine or Vedel (see Bibliography).

Descriptions Lastly, I would again draw your attention to Chapter 12 on the use of words and the glossary of tasting terms. These not only give you a very wide range of commonly, and less frequently, used terms, but the definitions – which admittedly are on occasion subject to slightly different interpretations – strive to give readers not only a clear indication of their meaning but, in the case of terms like 'tannin', explain something of the physical or chemical background.

PRICE

Although not a 'tasting' quality, price is a factor that cannot often be ignored. It is certainly the common denominator of all wine trade tastings except those concerned solely with the wine's physical development or condition.

Only a real wine snob or hypocrite (often the same person) and perhaps the carelessly rich, need not heed the price factor, though this does not mean that 'pure' or abstract tastings, comparing one wine with another, are not desirable and valuable. But for most purchasers and consumers of wine, price *is* the final arbiter, in the sense that value for money is sought and appreciated, as much as, if not more than, pure quality.

Recent years have witnessed an escalation of fine wine prices that appeared to be out of all proportion. For a time, we had a simple supply-and-demand situation – surging world demand for wines in geographically limited supply. Unhappily the speculator added pressure to the naturally increasing demands of opulent civilizations cultivating more and more wine enthusiasts. There was one consolation: the previously often impoverished wine grower at last received a return on his capital, using his new-found wealth to replant derelict vineyards, replace old vines and renew his equipment.

Increased production, the flight of the speculator – dumping stocks en route – and a recession then combined to reverse the market situation. For a while the price of wine dropped to levels which made sense to the drinker but which were unfortunately painful to the producer and trade. Now, I believe, the main culprit of rising prices is inflation, which is forcing increases in the cost of production and distribution.

What is really needed is a curb on the constant devaluation of all our currencies, linked with a healthy balance between consumer, merchant and producer. If an appreciative consumer is prepared to pay a respectable merchant or restaurateur a reasonable price, this will in turn allow the vineyard owner and wine maker a fair return for their labours, the risks and vicissitudes.

It should be remembered, however, that, historically, the finest wines have never been cheap. They were originally the sole province of the aristocratic, wealthy and privileged classes, and I dare say that quite a few didn't really appreciate them to the full – then as now!

At least, by increasing our awareness and appreciation we will not waste the opportunities of tasting fine and rare wines when, as they surely will, they present themselves for our delectation.

VI

ORIGIN OF TASTE CHARACTERISTICS

Rem tene, verba sequentur (Stick to your subject, the words will follow) **Cato the Censor**

I now propose to deal briefly, and necessarily inadequately, for it is a huge subject, with those factors at the growth and production end which create and influence the taste of wine.

It could be argued that this should have been dealt with first. However, tasting is primarily an end-product exercise, and it is the art of tasting and not vine growing and wine making which is the least documented of all wine knowledge and, after all, the subject of this book.

Background knowledge

We should, however, concern ourselves with grape varieties, with soil, climate, methods of cultivation and wine making, if only for one reason: the knowledge of the effects they all have on colour, bouquet and flavour. All this is not, however, necessary for the simple appreciation and enjoyment of wine, so don't please think that you *have* to read about, let alone master, this subject in order to be numbered amongst the world's happy band of wine lovers.

But if you do want to learn more, where do you begin? What has the greatest bearing on the style and flavour of wine? The variety of grape. Is this constant? No, it depends on the soil upon which it is grown. Is this combination constant? Again, no; the latitude, climate, the care of the vine and length of fermentation and, of course, the level of human skill at every turn: all these have a bearing.

However, before going into more detail it is important to realize that although it is convenient to break these elements down and study them separately, they can never, in practice, be completely isolated. They interact to create the final end-product.

GRAPE VARIETIES

Grape varieties are all-important. They have to suit the soil, the climate and the economy of the region. Many good wine books name and describe the main species and varieties, some also deal with vine diseases and pests, grafting and so on; but only a few relate all these to end-taste. What I propose to do here is to list the main varieties in alphabetical order (denoting the most important 'noble' varieties with a star), giving examples of the wine they make, but before I do so, there are a few points worth bearing in mind.

First of all, it is important to remember that the bulk of the world's wines are of ordinary quality, made from comparatively easy-to-grow, high-yielding vines. Grapes from different varieties may be blended, just as final wines may be. The resulting appearance, smell and taste are usually unremarkable and un-noteworthy.

Secondly, the great wines of the world, i.e. those with

exceptionally distinctive and refined taste characteristics and quality, are made from a limited range of noble grape varieties, the four leading ones being *cabernet-sauvignon*, *riesling*, *pinot* and *chardonnay*. These are produced mainly on difficult, sometimes almost barren, soils and terrains, in delicately uncertain, not to say risky, climates†. Familiarize yourself with these; they give the highest satisfaction to the senses, and their characteristics, once mastered, can be more easily memorized than those of lesser varieties. The latter may well be interesting and pleasant, but the fact is that they rarely merit a second glance. Their role is to provide an agreeable accompaniment to a well-cooked meal.

Finally, a highly important factor and one that is often overlooked is the age of the vine. It is commonly known that a newly planted vine does not bear wine-making fruit for 3 years. Thereafter the quality of the fruit increases steadily with age as the roots grow deeper down through soil and sub-soil; then for a period the vine combines high quality and substantial yield. Eventually the plant hardens and tires, and its production falls to uneconomic levels.

Aligoté White grape producing minor white wines in Burgundy. Pale; pleasant but undistinguished aroma; dry, light, pleasant acidity.

Alvarinho The principal vinho verde grape, only noticed as a crisp dry stylish wine in the better quality brands.

Aramon Prolific 'ordinaire' grown too extensively in the Midi.

Blanc-fumé See *sauvignon-blanc*.

Bual White grape making one of the richer madeiras.

Cabernet-franc One of the main Bordeaux varieties. A close relation to the *cabernet-sauvignon*, fairly similar in style. Known as *bouchet* in St-Emilion.

★Cabernet-sauvignon Without hesitation, I put *cabernet-sauvignon* at the head of the great red wine grapes of the world, not because I am dogmatic enough to place the finest claret, which it produces, above the finest burgundy, but because it maintains a recognizable style and character even when transplanted out of its classic home region, Bordeaux. For example, a well-made 'cabernet' from Australia, California or Chile will have a basic family resemblance despite overtones produced by differences of soil and climate.

The *cabernet-sauvignon* gives red Bordeaux (claret) its quality; its depth and richness of colour, aroma and wealth of bouquet; the firm, hard, keeping qualities and length of flavour. The three keys to its recognition are its deep colour, its characteristic aroma of fresh blackcurrants or cedar, and its particular concentrated fruity flavour combined with tannin and acidity. These may all vary in strength and intensity, not only because of differences of soil and microclimate within the Bordeaux area, but because the *cabernet-sauvignon* is rarely used alone but grown alongside and combined with other Bordeaux grapes, mainly *cabernet-franc* (similar but slightly less distinctive) and *merlot* (softer and plumper).

I think it is useful practice to familiarize oneself with the *cabernet-sauvignon* characteristics at their most pronounced.

---

†'Many centuries of experience indicates that only relatively few of the several hundred grape varieties used in making the world's wines are capable of developing the complex aromas and bouquets of the ideal, perfect wine.' Professor A. Dinsmoor Webb, of Department of Viticulture and Enology of the University of California, Davis.

If you are well off, try a good vintage Château Mouton-Rothschild. It has an opacity of colour, opulence of bouquet and concentration of flavour that make it almost a caricature of a great claret. If your finances don't permit you to run to a first growth try, for grape character, Malescot-Margaux or Lynch-Bages of a respectable year. Memorize the grape aroma in particular.

Carignan Prolific and rather neutral red wine grape (France, North Africa and elsewhere).

*Chardonnay This is the white relation of the *pinot* and makes the great white burgundies of the Côte de Beaune and Chablis (not to forget Champagne). It also produces some of the finest varietal wines in California.

It thrives on chalky soil and it produces a wine varying in colour from very pale straw to a fairly pronounced straw-yellow (a feature of many Meursaults and Californian wines). A good example will have a fresh, crisp, sometimes smoky, fruity (but not grapey) bouquet – very hard to describe. It will be dry; from the firm steely dryness of Chablis, and to some extent of the Puligny-Montrachet, to the softer dryness of Meursault, and the nutty dryness of Corton-Charlemagne. It will have a fair amount of acidity and body, and a subtlety and austerity of flavour that understandably, but paradoxically, attracts claret lovers.

High-quality white burgundies have a rich yet understated flavour; poor ones can be thin and dull. Louis Latour makes consistently fine Corton-Charlemagne, as does the Domaine Leflaive good steely Puligny-Montrachet. In California, there are dozens of outstanding wineries; amongst the top: Chateau Montelena, Chalone, Freemark Abbey and the pioneer Stonyhill; in Australia, Tyrrell, Max Lake and Brian Crozer of Petaluma are the most successful wine makers.

Chasselas Another neutral and prolific vine. White.

*Chenin-blanc A major variety making the dry-to-medium-sweet white wines of the mid-Loire. A pleasant waxy aroma, plenty of refreshing acidity. Also grown in California, Australia and South Africa (known as *steen*).

Cinsault Good red grape of the Midi, used for the better Tavel and Châteauneuf-du-Pape.

Fendant The same as *chasselas*. Grown in Switzerland.

Folle blanche White and ordinary.

Fumé-blanc Californian version of *blanc-fumé*; *sauvignon-blanc* varietal character.

Fürmint Hungarian white grape producing one of Europe's least-known great classic wines: Tokay. Straw-coloured wines, with a distinctive old-apple-like aroma when young, richly honeyed when aged. Ranging from dry to sweet, finally to concentrated 'essence'.

Gamay This is not a noble grape, but in one region, Beaujolais, it excels and produces a wine of such distinct character that it ranks only just below *pinot* in flavour. The *gamay* mainly produces a light red wine; often lightish pink-purple in colour and certainly light in alcohol and extract. Its most marked characteristics are a charmingly forthcoming and fruity bouquet, unique in character – difficult to describe but fairly easy to recognize. Lightweight and fresh in the mouth, with little tannin but quite a lot of acidity.

Grocers' beaujolais won't do: if you want a fair specimen, choose an unblended single-vineyard wine. Such wines are still not expensive, and most enlightened merchants stock one or two.

*Gewürztraminer In some ways, the most disregarded of the noble grapes. Yet it has an immediately attractive and recognizable style, easy, perhaps too easy, to appreciate and drink, for its opulent flavour tends to overplay its hand and then begins to pall; a white wine, at its best in south Germany (the Palatinate particularly) and Alsace.

In colour it is sometimes deeper and more yellow than the *riesling*; its most noticeable feature is a scented aroma, reminiscent of lychees, herb-like and spicy (*gewürz*). It ranges from fairly dry to medium-dry; has an equally flowery flavour but is soft and almost velvety, lacking the tinglingly refreshing acidity of the *riesling*.

Once again, for a copybook example try an estate-bottled Alsace of a recent good vintage. The old classic *traminers* of the Palatinate have never been very popular outside Germany and are even losing favour there, being rather earthy, heavyweight, and sometimes clumsy in style. They can, of course, be magnificent. Better to take the advice of a specialist Rhine-wine shipper if you want to taste a good example.

Grenache Fruity, pleasant red wines: lightish in colour but not in alcohol; agreeable, lightly fruity aroma. Grown in the southern Rhône, the Midi, California and Australia.

Gros plant A synonym for *folle blanche*, making a useful, rather neutral, dry wine in the lower Loire.

Grüner veltliner Milk-soft, dry white wine from Austria.

Kadarka Red grape grown in Hungary (principal ingredient of Bull's Blood); also in Austria and Yugoslavia.

Malmsey White grape grown in Madeira making a deep amber-brown sweet dessert wine with characteristic 'warm', tangy bouquet.

*Merlot A major variety grown in Bordeaux, giving claret flesh and roundness, complementing *cabernet-sauvignon*; dominant in Pomerol (Pétrus is a supreme example).

Müller-Thurgau A now well-established *riesling-sylvaner* cross producing a pale-coloured, grapey scented white wine of easy and attractive character in most German wine districts, particularly in Rheinhessen. Also grown in England.

Muscadelle A familiar-sounding grape name. One might expect it to be raisiny in smell and flavour, and it is. Usually of very pronounced character, it is used to add particular savour, in sparing quantities, to sweet white Bordeaux.

Muscadet Name of grape and type of wine: pale, bone-dry, white, from the lower Loire. Somewhat neutral.

*Muscat Rich, amber-coloured fortified dessert wine, with rich, tangy aroma and madeira-like acidity. Grown in several parts of the world but reaching its summit in north-east Victoria (Australia).

Muscat (*d'Alsace*) This is a somewhat unusual relation of *muscadelle*. It looks like any dry white wine, smells overpoweringly grapey and sweet, but is usually bone-dry on the palate. The best (Hugel produces some fine examples) seem to combine the grapeyness and richness of a *traminer* with the dryness and crispness of a *riesling*.

Nebbiolo One of the great red grapes of Italy, making the deep, powerful, firm and classic Barolo – try one of Marcarini's or Prunotto's; also Barbaresco.

Palomino The sherry grape: pale, dry, refined. With *flor* culture develops characteristic zestful bouquet, unmistakable but difficult to describe.

Pedro Ximenez Classic sherry grape used for blending. In

Victorian times drunk as a dessert wine: brown, almost opaque; rich, burnt, tangy nose; excessively sweet, rich and heavy.

Petit verdot Often used as the fourth component, albeit in a small proportion, of red Bordeaux. Slow ripener. A somewhat acidic grape which tends to be 'green' and tart in lesser years.

*__Pinot__ I place the *pinot* second amongst the red grapes of the world, for though (at its best) in Burgundy it produces wines of sublime richness and quality, it does not seem to make wine of so marked and recognizable a character when grown in other districts, whether elsewhere in Europe or in other continents. Perhaps I should mention here that it is also (with its white counterpart) *the* grape of Champagne.

A ripe *pinot*, vinified in a traditional way, from a good *climat* in the Côte de Nuits will have a velvety depth of colour (true 'burgundy red') with pronounced viscosity ('legs'). Its bouquet will be sweeter and more opulent than the *cabernet-sauvignon* in Bordeaux; and it will have a consistency on the palate that is both full and soft, alcoholic and velvety. The first main recognition signal is detected by the nose, in particular the *pinot* grape aroma which I, personally, find impossible to describe (though the head of a school of wine once suggested boiled beetroot as a memory trigger). The *pinot* smell must be identified, isolated and memorized. It is only from ripe grapes that the true *pinot* aroma emanates.

The next key factor is the weight of the wine, allied to softness. There is much less of the searingly mouth-drying tannin of its great rival, produced by the *cabernet-sauvignon* – a characteristic which makes a *pinot* much 'easier' to drink.

It is the hardest thing in the world to recommend perfect examples in the modest to middle-priced ranges; perhaps a bit easier in the pricier realms. To discover the flavour and character of a good *pinot* from the Côte de Nuits buy a fine vintage wine bottled by a leading grower such as de Vogüé, Daü, Rousseau or the relative newcomer, Domaine Dujac; or a good Côte de Beaune, from the Domaine Louis Latour or Drouhin; the higher-priced wines of shippers like Jadot or Faiveley; or, if you are rich, La Tâche of a great year.

Pinotage A red grape, a cross between *pinot* and *hermitage*, grown in South Africa, producing a rather jammy, inelegant, alcoholic wine.

Pinot blanc Once confused with *pinot chardonnay* but although of similar style, less distinguished.

Pinot grigio The dry Italian version of *Pinot gris*.

Pinot gris Makes a rather four-square, somewhat undistinguished, white wine.

*__Riesling__ German wine lovers may place the *riesling* first, but I place it second (to *cabernet-sauvignon*) in the hierarchy of noble grape varieties. It is certainly the most versatile and ubiquitous fine white grape, being grown in several European wine districts as well as in almost every major region on other continents. Like the *cabernet-sauvignon*, it has consistent strength of character which shows through even after transplanting.

The *riesling* makes a wine with a colour ranging from very pale straw with a hint of green, through pale yellow to deep gold (the latter would be a rich dessert wine, particularly with bottle-age). Its bouquet will be fruity but not grapey, forthcoming, refreshing and clean as a whistle; sometimes flowery, honeyed, and, when made from fully ripe grapes, almost *muscat*-scented. Most *rieslings* are dry to medium-dry but – another proof of its versatility – it can make the richest and sweetest dessert wines of the world. Another marked feature is a firmness, almost steeliness, of body, and fresh, crisp fruity-acidity. In Germany it is never very high in alcohol but has an excellent balance and finish.

The *riesling* scales the greatest heights in the Rheingau, Pfalz and Mosel districts, but can often be seen at its most recognizably straightforward in Alsace.

If I were to suggest a copybook specimen I would choose a *riesling réserve spéciale* or *exceptionnelle* bottled by one of the better Alsatian growers and shippers, like Hugel or Trimbach. They are remarkably pure wines and very good value.

If you want to take a more opulent hock as an example, I would choose a *riesling spätlese* or *auslese* of the 1971 or 1976 vintages from one of the several distinguished growers such as von Simmern, Dr Weil, von Buhl, Matuschka-Greiffenclau or Bürklin-Wolf. These wines are not cheap but, bearing in mind the price of other top-class wines (e.g. champagne, claret and burgundy), they are much less extravagant than you might think.

Rülander Synonym for *pinot gris* making a pleasant, slightly innocuous white wine in the Rhinelands of Germany. Pale-coloured, grass-like aroma, mild.

Sangiovese Of the noble grapes of Italy, the principal variety making Chianti. Firm, full, long lasting and with a distinctive dry, almost bitter finish. Try the Nozzole, or an old Frescobaldi wine.

*Sauvignon-blanc A curiously attractive variety; in bouquet and flavour something of a cross between *cabernet-sauvignon* and *traminer*. In other words, it combines a spicy blackcurrant aroma, with a mouth-wateringly refreshing acidity. Fashionable, but can be thin if poor.

It is grown under this name in Bordeaux, and is one of the components of Barsac and Sauternes, adding the necessary crispness and acidity. Of the same grape family but called *blanc fumé* it is responsible for the wonderfully crisp, dry, fruity wines grown at Pouilly-sur-Loire and for the wines of similar style over the river at Sancerre.

Scheurebe A successful crossing used in Germany, particularly in Rheinhessen and the Palatinate, producing a dramatically grapey aroma and rather facile flavour to match. Lacks the firmness and balance of the *riesling*.

*Sémillon A white grape, one of the major components of Sauternes and Graves. It has quality and style, a soft 'lanolin' nose, but somehow lacks fruity acidity, which is why it is usually vinified alongside the *sauvignon-blanc*.

Sercial Originally the *riesling*, making the palest and driest madeira.

Seyval blanc A white hybrid quite widely grown in England and making a clean, dry, somewhat neutral, ungrapy, wine.

Shiraz A red variety extremely at home in Australia and South Africa, making deep-coloured, swiftly maturing yet long-lasting, soft but alcoholic wines reminiscent of the Rhône, with an unmistakable and, at first, strange, tangy aroma aptly described as 'sweaty saddle'.

Siegerrebe Another somewhat exotic, grapey-smelling white wine grown in Germany.

Steen A long-planted variety, similar, probably identical, to the *chenin-blanc*. Grown in the Cape vineyards of South Africa and certainly making their best and most characteristic dry white wines.

Sylvaner Though making a familiar Alsatian wine type, *sylvaner* is not a 'noble' grape. It is a more humble but nevertheless distinct variety. It would be both unkind and misleading to describe it as 'the poor man's *riesling*', but it makes a useful dry hock-style wine of less marked character. The *sylvaner* is also grown in Germany, producing a second-rank wine, lacking the finesse and crispness of the *riesling*, except in Franconia, where it produces great Steinwein.

Syrah A fine variety grown in the Rhône valley, responsible for red Hermitage: deep, firm long-lasting wines (Paul Jaboulet makes wonderful examples). Also used in Châteauneuf-du-Pape.

Tokay Synonym for the *pinot gris* grown in Alsace. A firm white wine with few marked characteristics. Do not confuse with Hungarian Tokay.

Traminer See *gewürztraminer*.

Trebbiano A major Italian white wine grape used in Soave, Orvieto, Chianti and elsewhere, the style depending on the vinification but mainly straw-yellow in colour, with a waxy, rather unfruity, nose; dry, four-square and rather unexciting flavour and finish.

Viognier An unusual grape which in Condrieu, notably at Château Grillet, in the Rhône makes white wine of crispness, style and distinction.

Zinfandel A grape peculiar, and well-suited, to California making red wines of considerable distinction, many with potential staying power.

SOIL

The taster can comfort himself in the knowledge that convention – historical trial and error – and more recent research work have firmly established exactly what variety of vine flourishes in which type of soil (at any rate in the classic European districts). It is of interest for us to note that the best wines are made from vines grown in uncompromising terrain; often upon ground too poor to support any other crop: schistous rock (port), gravel (claret), slate (Mosel), large pebbles (Châteauneuf-du-Pape) and so on.

It seems that soil plays a major but subdued supporting role, at best when unobtrusive, supplying *just* those minerals, storing moisture and so forth, to allow the vine to struggle for existence but no more. Certainly good fertile soil encourages the vine to become over-prolific, producing quantity at the expense of quality. Excess use of fertilizers has a similar effect and, in addition, gives undesirable off-tastes to the vine.

Planting a vineyard and making wine is a gentleman's occupation, and the highest type of agriculture. **Frona Eunice Wait,** Wines and Vines of California, 1889

Fine *white* wines, requiring freshness and acidity, thrive on chalk (e.g. fino sherry and champagne). In Burgundy, along the Côte de Beaune, the natural adaptation of vines to soils can be seen dramatically by walking from the red wine *climats* of Corton round to the chalky slope of Corton-Charlemagne, where only white grapes are grown.

Some wines – red Graves, some Rhône and Palatinate wines – smell and taste 'earthy'. Some, as in parts of St-Emilion, reflect the high iron content of the soil by having an iron taste (if you've ever had an iron tonic or some of the more medicinally reminiscent Australian 'burgundies', you will recognize this feature). The Napa Valley soil gives its red wines a distinct and recognizable volcanic richness and earthiness.

Sub-soil

The importance of the sub-soil cannot be overstressed. Much of the richness and extract of a fine wine is drawn from the right sort of sub-soil by the deeply thrusting roots of the mature vine.

There are often subtle and complex differences between two red wines made in the same way, from the same grapes, but from neighbouring vineyards. These differences of flavour and bouquet are mainly due to the make-up of soil and sub-soil (almost certainly more important) and the balance of minerals. The drainage and the aspect also play a part, mainly in the disposition of moisture and the retention of heat.

Rarely, however, are the effects of soil on taste direct, and when they are these tend to be in the nature of 'overtones' of bouquet and taste, which makes their origin the more difficult to pin down. I readily admit to being ill-equipped to delve deeply into the fascinating sub-strata of soil and mineral tastes. At least the taster should be aware of their presence and indubitable influence, and should try to recognize those soil characteristics that are pronounced.

CLIMATE

After the indefinable complexities of soils, the effects of climatic variations are more frequently documented and more easily understood. Like soil, though, climate influences the taste of wine through its effect on the grape. Understand the reaction of the grape to sun, cold and rain, and it is easier to recognize the end-product of a given vintage.

Geographical influences – the limits of latitude, proximity of rivers and bodies of water and height above sea level – can take a back seat, from the taster's point of view. The wines we normally come across will not be grown in unsuitable areas. This is not our problem. Climatic variations, however, are of considerable interest and significance.

There are three broad aspects of climate in so far as they affect wine:

Zones The first concerns the consideration and comparison of the effects of two quite different climes: the gentle but significant variations in a temperate zone (the northern half of Europe, for example) and the less variable, hotter and drier zones exemplified by North Africa, the uplands of South Africa, the irrigated areas of South Australia and southern California * The comparative uniformity and reliability of the warmer areas make life less hazardous for the grower but somewhat less interesting for the discerning drinker, as the wine is of a more even quality, with fewer surprises, and rarely, if ever, scales the heights. The motto of fine wine could well be *nil sine labore*, for it is the struggle against the elements that kindles quality.

Annual differences The second aspect of climate is confined to the temperate zones. It consists of the annual variation and is of enormous importance to the entire concept of vintage wines. This aspect will be dealt with in some detail below.

*California has been scientifically divided into five climatic regions based on average sun/heat levels.

Micro-climate The third aspect is the micro-climate; the variations due to the lie of the land – sun traps, the susceptibility to pockets of frost and fog, etc. – which occur within wine areas and from vineyard to vineyard.

The connoisseur will mainly be concerned with the second aspect, vintage variations, but in the process of describing the general effects of too much sun and too much rain, the implications will throw light on the extremes of the first aspect: that is to say, the character of wines made at the edges of the permissible vine-growing latitudes will reflect the characteristics outlined below.

Variations Too much sun and too little rain (in a given year or in a particular part of the world) will reduce the quantity of juice in the grape and thicken the skins, thus producing excess colouring matter and tannin. In some northern zones, at the end of the ripening period the skins may shrivel and crack, letting in undesirable ferments. The first fermentation may be hard to control, risking spoilage. (Choice of grape, soil, irrigation and vat cooling systems are counter-factors in hot, dry areas.) As a result, the wines, if red, will be full of colour, alcohol and tannin, heavy, coarse and hard. If white they will lack acidity and, in consequence, be heavy, flat, flabby, charmless, and with little bouquet.

Too much rain and insufficient sun will increase the volume of juice. However, the grapes won't ripen fully, so the sugar content will be low, and the wrong sort of acidity high. This will result in a low alcoholic content and pale colour (if red). The wine will be thin and tart, unbalanced and short-lived. If steps are taken during vinification to increase the sugar content artificially, and to stabilize the wine, it can be made into a tolerable beverage but will never be fine.

Vintage charts

Those much-maligned aids, vintage charts, do at least provide a handy *aide-mémoire*, for their ratings, in effect, summarize quite accurately the overall weather conditions which have affected a particular area in a given year. For example, the year 1963 rates 1 out of 7 under the 'Claret' heading of the current Wine & Food Society Vintage Chart. This low rating reflects the poor weather prevailing that year in Bordeaux, resulting in equally poor wine. However, the north of Portugal enjoyed an excellent combination of sun and rainfall in 1963. Under the heading 'Port' it justly rates 7 out of 7.*

It is with vintages like 1964 that generalizations become dangerous. Heavy rain-storms in the middle of the vintage were disastrous for those Bordeaux growers who were holding on for further ripening. The early, pre-rain pickers like Château Latour were fortunate. The late pickers, including Lafite, Mouton-Rothschild, Calon-Ségur and Lynch-Bages, made comparatively puny, wishy-washy wines. Over the river, in St-Emilion, the rain was not as severe as in the Médoc and the wines were uniformly more successful. Charts *can* be useful, but watch out for the exceptions. Better a generalization than no information at all.

My tip for beginners is not to be bamboozled and bedazzled by airy-fairy vintage talk. Forget the bottle and label for a minute and remember that the precious liquid inside stems from a crop affected by weather conditions like any other

*This important subject is exhaustively covered in *The Great Vintage Wine Book* by Michael Broadbent (Mitchell Beazley).

crop. It would all come more naturally, for the English at any rate, if we were to realize that on the occasions when we have enjoyed a stunning summer the odds are that the rest of Europe has too, and that the vintage will probably be good.

WINE MAKING

Whereas the care of the vine – the annual toil in the vineyards – can vary in degree and attention from grower to grower, we can reasonably assume a tolerable standard, to enable the owner to earn a living. His husbandry will affect quality and quantity; the over-use of certain fertilizers may also affect the taste, but it is when we come to wine *making* that the skills and particular techniques of the owner, grower, wine maker or cellar-master will have the most direct bearing on the colour, bouquet and flavour of the wine which he produces.

Improvements

Thanks to the activity of schools of oenology and viticulture, to governmental and local institutes and advisory bodies, much less bad wine is made these days. It is, however, totally untrue for them to claim that without their help and advice no good wine would be made. Great wines were made before oenology, as an exact science, was conceived; just as wine was sold before marketing concepts were devised. The sciences and pseudo-sciences are servants and modern aids; rarely the originators, never the masters.

In the more ignorant and uncontrolled days of the past, galloping fermentation by wild yeasts would frequently give an off-taste to the wine, over-hot fermentation might breed microbes in the absence of sulphur dioxide and the heat would usually 'cook' the wines; sulphur would be over-used, and so on.

All these errors and omissions would spoil the smell and taste in some detectable way. Nowadays, so far as red wines are concerned, the principal worry is that the demands of commerce – wines for quick maturing and quick turnover – are being met by speedier fermentation and increased blending. The former leads to paler-coloured red wines with less tannin and extract, the latter to neutralization of character and quality (see Chapter 2).

Care

Care of the wine prior to bottling – or the lack of it – can have a direct effect on taste. For example, the woodiness which comes from wines being kept too long in new casks, or too long in cask at all; the acrid effect of over-sulphuring; the sour overtones of a wine left on the lees too long, and the vinegary smell of a 'pricked', probably neglected, wine.

THE EFFECT OF AGE

It is a useful over-simplification to say that 'wine is a living thing'. It implies, quite correctly, that wine, once made, is in a constant state of change and development, first in cask, then in bottle. Again, for simplicity, I am ignoring the use and effects of glass-lined vats, ionization, pasteurization, refrigeration and all the sophisticated tools and techniques employed these days by large undertakings to keep their wines as stable as possible. My terms of reference here are limited to the ageing of *quality* vintage wines, in so far as they affect taste.

Quality and maturity

Perhaps I should define 'quality vintage wine' or *vin de garde*. It is a wine of one good vineyard* of one vintage whose raw young components are present in strength and balance, so that over a period of years, first in cask, but mainly in bottle, these components will 'marry', settle and soften into one harmonious but characterful whole.

Red wines Young red wine will start life with a full colour, plenty of tannin, acidity and alcohol. Over a period of time, depending on the strength and degree of these basic elements, the colouring matter will be precipitated by the tannin (see 'Colour or Hue', p. 26), which itself gradually loses its harsh dryness. The acidity will tone down, and the whole ensemble will look more mellow, smell sweeter and richer, with subtler overtones and scents, and the effect in the mouth will also be soft, mellow and harmonious – no discordant edges – with layers of flavour and a long finish and fragrant aftertaste.

Red wines repay keeping best. But do *all* red wines repay keeping? The answer is no. Cheap branded wines, non-vintage blended wines, and very minor clarets and burgundies will probably improve with just 3 months' to a year's bottle-age in your own cellar (do not rely on the merchant to give an ordinary wine bottle-age, he will endeavour to sell it soon after bottling). Even well-made but minor *bourgeois* wines, claret in particular, are not worth holding over-long. It is important to keep things in perspective and realize that a 20-year-old *bourgeois* claret will not have improved to 'classed-growth' quality simply by keeping. It may have mellowed nicely, but in the final analysis it will only taste like a minor claret, just older, tireder and possibly sadder!

White wines It is commonly accepted that *dry* white wines are not meant to be kept, but to be drunk whilst young and fresh. What is little known is that the really good dry whites, particularly from classic districts, not only keep well but will develop with bottle-age quite distinctive qualities of colour, bouquet and flavour. For example, a 1952 Montrachet, a 1949 Corton-Charlemagne, a 1947 Vouvray, many 1959 Rhine wines of quality, from a good cold cellar, can still be on the 'plateau of perfection' now, in the early 1980s. In financial terms, unlike their red equivalents, they may not have appreciated proportionately in value; but in sensory terms they can be a revelation. Which really is what tasting is all about. . . .

Elders and betters? Summing up, don't expect age to confer upon an ordinary or middle-class wine qualities it never had to begin with. The only wines that will keep and blossom in interest and character over the years are the 'pedigree' wines: first-growth claret and some of the other classified growths; single-vineyard burgundies bottled at the *domaine*; the rare aristocratic Chiantis and Barolos; the great dessert wines like vintage port, a rich Tokay *aszu*, the great sauternes, sweet Loire wines (particularly Coteaux du Layon) and Rhine and Mosel wines of *auslese*, *beerenauslese* and *trockenbeerenauslese* quality; and also the top-quality premium wines of Australia and California.

---

*A particular *marque* of vintage port may stem from one or more vineyards, but will be made under the control of a single shipper.

VII
COLOUR VARIATIONS
IN SELECTED WINES

The appearance of wine can be most meaningful. Fill a generous tasting glass to about a third full with a good wine. Observe the depth of colour at a 45-degree angle. Then, holding the glass by its stem, tilt it over a white background to check the actual hue of the wine at the deepest point of the bowl and the gradation of colour towards the edge. Note the tell-tale intensity of colour at the rim. Finally, hold the glass up to a light to judge its clarity and brightness.

Under the heading of 'Appearance' on p. 26, there is a detailed description of the various points to look for when examining a wine. The following examples of actual wines have been selected to illustrate a wide range of colour combinations rather than to represent every major wine district. They will help the reader to pinpoint the most significant areas of depth and hue. The seemingly endless number of variations that can occur are due to differences of district, grape, quality of vintage and age of wine and are part of the fascination that a truly fine wine holds for the serious taster.

The intensity of colour at the rim or meniscus is indicative of richness, concentration and age

Towards the rim: look for signs of maturation and evenness of gradation

Mid-colour, brightness observed here

Full depth of colour revealed at widest point of bowl

Immature Red Bordeaux

A classed-growth Médoc of good vintage (sample drawn after 1 year in cask)

Fairly intense at rim – immature purple or violet colour is clearly visible

Good depth of colour maintained from centre to edge

Deep mulberry colour, almost opaque in centre

Maturing Red Bordeaux

Top-class château of great vintage, beginning to mature after 9 years

Outer rim red-brown indicating some maturity

Fine claret red, the initial youthful purple now lost

Still deep in colour but no longer opaque

Perfectly mature 26-year-old claret of excellent château and outstandingly elegant vintage

Fine Mature Red Bordeaux

Edge has distinct mahogany tinge indicating full maturity

Mellow, glowing red-brown colour in even gradation from centre to rim

Moderate depth of colour

A good château and good vintage but after 55 years beginning to deteriorate

Overmature Red Bordeaux

Amber at rim, no more life

Lacks healthy red glow

The whole spectrum has a drabber, browner shade

Deep colour now due to oxidation

Five-year-old White Graves

Produced by a château known for both its white and red wines

Most dry white wines have a colourless rim

Gradual thinning of colour

Pale lemon colour will deepen slightly with age

Maturing 8-year-old Sauternes

From one of the top châteaux, a classic wine of a good, medium-weight vintage

Yellow tapers off to a virtually colourless rim

Appealing rich yellow colour Initially deeper in colour than dry whites, sauternes becomes darker as it matures

Mature Great Sauternes

From the greatest of all the Sauternes châteaux, a very good vintage, 12 years old, approaching its peak but capable of further development with a long life ahead

Beautifully graduated to the palest yellow at rim

Looks rich and sweet: the colour of 21-carat gold leaf

The initial bright yellow-gold is now a deeper burnished gold

Very Old Classic Sauternes

Just over 50 years old, a first-growth Barsac of great vintage

The bright yellow-gold colour presses up against the meniscus

The rich, warm, umber-gold is enhanced by candlelight, giving the wine taffeta-like highlights

Beautiful, translucent old-gold colour of a perfect wine

Young Beaujolais

A year-old village wine of some quality and very good vintage. For early drinking

Very little colour at rim

Pale mauve reveals the wine's youthfulness

Fresh-looking, with a distinct pink-purple hue that will change to a pale burgundy red with time; however, this wine lacks the body and balance to warrant keeping

The colour is never very deep even when young

Maturing Burgundy

A 3-year-old Côte de Nuits, of good vintage, starting to mature

The slightly purple rim indicates immaturity; with age this will become more brown

Trace of red-brown near the edge is a hint of development

True burgundy red

Reassuring depth of colour; other burgundies of the same vintage may be slightly deeper or paler

A 30-year-old Côte de Nuits, of excellent vintage and from a moderately good shipper

Mature Burgundy

Palish mahogany red, impressively rich up to amber rim

A plummy burgundy red, shading off gradually

Has maintained a good depth of colour

A 60-year-old, fully mature *grand cru* burgundy of a classic vintage

Very Old Burgundy

Rich, amber rim

Warm mahogany colour towards rim

Beautiful red-brown colour, but predominance of brown suggests overmaturity

Richness of 'robe' that is the hallmark of a great old burgundy

Manzanilla Sherry

Young, lightly fortified wine, best drunk freshly bottled. Dry and zestful

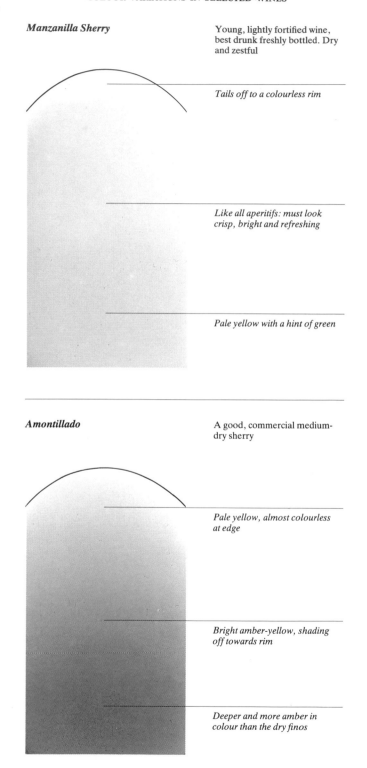

Tails off to a colourless rim

Like all aperitifs: must look crisp, bright and refreshing

Pale yellow with a hint of green

Amontillado

A good, commercial medium-dry sherry

Pale yellow, almost colourless at edge

Bright amber-yellow, shading off towards rim

Deeper and more amber in colour than the dry finos

A high-quality oloroso sherry, cask-matured in Spain, bottled in Bristol 25 years ago

Old-bottled Oloroso

Rich yellow-amber rim

Fairly deep colour to begin with, it has now developed with age a warm burnt amber hue with a hint of orange and brown

Deeper and heavier in style than amontillado

Old-fashioned style of sherry, very sweet and concentrated in flavour after considerable age in cask

Finest Old Brown Sherry

Pronounced amber-brown rim with faint green tinge

Suffused with orange towards the edge

Rich, 'toasted', translucent brown, indicative of age and quality

Deep brown, often opaque at centre

Immature Vintage Port

Taken from a sample 2 years in cask. Classic shipper, great vintage. Will take 15 years to soften and mellow; capable of lasting 50 years or more

Purple colour presses right up to meniscus

Deep and purple, graduating to an immature violet shade

Virtually opaque – 'black as Egypt's night'

Fine Ruby Port

A young ruby port of high quality, matured in wood, newly bottled ready for drinking

Pale plum colour at rim, with a touch of red-brown

Bright ruby

True 'ruby' red; only a faint hint of purple betraying youthfulness

Good depth of colour

Mature Vintage Port

A great vintage from a top shipper; shipped in cask and bottled after 2 years; matured in bottle for 30 years. Ready now but will keep

Pale orange-brown rim

No sign of purple anywhere; instead it is a warm tawny red

Totally different from a young vintage port: the initial opacity is lost, together with a considerable fading and softening of colour

Finest Old Tawny Port

Matured in wood, then bottled in Oporto at its peak of maturity. Perfect now

Pale, amber-tawny rim

Genuine old tawnies, aged in wood, are usually fairly pale with gentle gradation of colour

Warm, tawny-red with a ruddy glow, sometimes with a slight orange hue

Young Rhine Wine

A 3-year-old Riesling Spätlese of very good vintage from a top vineyard in the Palatinate district

Fades to a colourless rim

Pale lemon, with a mouthwatering hint of green; this wine can be drunk now or kept for further development

Still pale, even at its deepest, but will gain colour with age

Mature Rhine Wine

A 26-year-old, great, fully ripe vintage, from a leading estate in the Rheingau

Pale rim

Deep buttery yellow due to bottle-age

Some depth of colour, but attractively pale for its age. No hint of drab overmaturity

From a great and classic vintage, but after 34 years it has lost its initial zest, becoming rather flabby

Overmature White Burgundy

Insipid rim

Colour of old straw, with a faint orange tinge; dull, lacking sheen

Noticeable depth of colour; almost drab, with a touch of brown

An intensely sweet, fortified dessert wine from north-east Victoria, long aged in cask

Australian Muscat

An intense, green-gold rim indicates age and quality

Neither tawny nor ruby, it has a warm russet colour, not found in other wines

Fairly deep and rich

Napa Valley Zinfandel

Almost a caricature of a great Californian red: a 3-year-old late-harvest Zinfandel, high in strength, slightly sweet and with a long life ahead

Colour rich to rim, with immature violet tinge

Deep blackberry hue; high alcoholic content and 'extract'

Virtually opaque, almost like young vintage port

Napa Cabernet-Sauvignon

The best vintage of the 1970s from a relatively new winery. At 5 years of age, it has a long future during which colour loss and change will be very gradual

Intensely red at rim, indicative of 'extract' and quality

Initially opaque, it is now a translucent, finely graded shade of ruby red

Deep ruby at centre

The big classic Rhône wines are
becoming increasingly rare;
this is a 10-year-old example
from one of the best vineyards

Semi-mature Châteauneuf-du-Pape

*The red-brown rim is the only
visual concession to maturity*

*Good, rich mid-red – still
youthful for its age*

*Depth of colour reflects high
alcoholic content, body and
'extract'*

A 4-year-old 'claret'-style wine
from one of the oldest-
established wineries in the
Barossa Valley

Maturing Australian Red

*Considerable purple intensity at
rim suggests richness, body and
immaturity*

*Still a distinct, somewhat
youthful plummy-purple colour*

*Noticeable 'hot-country' depth
of colour; probably has a high
alcoholic content*

Sercial Madeira

A standard commercial blend of sercial from an old-established Madeira shipper. Has acquired some cask age, but does not improve in bottle. For immediate consumption

Colourless rim

Tails off to a pale yellow

Straw-yellow, looks 'dry', but the colour is warmer than that of dry sherry

Pure amber, with a faint orange tinge

Old Vintage Madeira

A 'straight' vintage from pure *Bual* grapes, with at least 50 years in cask, 40 years in glass demi-johns and about 15 years in bottle. Magnificent wine

Glowing colour extends right up to the rim, with a hint of green associated with age and quality

Pure golden amber

Warm vibrant amber shot with gold and orange – one of the most beautiful colours in the wine spectrum

Deep, 'toasted' amber

VIII
MAIN REGIONAL
CHARACTERISTICS

This chapter is an attempt to bridge the gap between tasting techniques and specific types of wine, to give the reader some indication of what to look for when faced with a wine from a major region or district or type.

Rather than give a 'blow by blow' description of each wine, which would require an encyclopedia not a chapter, I will endeavour to point out those salient features which are most characteristic, most distinctive or unusual. It might be helpful to keep one thumb in the 'Grape variety' section of Chapter 6, and the right hand in the Full Glossary of Tasting Terms. The arrangement is by country, district and type. Good, bad and indifferent vintages are listed, and finally, in chart form, there is a breakdown of wines into dry, sweet, light and heavy.

If the structure is rather rigid and the generalizations too broad, I nevertheless feel that some guidance is better than no guidance at all. As tasting is so subjective, it is up to you, the reader, to develop your own pattern of knowledge and to clothe it with your own tasting experiences.

FRANCE

Red, white, dry, sweet, sparkling, fortified with brandy, *liquoreux*, spice-augmented, common-or-garden to finest and rarest: France produces the whole gamut. A brief description of the major districts follows.

BORDEAUX (RED)

Claret is thought of as a light table wine. It can, however, vary from deep-coloured and heavy to 'clairet', palish and light, depending on district, vintage weather, vineyard site and vinification.

Médoc
The classic claret area: firm dry wines, purple and tannic when young, elegant and harmonious when mature. Life-span depends on vintage, weight and class of wine. These are the main districts:

Pauillac Depth and concentration of colour, opaque and purple when young, pronounced and concentrated *cabernet sauvignon* aroma and flavour (see p. 39), marked tannin and acidity when immature. The greatest wines for keeping and development. Home of three first growths: Lafite, Latour and Mouton-Rothschild.

St-Estèphe Deep colour; stark raw fruity nose, *cabernet* less marked; full, firm, tannic. Slow-developing, solid wines, from heavier clay soil.

St-Julien Copybook claret. Lighter; more cedary bouquet; balance, elegance, harmony. Not the longest-living but capable of great finesse.

Margaux Quite variable in style but on the whole similar in colour and weight to St-Julien; bouquet varietal, complex and fragrant. Develops well.

Moulis, Listrac, Soussans and St-Laurent These middle-Médoc and hinterland districts, noted mainly for good *bourgeois* growths, produce fruity and dry wines but without the strongly marked characteristics of greater districts and vineyards. Will keep, but not worth keeping too long.

Graves
Similar weight to Médoc but develops more quickly. Garnet-coloured, showing red-brown tinge sooner. Bouquet and flavour notably earthy, both being loose-knit, soft and rounded.

Pomerol
Two styles: one deep and firm but with full, silky *merlot* richness, slow developing; the other lighter in colour and weight; sweeter, more gentle and quick-maturing. Each style has a noticeable velvety texture in the mouth. Lighter vintages develop quickly.

St-Emilion
Again has two styles: from the 'Côtes' around the town, deepish but quick-maturing wines, loose-knit, sweeter on bouquet and palate; easy, flavoury. From the 'Graves' plateau next to Pomerol, firm fine fruity wines with depth of colour and flavour, with hint of iron/earth character detectable on nose and palate.

Fronsac
Good deep-coloured wines; hard, fruity bouquet and flavour, tannic and needing bottle-age though rarely capable of great development. Like a firm hard Pomerol. Austere but pure and characterful.

Bourg and Blaye
The poor man's Médoc – if I may so categorize without wishing to give offence. Dry, straightforward, rather coarse wines: plain but honest. Need a little bottle-age but not worth cellaring for 10 years – all you will have is a still somewhat coarse minor wine, 10 years older.

Claret vintages
Great years: 1928, 1929, 1945, 1947, 1949, 1953, 1959, 1961, 1966, 1970, 1975, 1978, 1982. *Good years:* 1933, 1934, 1943, 1948, 1950, 1952, 1955, 1962, 1964, 1971, 1976, 1979, 1981, 1983. *Indifferent or variable years:* 1937, 1954, 1957, 1958, 1960, some 1964, 1967, 1969, 1972, 1973, 1974, 1977, 1980. *Poor years:* 1951, 1956, 1963, 1965, 1968.

Maturity-span
Great wines: 12–30 years; *good wines:* 8–20; *lesser wines:* 5–10.

BORDEAUX (WHITE)

Ranges from very dry to medium-dry, from medium-sweet to very sweet; colour from very pale yellow-straw (more yellow in a hot vintage), golden-tinged with bottle-age, to the deep old-gold of venerable sauternes. The common denominator on the nose is the soft 'lanolin' fragrance of the *sémillon* grape, fresh and mouth-watering when young, deep, rich and honeyed when fully mature.

Graves
Colour range pale to straw-yellow. Very dry to medium-dry, with more body and less of the mouth-puckering acidity of Loire whites, less fruity-fragrant than hock. At best, refined;

improves with 5–10 years' bottle-age. The less-than-best are often dull, stodgy, uninspiring.

Sauternes

Deep, more golden in colour. Characteristic honeyed over-ripe grape smell from *pourriture noble*. Essentially sweet, luscious and full-bodied though varying in weight and richness, depending on year, and neatly counter-balanced by acidity. Note particularly the concentration and aftertaste of the really great wines. Fine sauternes not only keep well, they really need bottle-age.

Barsac Similar in style and content though sometimes paler, green-tinged when young; often more refreshingly forthcoming bouquet; slightly lighter in body and less rich, particularly in minor vintages.

White Bordeaux vintages

Great classic years: 1921, 1928, 1937, 1945, 1947, 1949, 1955, 1959. *Good years:* 1929, 1934, 1943, 1948, 1950, 1952, 1953, 1962, 1967, 1970, 1971, 1975, 1976, 1983. *Fairly good, slightly lighter years:* 1957, 1961, 1966, 1969, 1973, 1979, 1981, 1982. *Variable or poor years:* 1951, 1956, 1963, 1964, 1965, 1968, 1972, 1974, 1977, 1978, 1980.

Maturity-span

Great sauternes: 10–100 years; at peak 20–30. *Good sauternes:* 8–40; at peak 10–20. *Lesser wines:* 3–10; peak 4–8. (The finest Graves of great vintages have a 10–30-year-old span; even longer.)

BURGUNDY (RED)

It is difficult to generalize about burgundies. Often the dominant factor is a grower's or merchant's style. Nevertheless, burgundy is essentially different in style, weight and development from claret, and subject to great variations of colour and body (and quality). At best, deep, rich colour, fine ripe *pinot* aroma and fragrance, fairly alcoholic yet velvety, and quicker-developing thanks to a lack of tannic astringency, the result of grape variety, climate and vinification methods.

Côte de Nuits

The main classic red burgundy area producing full, firm long-lasting wines. By *commune* or village-district:

Gevrey-Chambertin At its best – good vintage, great vineyard, top grower – deep-coloured, inimitable bouquet: rich, masculine, complex, with 'meaty' *pinot* aroma; full-bodied, firm yet velvety and long-lasting.

Chambolle-Musigny Almost the opposite: lighter, more gentle, feminine, elegant; noted for fragrance of bouquet. The 'Margaux' of the Côte de Nuits.

Morey-St-Denis Two styles: one big and fruity, the other lighter and looser-textured. At best firm and elegant. Sometimes 'fluffy' and short-lived.

Vougeot The famous Clos is much sub-divided, and variable. Hope for a fairly full, firm, flavoury, long-lasting wine.

Echézeaux Just above Vougeot, more close-knit and elegant; refined, some delicacy.

Vosne-Romanée The centre, the heart of the Côte de Nuits. Colour variable in depth; bouquet rich, fragrant and capable of extraordinary opulence, even spicy. On the palate, deep, rich, velvety but not heavy. At best the epitome of burgundian elegance and style.

Nuits-St-Georges and Prémeaux At best 'copybook', but without the majesty of Chambertin or regal opulence of Vosne-Romanée. Agreeable, fullish, firm, flavoury. Note the smoky oak-reminiscent *pinot* aroma and flavour of some of the finer *domaines* such as Henri Gouges.

Côte de Beaune
Generally more loose-grained, less concentrated and shorter life-span than Nuits. Easy and agreeable, but as with all burgundy, only the best *domaines* will give a true picture of the *pinot* grape and district styles.

Aloxe-Corton No more than pleasant, medium-weight wines except for Le Corton and the top vineyards which sometimes match Chambertin in weight, with full, meaty, slightly roasted *pinot* aroma and flavour. Long-lasting.

Beaune The centre, geographically and in style. At best, not too full, elegant, good *pinot* flavour and balance.

Pommard Not dissimilar, but in Epenots and Rugiens make distinguished, fruity wines which develop and keep well.

Volnay Lighter in colour and style; firm, elegant, a certain delicacy. Equivalent to Chambolle-Musigny in the Côte de Nuits, but lower-keyed.

Santenay The most southerly of the Côtes, and relatively minor. True Santenay is light in colour and frankly no more than pleasant. Do not expect great depth or finesse.

Red burgundy vintages
Great years: 1911, 1915, 1919, 1923, 1928, 1945, 1947, 1949, 1959, 1971, 1978. *Good years:* 1924, 1926, 1929, 1933, 1934, 1937, 1948, 1952, 1953, 1955, 1961, 1962, 1964, 1966, 1967, 1969, 1970, 1976, 1981, 1982, 1983. *Fairly good years:* 1954, 1957, 1972, 1973, 1974, 1977, 1979, 1980. *Poor years:* 1951, 1956, 1958, 1960, 1963, 1965, 1968, 1975.

Maturity-span
Great wines: 8–30 years. *Good wines:* 6–15. *Lesser wines:* 3–8. (Some top-class wines of the 1920s are still most attractive. It is hard to generalize.)

BURGUNDY (WHITE)

Virtually all white burgundy is pale in colour, and dry. Exceptionally hot vintage years, like 1959 and 1964, will produce a deeper colour, more body and very slight sweetness, and wine from top-class vineyards in other fine years may also have more colour and richness.

Chablis
Noted for its appealing pale straw-yellow colour with greenish tinge; firm, steely bouquet; and in particular, for its dryness and crisp, rapier-like, quality: austere yet subtle and long-flavoured.

Côte de Beaune
Puligny-Montrachet In weight and style not unlike Chablis but the best have a noticeable and very fragrant smoky *chardonnay* aroma. Firm, crisp, refreshing on the palate. 'Copybook' white burgundy. Leflaive is supreme.

Le Montrachet Rich, yellow colour, shot with gold as it matures; deep, complex, rich, 'smoky' bouquet. Dry, warm, nutty, long flavour, fragrant aftertaste.

Bâtard-Montrachet Fine, full, dry, oaky. Substantial and of high quality.

Chevalier-Montrachet Refined, lighter, elegant.
Chassagne-Montrachet Not unlike its neighbouring *commune*, Puligny, but perhaps slightly less elegant, less austere. (Also produces excellent red wine.)
Meursault Often yellower in colour; fine bouquet; broader texture and character.
Corton-Charlemagne Noted for its full, nutty, vanilla-oak aroma and flavour. Full-bodied, long-lasting.

White burgundy vintages

Great years: 1952, 1967, 1969, 1971, 1978. *Good years:* 1953, 1955, 1959, 1961, 1962, 1964, 1966, 1970, 1974, 1976, 1979, 1981, 1982, 1983. *Average years:* 1957, 1972, 1973, 1975, 1977, 1980. *Poor years:* 1956, 1958, 1960, 1963, 1965, 1968.

SOUTH BURGUNDY

South of the Côte d'Or, between Chagny and the outskirts of Lyon, are a string of relatively minor districts producing pleasing, fairly distinctive but not particularly distinguished wines.

Chalonnais

Rully and Mercurey make stylish medium-light red wines of a generally burgundian character; fruity, and best drunk fairly young. Montagny makes good, well-balanced, dry white wine, pleasing but not great.

Mâconnais

Mâcon rouge and Mâcon blanc are at best agreeable, clean, wholesome lightish red and dry white. Do not expect more. Pouilly-Fuissé, though a cut above, is over-rated and over-priced. At best it is pale, dry, clean and crisp; no great subtlety or memorable distinction.

BEAUJOLAIS

There are two sorts of genuine beaujolais: the currently fashionable, modern-vinified wines which take a lead from *beaujolais nouveau.* Their characteristics are a palish, pink-red colour; very pronounced, almost scented *gamay* aroma; dry, very light (thin in poorer years), flavoury and with marked, refreshing acidity. To be drunk young. However, the finest, worth seeking out, are still the unblended single-vineyard wines made by older methods: deeper and more substantial in colour and body, with a deep, elegant, more vinous *gamay* bouquet and flavour, which improves with some bottle-age. (Not to be confused with the plummy, stewed, characterless, commercial 'grocer's' beaujolais.)
  Beaujolais blanc is pale and dry, often with slightly more body than Mâcon blanc or even Pouilly-Fuissé.

Beaujolais vintages

The rare recent classic years: 1967, 1969, 1970, 1971, 1973, 1976. Avoid poor years. Though made every year it is not consistent. Beaujolais can be thin, feeble and bitter. Much of late has been undistinguished and over-priced.

RHÔNE (RED)

The main characteristics of the Rhône reflect the nature of the terrain, and sun. Deep and very purple when young; full, heavy, alcoholic, less elegant, less acidity than burgundy. Bouquet the least interesting feature.

Châteauneuf-du-Pape
Most people's idea of a Rhône wine: deep-coloured (unless a poor year or speedy vinification), four-square, hefty, fruity, soft yet good balance. Bouquet vinous, but no strong varietal aroma owing to the *mélange* of grapes. Tannin and acidity less marked than in Bordeaux.

Hermitage
Although deep and purple when young, a contrast to Châteauneuf in style: less heavy, with finer bouquet, considerable fruit, more refinement and balance. Sometimes claret-like. Improves with maturity.

Côte Rôtie
Some of the weight and 'heat' of Châteauneuf, with the style and elegance of Hermitage. Fine, long-lasting.

Lirac, Ventoux, Gigondas
Although from the hot southern Rhône, making lighter, almost beaujolais-like wines, at best delightful, fruity and not too serious; often lacking depth and finesse.

Tavel rosé
The nearest rosé to a red wine. Tavel's most notable feature is its dryness, body and certain austerity. Less frivolous than most rosés.

RHÔNE (WHITE)

Palish in colour, more body than white burgundies, and less acidity. Bouquet not very marked save for really good Hermitage blanc, Condrieu and Château Grillet.

Châteauneuf-du-Pape blanc
Not often seen, but in a good year slightly sweet and with unusual character. Fullish colour and body; deep, rich.

Hermitage blanc
A lemon-tinged straw colour; a squeeze of lemon peel in the often stylish bouquet and flavour. Dry, often refined.

Château Grillet
Unusual, and deserving its unique appellation. In a good year (e.g. 1969) deep yellow in colour; vinous, rich, slightly smoky bouquet; dryish, fairly full, rich, stylish, original, slightly caramel-tinged flavour.

Rhône vintages
Very good years: 1929, 1949, 1952, 1953, 1955, 1957, 1959, 1960, 1961, 1962, 1964, 1966, 1967, 1969, 1970, 1976, 1978, 1979, 1982. *Moderate years:* 1971, 1972, 1974, 1977, 1980, 1981. *Poor years:* 1956, 1963, 1965, 1968, 1975.

LOIRE

Total contrast to Rhône. Mainly white, very dry to medium-dry; lighter, with pronounced refreshing acidity.
Sancerre and Pouilly-Fumé Both pale, slightly green-tinged; forthcoming, piquant, raw blackcurrant *sauvignon-blanc* aroma; very dry, light (thin in poor years), a piquant fruitiness and high acidity. Over-fashionable.
Vouvray Although with high acidity, much broader in style than Sancerre, with pleasant, not very pronounced, waxy-vanilla aroma. Both dry and medium-sweet (*demi-sec*). The latter can be long-lasting, developing honeyed richness. Also pleasing *pétillant* and sparkling wines.

Saumur Thin but flavoury whites and red (Champigny). Excellent sparkling wines, lively with attractive grapey aroma, medium-dry, light and clean.

Chinon and Bourgueil The two main red wine districts. Medium, beaujolais-like colour: violet when young. Marked piquant raspberry-like aroma. Dry, light, very flavoury and fruity, but tart and thin in lesser years.

Savennières Yellow; elegant waxy bouquet; dry, firm, elegant and finely balanced.

Coteaux du Layon Yellow; rather underplayed lanolin aroma that deepens and improves with age. Main features: semi-sweetness, rich ripe attractive fruitiness and marked acidity. Bonnézeaux and Quarts-de-Chaume keep magnificently, indeed need bottle-age. Good summer pudding wines.

Muscadet Near to nondescript in colour and bouquet; pretty low-keyed in flavour too. Main feature bone-dryness, but clean, zestful, the best refined.

Loire vintages

Great classic years: 1921, 1937, 1947, 1959, 1964, 1983. *Good years:* 1969, 1970, 1971, 1973, 1974, 1975, 1976, 1978, 1979, 1982. (Only the finest Vouvrays and Coteaux du Layon will last 15 years or more. The very dry whites are thin and over-acid in the poorer vintages and do not keep well.)

ALSACE

In Alsace, the wines are named after grape variety and not district. Virtually all are white, most are dry; overall honest and reliable.

Riesling Main feature: firm fruit and steeliness of flavour; dry, crisp acidity.

Gewürztraminer Main feature: spicy-grapey bouquet and flavour. Soft, fatter, less acid.

Muscat Assertive grapey bouquet, but surprisingly dry, light, sometimes austere.

Tokay, Pinot Somewhat indistinctive dry wines overshadowed by the first two classic grapes.

Sylvaner Lower-keyed, less pronounced characteristics. Dry, mild.

Alsace vintages

Good years: 1966, 1967, 1969, 1970, 1971, 1973, 1976, 1979, 1981, 1982, 1983. *Moderate years:* 1974, 1975, 1978, 1980. *Thin years:* 1963, 1965, 1968, 1972, 1977.

CHAMPAGNE

All-important is the name of the *marque*, though most major champagne houses produce a de luxe blend of some refinement and distinction. Whether the full, meaty classics (like Krug and Bollinger) or pale, light *blanc de blancs* (Taittinger for example), essential characteristics of a fine champagne are:

APPEARANCE: appealing palish colour with a steady, continuous flow of small, evenly spaced bubbles. With age the colour deepens to gold, sparkle less lively.

BOUQUET: the next major feature is a firm vinous bouquet, with either a rich meaty style or a nutty, smoky-charred *pinot chardonnay* aroma.

PALATE: bone-dry to dryish; light and firm to full, depending on the house style. What distinguishes fine champagne from other sparkling wines is finesse, elegance, length of flavour and crisp, positive finish.

Champagne vintages
'*Declared vintages*': 1923, 1928, 1937, 1943, 1945, 1947, 1949, 1952, 1953, 1955, 1959, 1961, 1962, 1964, 1966, 1969, 1970, 1971, 1973, 1975, 1976, 1978, 1979, 1982.

CAHORS

Although recently upgraded, the wines from this famous old area are rarely seen outside France, and the 'black' Cahors almost never. At best deep characterful substantial reds, soft, fullish, long-lasting.

MIDI

The Gard, Hérault and Aude areas produce a vast amount of white and red – but not for the connoisseur to linger over. At best they make agreeable table wines. Some, like Fitou, have character and flavour. However, perhaps the most interesting, but little seen outside France, are the classic *vins doux naturels*: 'muted' sweet dessert wines such as Lunel, Muscat de Frontignan and (in the Rhône) Beaumes de Venise. All have a palish tawny colour, an attractive, muscatelle-grapey aroma and are sweet and fullish but not heavy like port; easy, raisiny-flavoured wines with refreshing end-acidity.

PROVENCE

Solid, respectable but stodgy reds; dry, rather unexciting whites; and dry, rather zestless rosés, the main attraction being a fancy bottle. Fine for drinking on the spot. Affords the peripatetic wine lover happy explorations to discover the occasional outstanding *domaine*, such as Ott (a rosé best served at room temperature) and Vignelaure (deep, distinguished red). Bandol can be good.

JURA

Frankly, the red, white, rosé and sparkling wines from this area, with a few exceptions, are sound, quite appealing but commercial, bland and fairly undistinguished. The Jura is, however, the cradle of one of the most original wines in the world: the *vin jaune* of Château-Chalon. Yellow in colour, with strange, nutty bouquet; dry, austere, fairly full-bodied: a cross between an old fino sherry and Tokay *szamorodni*.

The white wine of Etoile is very dry, straw-flavoured and of good quality. Nearby, Château d'Arlay makes dry white wine of rare distinction.

GERMANY

From the point of view of the connoisseur, German wines are white, ranging from dry and light to exceptionally sweet and rich; in quality and style between insubstantial and short, to deep, rich, refined and long-flavoured. There is much bland commercial wine.

The range, thanks to oenology and the new German wine laws, is infinitely less varied than of old. Real character and quality depend on dedicated growers. Happily, there are still quite a few left.

The essential thing to bear in mind is that the German wine-makers' ideal is 'fruity-acidity': a combination of delicacy, ripe-grapey quality, fragrance and refreshing acidity. However, thanks to advanced wine-making techniques and a rather contrived efficiency, quality standards are levelling out and the grape style, sweetness and consistency seem to mask district, soil, micro-climate and other local variations. Perhaps the 'ideal' is now too easily reached at the expense of character and individuality. Nevertheless, the great estates in the classic areas continue to produce fine wines. Quality and vintage variations are still very important.

The German wine enthusiast will be interested in the clearly defined fine wines (*Qualitätswein-mit-Prädikat*):

- *Kabinett:* natural, unsugared wines of some quality.
- *Spätlese:* late-picked, i.e. ripe, grapes. Intensity, weight, character and sweetness vary from district to district, grower to grower, year to year, but generally speaking, palish in colour, dry to medium-dry.
- *Auslese:* from selected riper bunches. As with *spätlesen*, variations of sweetness and body depend on place and vintage. *Auslese* wine is richer, riper, usually, but not necessarily, sweeter, and of fine quality.
- *Beerenauslese:* from individually selected very ripe grapes. Usually a fuller yellow-gold in colour; most characteristic bouquet: rich, ripe, honeyed scent of *edelfäule*. On the palate: sweet, fullish, rich, ripe, often grapey, with fine balancing acidity. Becomes softer and more complex with age. Long-lasting.
- *Trockenbeerenauslese:* from select, over-ripe, shrivelled grapes. Yellow-gold, deepening to fine old-gold with age; concentrated essence-of-grapes aroma, often raisiny but when immature less assertive than the smell of *beeren-auslesen*. Very sweet, very rich, highly concentrated; often with low alcohol but high degrees of sugar and acidity. The world's rarest and richest dessert wines. Very long-lasting.

RHEINGAU

Riesling reigns supreme in this district and produces fine, firm, steely wines with intense bouquet and fragrance; dry to medium-dry, long finish. Also, in suitably fine years, outstanding dessert wines with incredible concentration, richness and refinement. Long-lasting. Districts provide thematic variations: for example, Eltville wines are light but firm and elegant, Rauenthal rich, almost spicy, Hochheim masculine, four-square, more earthy.

RHEINHESSEN

Generally softer, more 'open', less condensed, attractive ripe fruity wines.

PFALZ (PALATINATE)

Germany's most southerly great wine district, just north of Alsace. Essentially more substantial, deep grapey wines. Even the dry rieslings have a touch more body and richness; the more old-fashioned Pfalz wines have a weight and earthiness of their own. Under-rated.

NAHE

Fruit-salad bouquet; firm, medium-light, crisp-bodied. Can be quite dry. Half-way, geographically and in style, between the Rheingau and Mosel.

MOSEL/SAAR/RUWER

Usually pale, green-tinged and often *spritzig* (very slight effervescence); fruity, light, 'high-toned' *riesling* aroma; dry to medium-dry, usually light, low in alcohol, but enormously appealing with its characteristic refreshing acidity. In exceptional years, *beerenauslese* and *trockenbeerenauslese* quality wines can be made.

In essence, both Saar and Ruwer are Mosel in style. Special characteristics: peach-like bouquet; often very dry and with fine, steely acidity, delicacy and subtlety. Thin, verging on tartness in lesser years.

BADEN

To the east of Alsace, Baden produces a large quantity of wine, both commercial and good, though rarely of fine quality. Rather four-square in style; agreeable bouquet and flavour but relatively undistinguished, unsubtle and lacking zest. The reds are not very deep in colour, lacking the character and firmness of their French counterparts.

FRANCONIA (WÜRZBURG)

Known generally as Steinwein: fine dry steely wines from Würzburg, like *grand cru* Chablis, yet with Germanic fruit and acidity. *Sylvaner* also thrives here, producing wines of unusual firmness and quality.

German vintages

Great years: 1949, 1953, 1959, 1964, 1971, 1976, 1983. *Good years:* 1955, 1961, 1966, 1967, 1975, 1979, 1981. *Light years:* 1962, 1970, 1973, 1974, 1978, 1980, 1982. *Poor, thin years:* 1956, 1960, 1963, 1965, 1968, 1972.

AUSTRIA

Although there is a family resemblance, it is a mistake to compare Austrian whites with German Rhine wines. They look similar, have variations of a delicate grapey bouquet and are lightish in style but soft-edged, the fine wines lacking that distinguishing fruity-acidity and length. The *grüner-veltliner* grape grown in the Wachau district typifies the soft, easy Austrian style. High-quality dessert wines, *beeren* and *trockenbeerenauslesen* are made, but again, though good, often lack the length and breed of the German equivalent (but they are half the price).

Some top-class individual growers and commercial firms. Worthy of greater attention, and good value.

HUNGARY

This once most characterful and varied wine country is now dominated by co-operatives. Doubtless overall quality has improved; certainly the wines are good value. The range of table wines is far wider than in Austria, amongst which the whites are best, though the highest quality they are allowed to attain is the equivalent of *spät-auslese*. Look for softness, almost milkiness of bouquet and flavour. The famous reds from Eger are robust and assertive but lack finesse – ideal for paprika dishes.

TOKAY

This area stands out; it is one of the unique classic wine areas of the world.

● *Szamorodni:* the natural white wine of the region. Pale yellow in colour, characteristic appley nose of the *fürmint* grape, either quite dry or slightly sweet. Unusual flavour, fullish, quite good length.

● *Aszu:* ranges in colour from straw to deep yellow, golden-tinged with age. Pronounced appley nose, unlike any other wine aroma. Graduations of sweetness up from two *puttonyos* slightly sweet, three *'putts'* roughly medium-sweet, four and five *'putts'* rich dessert wines. Fairly full-bodied but not heavy; rich, attractive appley flavour, good acidity and finish.

● *Essence:* no longer made for sale though an *Aszu-Essencia*, somewhat on a par with the former six *puttonyos*, is now marketed. Like an *aszu* but more luscious and rich.

Tokay Essence of old vintages varies from deep amber to deep tawny and has a very heavy sediment; a magnificent concentrated, raisiny, almost pungent nose (a cross between old Malmsey and a *trockenbeerenauslese*); very sweet on the palate, rich, concentrated, with high acidity and a penetrating, lingering flavour and aromatic aftertaste. They appear to have unlimited life.

SWITZERLAND

There are three main areas, the Suisse-Romande, the German-speaking areas and the Italian-speaking areas. They produce a variety of reds and whites, ranging from commercial to moderately good; for local drinking.

In the Suisse-Romande, the best reds, made from the *pinot noir* grown on the chalky soil of the upper Rhône, are soft, mild and of a burgundy character. The whites, from the *chasselas* grown on the shores of Lac Leman are often rather yellow, have fruit but tend to lack zest.

Reds from the German-speaking areas are generally light and unimpressive; the whites, from the *riesling* and *müller-thurgau* grapes are fresh and pleasant for early drinking.

The Italian-speaking areas produce wines of little interest except for a pleasant mild *merlot* from the canton of Tessin.

ITALY

An immense range of wines: all shades of colour, type and strength. Although quality can be high, connoisseurs' interest tends to be local except for the acknowledged classics.

CHIANTI

Made from four grapes, the balance, as in Bordeaux, can vary from district to district and year to year. What are the distinguishing features? First, a rich garnet hue, deep when young, warm brick-red when mature; second, a deep, slightly earthy and complex flavour with a characteristic 'upturned' finish: tannic and slightly bitter.

Chianti vintages

Great years: 1962, 1964, 1967, 1971, 1975, 1978. *Very good years:* 1945, 1947, 1949, 1952, 1955, 1957, 1968, 1969, 1970, 1977, 1979. *Good years:* 1950, 1958, 1959, 1973, 1974. *Quite good years:* 1946, 1948, 1961. *Average years:* 1953, 1956, 1960, 1965.

BRUNELLO

Brunello di Montalcino is widely regarded as one of, if not the greatest of, Italian reds. Of the Chianti family, but very deep brown-purple in colour, a 'hot' concentrated aroma and flavour and swingeing finish. Immense keeping power and longevity. Expensive.

BAROLO

The favourite amongst English connoisseurs, possibly because it is nearest to their idea of a classic red. Characteristics: fine deep colour, fruit and finesse on nose and palate; full-bodied, yet finely balanced. Tannic when young, needs ageing, keeps well.

Barolo vintages

Great years: 1947, 1958, 1961, 1964, 1971, 1978, 1982. *Very good years:* 1945, 1952, 1967, 1970, 1974, 1979, 1983. *Good years:* 1951, 1954, 1955, 1957, 1965. *Fairly good years:* 1946, 1950, 1962, 1968, 1969, 1976, 1980. *Average years:* 1949, 1956, 1959, 1966, 1973, 1975, 1981.

VALPOLICELLA

A lighter, elegant red from near Verona.

SOAVE

One of the best-known dry whites. They used to be yellow and flat owing to over-maturing in cask. Now they are fresher and altogether more pleasant and reliable.

MARSALA

One of the classic fortified wines of the world; deep, plummy-purple when young; sweet, meaty, almost malty nose; very sweet, full, rich, earthy/volcanic burnt flavour, with a tangy-acid, sometimes slightly bitter, finish.

PORTUGAL

A wide range of table wines, many with character and above-ordinary quality. The main districts and styles are:

MINHO

Vinho verde can be white or red. Both are light, with slight to marked effervescent prickle and very high acidity that can be raw, thin, even tart in the wrong context. Commercial wines are slightly sweeter, acidity toned down.

Madura Not a district but a 'mature' white wine, heavy and flat-tasting – strange to modern taste buds.

DÃO

Reliable reds and whites, the latter sound but rather dull and lacking character. The best red Dão is full in colour and body, with positive bouquet – classic, but a little earthy – and fine flavour and finish.

COLARES

Red, rare and worth seeking out. They hold colour and age well; deep meaty nose; rich but not heavy in style.

SETÚBAL

The Moscatel de Setúbal is an old classic grapey dessert wine. Pale tawny-brown in colour; light, clear muscatel-grape aroma and flavour; sweet, of course, but not heavy in style.

PORT

All port is fortified with brandy, full-bodied and with a high alcoholic content. Red port is sweet. These are the main styles:

Ruby Should be full and true ruby in colour; fruity 'peppery' nose, not unlike young vintage port; invariably sweet, full and fruity. Tends to be strapping and hefty.

Tawny A true tawny, aged in the wood, surprisingly pale in colour with an attractive amber-tawny hue and positive, sometimes lemon-yellow, rim; its next most noticeable feature is the soft nutty (cobnuts, brazils) bouquet – sweet and harmonious. Invariably sweet on the palate but not heavy, indeed usually lightish, with gently rich, soft but nutty, extended flavour, and fine aftertaste. Lesser tawnies lack these characteristics.

White Palish, yellow-tinged; nose somewhat characterless; rarely truly dry, usually medium-dry and a trifle heavy and dull. Pleasant though lacking the freshness of sherry and the rich tang of a dry madeira. Serve cold.

Vintage port Modulations depend on the vintage, age and shipper's house style; quality is reliably high amongst the major port houses.

Young vintage port is deep, very purple, often opaque; rather peppery, alcoholic and unyielding on the nose; very sweet, very full-bodied, fruity but slightly rasping.

Mature vintage port will have shed its colour and become medium-deep, much more tawny-hued; the bouquet will have ripened and developed overtones, sometimes liquorice-like. When very old the fruit fades leaving the brandy exposed. The maturing wine dries out, becoming lighter in body, softer and more harmonious. Styles range from Noval – generally soft, light, feminine and forward to Taylor – full, with firm 'backbone', great power, depth and longevity.

Port vintages

Generally 'declared' vintages: 1896, 1900, 1904, 1908, 1912, 1920, 1924, 1927, 1934, 1935, 1945, 1947, 1948, 1955, 1960, 1963, 1966, 1970, 1975, 1977. *Lighter or limited declaration vintages:* 1911, 1917, 1922, 1931, 1942, 1950, 1954, 1958, 1962, 1967, 1978, 1982.

Maturity-span

Great classics: 12–120 years, at peak 15–40. *Good vintages:* 12–30 years.

MADEIRA

One of the three really great and traditional fortified wines of the world. Range: fairly dry to very sweet. Essential characteristics: rich burnt-tangy bouquet and flavour, and fairly high acidity. The rare top-quality wines have remarkable longevity. Some commercial blends are dull. Basic styles are named after grape varieties.

Sercial The palest, deep 'fino' yellow, sometimes amber; the freshest, most mouth-watering aroma, but still with burnt-tangy character; dry to medium-dry, the lightest, but still with a fair amount of body.

Verdelho Varying amber-brown shades; nose deeper, richer, more tangy; medium-dry to medium-sweet, medium-full bodied, fairly rich attractive tangy wine with good acidity.

Bual Deeper, warm oloroso-type amber-brown; rich, more 'volcanic', meaty and assertive madeira tang; sweet, rich, fine-flavoured.

Malmsey Like Bual but sweeter and softer, with a rather more grapey-rich flavour added to the burnt-volcanic character. Intensely rich and attractive.

Old vintage and old solera

The many authentic old solera and vintage madeiras have a common denominator: great richness of colour, powerful bouquet and length of flavour. A true old madeira has a positive tawny-brown colour with ruddy hue in the middle and pronounced greeny-amber rim; strong burnt aroma, high acidity; sometimes sweetness fades, but maintains rich, complex flavour, with extraordinarily powerful tang and extended finish.

Life-span of the finest vintages and soleras

Longest-living after Tokay essence: 100 years or more.

SPAIN

The mass of Spanish table wine, red and white, is of ordinary to good commercial quality. Reds range from light to fairly full; whites are less appealing, the aroma of some being positively unattractive. Few will engage the attention of the connoisseur, though some do deserve it.

RIOJA

The major region producing wines of quality, particularly the reds which are of Bordeaux type but often more supple and attractive than all but the best young claret. Fairly deep in colour; agreeable, fruity, sometimes classic, almost cedary, aroma; dry but not over-tannic, pleasant medium-weight, soft through cask-age; fine balance and flavour.

Penedès One family firm, Torres, is making outstandingly good and moderately priced wines, both red and white.

SHERRY

Basically dry white wine, but with a wide range of styles within the two basic 'families': fino and oloroso. The former are usually dry and the latter, though starting dry, generally have sweetening wine blended in.

Fino Characteristics: paleness of colour, fine lemon straw-yellow; refined, positive fresh *flor* aroma (less marked on lower quality wines); dry, light, fresh, with long crisp finish. Not very alcoholic.

Manzanilla A fino from Sanlúcar, usually very dry and with a fine tangy flavour.

Amontillado Deeper in colour; light amber-brown. Fine-quality amontillados have a very slight fino-reminiscent smell but are richer and distinctly nutty. Dry to medium-dry, slightly fuller in body and nutty flavoured.

Palo Cortado A rarer and refined version of amontillado: similar colour and weight; dryish but a certain richness, nuttiness, vinosity and length of flavour.

Oloroso Total contrast to fino: deeper in colour, ranging from deep amber to warm amber-brown; complete absence of *flor* tang; softer, sweeter on nose and palate. Medium to full-bodied. The perfect mid-morning wine.

Cream An extension of oloroso, sometimes paler; certainly very sweet and soft.

Brown Now almost totally out of fashion. Deep and brown, with a burnt oloroso aroma; very sweet, heavy.

Pedro Ximénez The ultimate brown sherry: opaque colour; powerful, tangy, burnt-grapes aroma; very sweet, heavy, highly concentrated but fine acidity. Magnificent in its way but rarely offered commercially now.

UNITED STATES

Once condescendingly known as 'domestic' and lacking the snob appeal of 'imported' wines, the tables have turned. The development over the past 10 years has been astonishing.

CALIFORNIA

The scale, variety and quality of Californian wines are not to be underestimated: red, white, rosé, sparkling, fortified and 'flavoured'; mass-produced, sound, commercial, refined, even rarefied. Amongst the fine wines, grape variety takes precedence over area. Even though the Napa Valley is undoubtedly the 'Mecca', other districts are also known to possess actual or potential 'classic' vineyards. The wine maker is all-important.

Cabernet sauvignon The finest red, widely planted. Tends to be used alone, unblended. Characteristics: more consistently deep-coloured than in Bordeaux, often opaque and very purple when young, maintains its depth of colour better than claret with age; often a pronounced blackcurrant, recognizably *cabernet*, aroma but usually with earthy/volcanic overtones; slightly less dry than claret, often full-bodied, hefty wines full of fruit, rich in iron and quite tannic. Can be magnificent; long-lasting.

Zinfandel Unique to California: variable, but mainly satisfactory red, not unlike *cabernet* in weight, character and longevity. Possibly nearest to a Barolo in style.

Pinot Not to be compared with burgundy. *Pinot* in California produces a deepish-coloured, full-bodied, rich, rounded wine but with a 'stewed' and earthy quality. Most are devoid of the classic *pinot* aroma and flavour. Improvements are being made.

Chardonnay Outstandingly the most successful varietal in terms of true classic style and quality. Colour ranges from palish to buttercup-yellow; remarkable *chardonnay* aroma: oak-vanilla tang, richness and freshness; dry to medium-dry, never very light—more like a Corton-Charlemagne or Bâtard-Montrachet in weight and style. The best have a remarkably clean true varietal flavour and quality, length and aftertaste.

Johannisberg riesling Palish, fairly fruity, medium-dry and of general Germanic character but often, of course, lacking the inimitable freshness and fruity-acidity of a Rheingau. However, some outstanding sweet wines are now being made with *botrytis*-induced grapes up to finest *beerenauslese* quality, also some early-picked dry wines.

Emerald riesling Pale, clean, attractive grapey aroma; medium-dry, fairly light, clean and fruity. Not a refined wine but consistently attractive.

Fumé blanc Although not absolutely comparable with the light acidic *blanc-fumé* of the Loire, Robert Mondavi produces a consistently successful version: pale; refreshing, fruity aroma; dry, appetizing and with crisp finish.

Gewurztraminer Some of the spiciness and softness of the Alsace prototype but lacking complexity and delicacy. Plenty of flavour.

Napa vintages

Exceptional years: 1941, 1951, 1958, 1959, 1964, 1966, 1968, 1970, 1973, 1974, 1978, 1981. *Good years:* 1955, 1960, 1961, 1965, 1975, 1980, 1982, 1983. *Moderate years:* 1962, 1963, 1967, 1969, 1971, 1972, 1976, 1977, 1979.

NEW YORK STATE

The home of jammy, boiled-sweet-like wines made from native American vines and hybrids. Until recently the only light in this wilderness was provided by a remarkable grower and wine maker, Dr Konstantin Frank. Other *vinifera* growers have recently followed suit and some excellent pure wines are now being made, notably *Johannisberg rieslings* and *chardonnays*.

AUSTRALIA

To the elder generation of Englishmen, Australian wine conjures up an iron-tonic 'burgundy'-type wine sold in flagons. The scene in Australia is totally different, the technology and enthusiasm resembling those of California but with far older traditions.

The range of styles and qualities is enormous. The practice of many big commercial firms, as well as small wineries, to produce a wide range, blending from different grapes and different regions, adds to the profusion – and confusion – of nomenclature.

HUNTER VALLEY

Perhaps the oldest classic district, in New South Wales, north of Sydney. The home of the *shiraz*, producing a rich, earthy burgundy/Rhône-style wine with the most evocative of all aromas: 'sweaty saddle'; also of the *semillon*, less interesting dry whites, and, a recent development, of the rare *chardonnay* (Tyrrell and Max Lake produce two notable examples). Good and big producers include McWilliams and the ubiquitous Lindeman's; Rothbury sets the pace, Tyrrell the standards.

BAROSSA

A vast and hugely successful wine valley in South Australia, north of Adelaide, with long-established family businesses like Yalumba and precocious newcomers like Wolf Blass; the enormous Kaiserstuhl co-operative (excellent *rieslings*); Seppeltsfield (fortified wines); and Saltrams and Orlando (producing *rieslings* of outstanding quality).

CLARE/WATERVALE

Also north of Adelaide, growing *cabernet*, *shiraz*, *rieslings* and making good *flor* sherries. Wineries include Quelltaler, Chateau Clare (new), Stanley Leasingham and Sevenhills.

ADELAIDE AND SOUTHERN VALES

In a suburb is preserved one of the great classic vineyards of Australia: Grange, whose Hermitage is deep, rich and magnificent, the Latour of the southern hemisphere. To the south of Adelaide are small family wineries like D'Arenberg Osborne and Kay's Amery; and large wineries like Seaview, Hardy's (magnificent ports) and the old Chateau Reynella, all producing a wide range of wines.

COONAWARRA

An extraordinary strip of red earth in the middle of nowhere, first planted early this century, only lately recognized as the 'Médoc' of Australia; magnificent *cabernets* and *shiraz* reds, some good *rieslings* produced by Wynn's, Brand's Laira winery and Redman's.

RUTHERGLEN AND N.E. VICTORIA

An old classic area making a variety of wines, but famed for its magnificent rich tangy *muscats*, the great classic dessert wines of Australia. Best producers include Morris's, Chambers' Rosewood, All Saints and Bailey's Bundarra. Browns at Milawa produce a fine range, including excellent *Rhine-rieslings* and *shiraz*.

Chateau Tahbilk

Nearer to Melbourne and worthy of special mention. Quaint old winery producing *marsanne*, *semillon*, *shiraz* and top-quality *cabernet sauvignon*.

SOUTH AFRICA

Perhaps the most beautiful of all winelands, the Cape, once the home of some very well-known dessert wines, went into a long decline and has only relatively recently pulled out. Its post-war reputation was built upon its excellent sherries, but now many fine wines are being made – magnificent *rieslings* at Nederburg and interesting reds at individual estates. The most at-home white is the *steen*, steely, fine; and, of the reds, the *shiraz*, an unusual style, not unlike its Australian counterpart. *Cabernet* has not yet achieved real distinction, but there are interesting developments.

ENGLAND

The resurgence of English vineyards has been remarkable. Pioneered by Sir Guy Salisbury-Jones and the late Colonel and Mrs Gore-Browne in the 1950s, small vineyards now abound in southern England, the best sweeping from Norfolk in the east to Wiltshire in the west. Unfortunately, the main hazard for the English grower is still the weather: grapes rarely ripen fully.

Several early ripening white grapes are grown, amongst which *müller-thurgau* has been the most popular, also *seyval* or *seyve-villard*. District styles have not yet clearly emerged, but top vineyards – making better and more interesting wines than many competitors in the Loire and other northerly European districts – include Adgestone, Felstar, Lamberhurst Priory, Pilton Manor and Pulham.

SUMMARY

I should like to end by making four points: first, that the wine lover should deliberately broaden his sights; second, in doing so, that he should make allowances for strange styles and flavours, and appreciate the context – for example, rich food and hot climate – that certain wines were made for and taste best in; third, as witnessed positively by Australia and California (and slightly negatively by Hungary), that wine is as good, and as fine, as the wine drinker requires it to be and will pay for (or the State will allow). Positive, active, articulate connoisseurship and enthusiasm, allied to thriving economies (which allow healthy discretionary incomes) encourage the wine maker to excel up to a point. For, and this is the fourth point, with all the will in the world, *great* wines cannot be made in unsuitable areas, which is why the connoisseur always returns with added appreciation to the well-tried and long-established classics.

IX

ON TASTING EXPERTISE

Although there is a marked difference between what is insipid and what pleases our taste, the interval is certainly not wide between what is acknowledged to be good and what is excellent. **Brillat-Savarin,** The Physiology of Taste, 1825

Experience – and the novice

There are, I believe, two general but little-understood points concerning tasting ability, and they are related. First, the more one has tasted, the less clear-cut may be one's reactions and the less dogmatic one's pronouncements. This is because the experienced taster (almost always a professional) has been exposed to such a wide range of closely related smells and tastes, and has met with so many exceptions to the rules. The corollary is an easily noted one: that the beginner and amateur having fresh perception and an uncluttered vinous memory, is frequently more certain of himself and sometimes more accurate in identification.

Second, a point which may probably be widely accepted but that is rarely admitted: successful 'guessing-game' experts almost always perform in the comparatively limited field of very fine wines and great vintages, the characteristics of which stand out in sharp black and white, compared with the half-tones of middle-quality wines or the bleak wash of the *ordinaires*. It is not uncommon for the highest scorers to be amateurs, for their greatest performances are usually set in an even more limited (however excellent) context, that of their own and their friends' cellars.

I do not wish to belittle the seasoned and discerning amateur palates, or spoil their fun. On the contrary, without such enthusiastic and enquiring attitudes, without lay scholarship, the precarious incentive to produce such wines would waver, to everyone's loss. I merely make these points to keep things in perspective.

Having cleared the ground, I would like to pursue the subject of tasting 'blind'.

Tasting blind

It is my firm opinion (one of the few these days unwhittled by doubts!) that to assess the qualities of a wine by tasting it completely blind, without any hint of what it might be, is the most useful and salutary discipline that any self-respecting taster can be given. It is not infrequently the most humiliating. The first thing it does is to concentrate the thoughts, and expose fresh and unprejudiced senses to the problem of analysing the colour, bouquet and flavour. To know what the wine is before one starts to taste is like reading the end of a detective novel first; it satisfies the curiosity but dampens the interest.

The occasion . . . Should blind tastings and guessing games be conducted at the dinner table? This is perhaps the most vexed question of all. I am sure that my colleagues in the British wine trade, particularly fellow Masters of Wine, will be the first to agree that it is one of the hazards of their occupation to be expected to 'perform' before an anonymous-looking glass of wine and before only too un-anonymous and hideously expectant hosts and fellow guests: to pronounce vineyard, vintage and the name of the cellar-master in 10 seconds flat. It is not that it *cannot* be done, even in this time. It can, but only in rare and exceptional circumstances, and I exclude all known methods of cheating, like bribing the butler. The point is that unless there is an immediate and quite positive 'click' of recognition, the only alternative is an extremely elaborate round-the-houses process of elimination, an intellectual exercise that takes time and may well be acutely boring for those waiting and watching. At a dinner party, particularly, the surest way of offending one's hostess is to undergo these mental contortions, letting one's meal go cold, and possibly even delaying subsequent courses.

. . . and the company Broad-minded professionals don't mind making fools of themselves in the company of others in the business. At least, they reassure themselves, their friends in the trade *know* how really difficult it is to identify wines, and they all have the comforting knowledge of their common manifold blunders. It is another thing to be exposed before, and caught out by, amateurs – perhaps their own customers – who simply don't understand the complexity and problems involved.

Dinner party tastings

I personally subscribe to 'blind' tasting, at least of the principal wines, at a dinner party, but only on the following conditions:

- that the occasion is an appropriate one – good and carefully planned wines with appropriate food.
- that the company should be like-minded, otherwise the whole thing becomes a bit tedious and unbalanced; off-putting for expert and non-expert alike.
- that reasonable time be allowed for thinking about the wine. The host and hostess must time the service of wine and food to accommodate this. Nothing is more irritating and fatuous, in my opinion, than for a host to say 'What is it?' and then blurt out the answer before one has had a chance properly to examine the wine.
- that the length of time is not dragged out and that one is never forced to a complete and final answer if one is not naturally forthcoming. Indeed, in mixed (not just 'genders', but professional and lay) company I think it probably tactless of the host to try to extract nearest answers in a competitive manner. If people want to be sporting, let them have a go. (This can be a good thing, for one is stimulated into thinking along fresh lines by hearing other people's reactions, and one finds perhaps a new point of view engendered.) It should be remembered, on the other hand, that some people can no more guess wines in public than they can stand on a table and sing; their minds become blank as panic sets in!

The dinner-party host has peculiarly difficult responsibilities. There is a danger of two extremes that can be disheartening and deadly, respectively. Disheartening if beautiful wines are produced and not noticed or commented on at all; deadly if too much of a rigmarole is made of the occasion. Even variations in the middle range can be unsatisfactory. It is little satisfaction for a wine-loving guest to enjoy the wine but not to know what it is. The very least that should be provided is a small menu card with the wines listed, to be taken away by the interested guest. Quite frankly, I carry a little note card and make notes furtively or blatantly depending on how well I know the host (or I scribble on the menu).

Menu and wine cards

How does one provide a menu card without revealing in advance the names of the wines? There are at least two ways. One is to provide a small folded card with a seal. When the seal is broken, the list of wines is revealed inside. (I came across this recently, charmingly done, by that most articulate of wine lovers, Tony Alment, one of that excellent breed of civilized medical men who seem to be the universal backbone of wine-loving fraternities.) The other is a variation I occasionally use, slightly more elaborate in that it reveals the identity of each wine in turn. I write the menu on the left-hand side of a stiff card, and the matching list of wines, well spaced, on the right. Each wine name is covered with a finger of paper held in place by a paper clip. Those who can't wait can quietly remove the covers. Those who want to rise to the challenge and persist until they have exhausted their memory banks can do so without keeping everyone in suspense.

The order of wines is in the inverse of that of the guests: the most respectable come last. **Cassagnac**

It is nice to be able to arrive, by deduction, at a district or vintage. But I believe the main benefit of not knowing the wine in advance, even at a dinner party, to be this powerful concentration of thought and appreciative judgment which is, for the professional, a good discipline and, for the amateur, a continual test of discernment.

Before leaving tasting mystique and expertise, I would like to comment on two interesting facets of blind tasting.

First impressions

One is the subconscious, evocative memory that enables a taster, presumably highly sensitive to smells and tastes, to reach a perfect, or at least remarkably accurate, 'answer' to a wine tasted blind. The value of first impressions is well known to tasters but its true significance is less well understood. As we have seen from Chapter 4 on the physical aspects of tasting, the sense of smell, though often a cinderella in development, is primitive and primal, and has the power of recalling a total experience from the memory, seemingly without the intervention of positive thought.

What is most frequently *not* comprehended is that if the memory-brain does not instinctively and immediately produce an intelligible reaction, the reliance on this for the wine in question must be abandoned, and conscious reasoning must begin.

Deduction by elimination

This second approach is totally opposite to the reflex action of the first impression; it requires the exercise of determined intellectual effort; the use of eyes, nose and palate to deduce the answer that the nerve cells and memory failed to conjure up at 'first go'. I personally, at this stage, try to detect the grape used, the regional characteristics and work out a rough age-bracket. Then, by the process of elimination, arrive backwards at the answer, or, at any rate, at an intelligent approximation of district and vintage, with a definite opinion of quality. All this takes time and patience. The results are rarely as spectacular as those produced by the evocative memory. Furthermore it may well bore the bystander, unless the reasoning is concise and thought out aloud to sustain interest. The next chapter deals in greater detail with these important methods and techniques.

No cheating!

The very last word on this subject is an appeal for honesty, tempered with consideration. Cheating and short cuts in the tasting game are self-defeating. The true taster puts his blinkers on, is honest with himself, and is not influenced and led astray by others. On the other hand, the pursuit of zealous tasting expertise should only be pursued in appropriate company, and then only with discretion; otherwise the whole thing becomes a bore.

X

APPRECIATION, RECOGNITION
AND DEDUCTION

The palate, like the eye, the ear, or touch, acquires with practice various degrees of sensitiveness that would be incredible were it not a well ascertained fact. **T. G. Shaw,** Wine, the Vine and the Cellar, 1863

Having covered first principles, the senses, the approach to tasting and, broadly, those elements which give rise to taste, the time has come to dig a little deeper.

Tasting is not just an isolated theoretical exercise; it is usually an assessment of physical attributes in relation to a particular wine or wines, with a specific end in view (see p. 14). It may well have one of the following purposes:

- to assess the quality, state of development and possibly the value of a *known* wine
- to assess the relative quality and value of a known type of wine – possibly one of a range of similar or even identically named wines
- to identify, from its physical taste characteristics, the style, region, quality and maturity of an *unknown* wine.

We might even reduce the taster's problems to a basic two:

- knowing the name and full details of the wine, to judge its true qualities, etc. This boils down to *appreciation* and *assessment.*
- knowing little or nothing about the wine, to find what it is, from an accurate assessment of its characteristics, by tasting alone. This is encompassed by two words: *recognition* and *deduction.*

Before embarking, however, I must stress that what follows must be seen in the context of a relaxed and informal group of like-minded *amateurs* (in the French sense) concentrating their attentions upon the merits of vintage wines. I am not writing about clinical laboratory tests to measure tasting thresholds, to isolate elements, to detect and quantify small differences in new wines made from experimental vines: these worthy endeavours we can leave to viticultural schools and oenological colleges.

Wine competitions

Equally out of court are those formally – and often excellently – organized tasting competitions, inter-district and international, where judges sit in splendid isolation to award medals to the best commercial entries. I am not trying to belittle either approach, though I confess I am confused and bored with some of the scientific approaches to sensory evaluation, with their emphasis on methodology, triangular tests, random numbers and abstruse mathematical formulae. Awarding gold medals can take on nationalistic or political overtones; some are like beauty contests, when it appears to the disinterested onlooker that the really lovely girls have stayed at home. The fact of the matter is that truly fine and great wines are not entered for such competitions, and if they were they would probably be wasted in such mediocre company.

(These remarks do not apply to Australia, where State wine competitions are immaculately organized and taken seriously by producer and public alike.)

APPRECIATION AND ASSESSMENT

Hedonistic approach

At its most elementary level, appreciation manifests itself in a positive liking (or not liking) for a wine, whether at a tasting or at a dinner party. At the same level, discrimination is expressed by a preference for one wine amongst a group of wines.

Wine merchants often find that even people fairly new to wine can be quite discriminating. Given two or three wines to taste, the customer will often express a marked preference for the best-quality wine of a group, price notwithstanding. However, the layman falters in trying to express the degree of quality, and in sifting and describing the individual characteristics which, in combination, have awakened his natural taste instincts.

Relative quality

Without wishing to be condescending, what I am trying to say is that appreciation and simple discrimination are relatively easy. The next stage, assessment, is more complex and requires some background knowledge and tasting experience. Take one very important element, quality, for example. Quality is always relative. Even the best Yugoslav Riesling will be on a lower-quality plane than a good classic Rheingau such as a Rauenthaler Wieshell Riesling Spätlese; the best sparkling Loire wine rates lower than a good *grande marque* champagne; and the best unblended beaujolais is below the peak of a *grand cru* Côte de Nuits. One has to know the relative quality strata before one begins.

Background knowledge

There is a whole kaleidoscope of tastes (and smells) that emanate from the physical characteristics of grape varieties, soil and climatic influences, wine-making techniques and effects of age (see Chapter 6). They reveal style, areas and maturity as well as quality. The greater one's understanding of all these factors, the more accurate and rapid will be one's assessment and final pronouncement.

RECOGNITION AND DEDUCTION

Imagine that you are confronted with a glass containing an unknown wine. The steps which follow the processes of recognition and deduction – are perhaps the most difficult a taster ever has to contend with. He will have to bring to bear *all* his critical tasting faculties and knowledge.

Guessing?

Guessing is not allowed. Or is it? Let's not be too dogmatic, for there is surely only a fine dividing line between the inspired guess and split-second recognition: both may stem from a subconscious signal from the evocative memory. However, what usually happens is that we are baffled and taunted by a half-familiar smell or taste that evades recognition. It remains 'on the tip of the tongue', literally in this case, and the harder we try, the less is revealed.

If there *is* failure of recognition at this stage, the only solution is to 'back out', start again and attempt deduction by a systematic examination of taste characteristics. This needs not just a good palate and a detailed knowledge of regions and vintages, but the ability to link the reactions of the former with the recollections of the latter. This is, unhappily, as difficult as it sounds. There are, however, two useful techniques to bring to bear: elimination and bracketing.

DEDUCTION BY ELIMINATION

The technique of elimination entails a mental exercise. Take the most positively identified characteristics of the wine, compare them with the known characteristics of other wines, and cross off those that do not remotely match up. In other words, first eliminate all the obvious wines it *cannot* be; then consider those it *could* be; finally deduce what it *must* be. This simple and effective method can be used to arrive at the grape variety, style and geographical area; even the district and vineyard. It is also useful to confirm or strengthen opinions previously half-held.

Method

What happens in practice is this: one picks up the glass of unknown wine and examines first its appearance, bouquet and flavour, sifting the normal, straightforward or 'classic' from the unusual or 'foreign'.

Take its appearance first of all. Is it unusually deep (this applies to either red or white) or abnormally pale (red mainly)? Is it strikingly young and purple, or 'sear and yellow'? Is it star-bright or murky or slightly *pétillant*? The important thing is not just to notice these factors but to work out what might cause them. For example, unusual depth of colour in a red wine might be due to a fine hot vintage year in a temperate area like Bordeaux, or might indicate its origin in a sun-baked section of the Rhône valley, or from a particularly hot region like the irrigated areas of South Australia, California or the Cape. It could also arise from the vinification – a long fermentation which extracts a good deal of colour from the skins. With unusually pale-coloured wines the reverse might apply. All these will be clues, pointers. It is vital in the early stages *not* to jump to conclusions, but to leave the tracks open, passing on to the bouquet and then to the taste for a further crystallization of impressions, and then on to the final confirmation. So, I repeat, get as many clues and leads from the appearance as possible; leave doubts hanging in the air and then pass on to the bouquet.

With bouquet, once again one looks for any unusual or outstanding characteristics. First of all, whether there is a distinctive grape aroma and whether it is from a classic region or not. If it is pronounced, and you can recognize the grape, the areas where this grape is never grown can be eliminated. Incidentally, strength of bouquet, in the sense of fullness and forthcomingness, is not the sole criterion, for a fine classic grape aroma can be subdued, even scarcely noticeable, particularly when the wine is young and undeveloped. What one is really looking for is clarity and purity of character. The more indeterminate, 'muddy' and neutral the smell, the poorer the quality.

The most important thing of all is to realize that the combination of appearance and nose can provide many if not most of the clues to a wine's identity. By spotting the main characteristics of each and eliminating all that the wine *cannot* be, one's conclusions can then be confirmed on the palate; or one is left with likely alternatives that remain for the palate finally to sort out and decide.

Confirmation

In what way can the palate aid and confirm? First of all, consider the major taste factors which are noted on the palate: sweetness (in white wine, mainly); the degree of tannin, acidity and alcohol; the extract; the continuity of varietal characteristics (i.e. flavour to match the grape aroma); finesse, breed and, above all, length and intensity of flavour and finish – in short, quality. It is the linking of these taste factors to the colour and smell which should firmly anchor the total impression and lead one straight, or more safely by elimination, to a logical conclusion.

It will be obvious now, if it wasn't before, that one can only eliminate on a broad 'taste front' by having a wide knowledge to match; on a narrow front by having a detailed knowledge. Take heart, for though considerable tasting experience is desirable, it is surprising how much can be achieved by limited experience aided by some theoretical knowledge of grape, district and age characteristics. By constantly reading wine books and articles one can, over a period, gain knowledge of what certain types of wine should taste like, and link the recollection of these characteristics to the actual taste of the wine in the glass. Indeed, I shall go one stage further and say that it is perfectly possible to deduce what a wine is even though one has never tasted it, or its type, before, simply by recognizing taste characteristics one has read or heard about. It would be rash for the taster in such circumstances to say that the wine *is* from such and such a vineyard; better to conclude that it *might well be*. Indeed, to be dogmatic at all in the field of tasting is both risky and tiresome.

What to expect

Now one of the difficulties facing the keen wine lover is finding out what a wine *should* taste like. Few of the many otherwise excellent books on wine actually help here. Nevertheless, if you read widely, an impression of the characteristics of the wines of various areas and districts will eventually be conveyed. A combination of reading, and visits (with tastings, of course) to wine areas is the best way of learning the salient characteristics. Chapter 7 should point the student in the right direction.

Over a period of time, one's memory will be usefully furnished with a library of names and tastes – together with the inevitable exceptions to the rules that ensure that one never has a dull moment!

DEDUCTION BY BRACKETING

To round off the 'technique' section, here is a short exposition upon the useful method of bracketing, followed by two examples of the blind tasting technique in practice. Bracketing also involves elimination. It is most useful when trying to assess the age of a wine.

Vintage deduction

Once again, some knowledge is required, this time of the

vintage characteristics of the area one assumes, or knows, the wine to have come from.* At one end of the bracket will be the oldest vintage it could possibly be; at the other the youngest. The bracket may extend over 10 or 20 years, or even longer in the case of really old wines.

The next stage is to jot down the most appropriate intervening vintages, eliminating the 'off-years' if the wine is robust, well made and 'classic' (and vice versa if the wine is light and feeble) until one is left with three or four possible vintage years. The final piece of elimination follows a thoughtful examination of the wine, comparing it against the known features of those singled-out vintages until, hopefully, one is left with just one inevitable choice of year. Incidentally, it is not sufficient merely to know that 1959, for example, was a big classic year in Bordeaux. It must also be borne in mind that not all the wines of the Bordelais are made in the same way, and that the types of grapes grown and blended can have different effects on the colour, bouquet and taste. One must know how the wines – at any rate the key wines – have developed in different districts, and be aware of the fact that the wines of St-Emilion, for example, and certain red Graves, develop more quickly than the firmer wines of the Médoc. Once again, this sort of information is 'bracketed' in one's mind, and a conclusion often reached by the process of elimination described.

EXAMPLES

The trouble about trying to explain in words techniques that are second nature to the experienced taster is that the whole exercise is made to sound impossibly difficult. This is certainly not the intention. There is nothing I dislike more than the academic use of long words where short ones would do, as if one had to surround oneself with an off-putting protective layer of super-professionalism. My aim all along has been to try and break down the barriers of the unknown into logical and progressive steps. If words are used that sound curious and stultified (or even pure 'winemanship') to the layman, let him remember that every specialist has his own peculiar vocabulary, whether he be a musician, lawyer, gardener or judge of dogs at Cruft's.

To help explain how elimination techniques work in practice, here are two examples of wines tasted blind at a 1970† Master of Wine study course. They were in a range of five unknown white and four unknown red wines. The approach and notes made were precisely as follows:

'Wine No. 1' (red)

Appearance Unusually deep, indicating hot vintage conditions, either naturally or of an abnormally hot summer and early autumn. In other words, from South Australia; or a big classic Bordeaux of a particularly good year, or from the Rhône valley. Just conceivably North African.

Actual colour a normal shade of red but with a marked purple edge to it, indicating immaturity.

*Once again, readers are referred to *The Great Vintage Wine Book* by Michael Broadbent (Mitchell Beazley, London), in which the salient characteristics of each vintage are described.

†As the same principles still apply, I do not see much is gained by updating these examples.

A noticeably heavy bead ('legs') indicating high extract and glycerol. If, as is likely, the wine is from France, the combination of depth of colour and immature purple rules out recent poor vintages like '68 and '65. It is unlikely to be '67; more likely '66 and just possibly '64 if from the Médoc. **Bouquet** 'Classic' and not 'foreign'. This rules out Australia, which often has a peculiar earthiness and 'hot' burnt smell. The grape aroma, however, is not easy to identify; certainly not *cabernet*, *pinot* or *gamay*, which rules out Bordeaux, and Burgundy north and south.

It smells 'sweet', slightly scented, and certainly a heavy-weight – the presence of considerable alcohol can be detected. Although young-looking there is an absence of raw, youthful, mouth-watering acidity on the nose.

By virtue of elimination, and the combination of great weight and lack of the usual raw acidity, one turns to Rhône or possibly North Africa.

Palate Very slight sweetness for a red (i.e. not austerely dry like many a Médoc). As full-bodied as it looks: heavy in the mouth, revealing considerable weight of alcohol, and full of extract. Robust yet curiously soft (lacking the excess tannin and acidity of a Bordeaux of the same weight and youthfulness). A nice, slightly scented flavour; still a little raw, and with a faintly bitter finish.

Conclusions A full-bodied, almost old-fashioned, Rhône wine from the south, around Châteauneuf. Good quality in its way; from an individual *domaine*, and of a recent big vintage, probably 1966.

(The wine was, in fact, Clos du Mont Olivet 1966. Estate-bottled: Reflets du Châteauneuf-du-Pape. Alcoholic content over 14° G.L.)

'Wine No. 2' (white)

Appearance Noticeably deeper than the other whites in the range. Deep, old-gold. Not very bright.

Distinctly an odd-man-out. From depth of colour could be a sweet dessert table wine or from some lesser region – perhaps Spain or southern Italy. Could also be due to considerable age in cask or bottle.

Bouquet Rich, honeyed. Clearly a dessert wine and, although not very distinct, sufficiently 'classic' to rule out Spain, Italy, etc. The honeyed overtones and richness would suggest *pourriture noble*, maturity and bottle-age. Probably a sweet Bordeaux, or just possibly a sweet Loire like Coteaux du Layon.

Palate The sweetness confirmed: in fact a medium-sweet dessert wine. Medium-full bodied. Certainly sauternes (a sweet Loire would have had more acidity and less body)

Clean, straightforward, but with a rather short flavour which rules out first-growth quality but better than an ordinary 'sauternes supérieur'. Balance quite good, indicating a soundly made wine of a fairly reasonable vintage with some maturity.

Conclusions A heavy Barsac or medium sauternes of *bourgeois* quality, 1962 or 1964 vintage.

(The wine was Château Pajot 1964, London-bottled.)

The ultimate test

After all this, it need hardly be re-stated that tasting blind – deducing a wine's precise origin and age – is the most severe test of a taster's true knowledge and ability.

Happily, however, it is not necessary to strive to reach, let alone to have reached, this stage of vinous ability in order to appreciate the taste of wine, and to enjoy drinking it. But if achievement in the higher realms of wine tasting *is* sought, it will now be apparent that a sensitive and trained palate alone is not enough: it has to be supported by real knowledge of areas and districts, of grape varieties, of styles and methods, and of vintage characteristics. And a good technique is helpful.

XI
HOW TO ORGANIZE
A TASTING

The buyer is recommended by Florentinus (Geoponica vii 7) *to taste the wines he proposes to purchase, during a north wind, when he will have the fairest chance of forming an accurate judgement of their qualities.* **Henderson,** A History of Ancient & Modern Wines, 1824

Experienced wine shippers and merchants know perfectly well how to run their own tastings. The aim of this chapter is to advise younger members of the wine trade, amateur wine societies and tasting groups what preparations are necessary and what pitfalls to avoid.

It is assumed that the purpose of a tasting is to present a range of wines in the most favourable light either to induce sales, or simply to learn more about wine.

The first thing is to decide what type of tasting it is to be, what and how many wines are to be shown, and how many people are to participate. Very often, consideration of the latter point will dictate the number of wines and the type of tasting, so this factor will be dealt with first.

How many tasters?

Generally speaking, the seriousness and the effectiveness of a tasting is inversely proportional to the number who attend. A large 'propaganda' tasting, attended by anything from 60 to 300 people, will require a large hall or cellar, a large staff and very careful organization. The consumption, *per capita*, is bound to be greater than at a small tasting; and even if, as is wise, the range of wines is strictly limited, the expense may be out of all proportion to the ultimate benefit.

Forty to 70 guests may be considered the maximum manageable number at a standard stand-up and free-roaming tasting; rather fewer if a lecture-tasting or tutorial is envisaged.

The aim of the tasting

If the tasting is planned to launch a new branded wine, it ought really to be limited to this alone. Rather like the press review of a new model at the British Motor Show, the aim will be to demonstrate the wine's desirable selling points, its drinkability, its price, the weight of supporting advertising and the attractions of the point-of-sale material. The gathering will generally be confined to salesmen, their customers and members of the press, who will be expected to extol the product's virtues. Frankly, this is hardly a tasting in the wine lover's sense, but is not an infrequent type in these days of sophisticated wine marketing.

More traditional are the tastings organized by the wine importer or merchant for his customers, presenting a range of wines of a new vintage or his current seasonal stock-in-trade. These are vital and informative tastings, that benefit both trade and consumer alike. Their proper organization is vital and the principles involved are discussed below.

Wine society or informal group tastings, usually aimed at the education and enlightenment of the members, who share the cost, can be similar in style to trade tastings, and most of the same problems arise. But if the object is to *learn* something about wine, then by far the best type of tasting is the controlled and seated variety in the form of a lecture, with carefully selected wines used as illustrations. An event of this type will stand or fall on the knowledge and ability of the lecturer, and is probably best handled by a professional. The financial virtue of this type of tasting is that it is the most economical in terms of the amount of wine consumed.

How many wines?

At a big trade tasting there may well be from 30 to over 100 different wines on show. It goes without saying that when there is a vast number of samples, the host expects his guests to discriminate, and also to spit out. After all, a trade buyer will only be in the market for wines of a certain type and price, and he won't waste his time, and cloud his mind, by tasting wines right out of the range of his own requirements.

The minute the public is let in, however, discrimination can go by the board. Whereas the wiser and more experienced lay-tasters will concentrate on those wines that interest them most, others will treat the whole thing as a sort of cocktail party and try to drink round the room – in the long run, wasting their time and the wine merchant's money.

It is far wiser for the organizers to be selective and to show only a limited range of say 10–20 wines as outstanding representatives of their type and for price (even fewer if they are fortified wines, i.e. port, sherry, etc.). However, if the types are mixed, do make sure they are grouped clearly and that they are tasted in the right order, heavy sweet wines last.

Horizontal and vertical tastings

For a small club tasting or a lecture-tasting, then six to ten different wines will usually be enough. They must be well chosen, however, and worthy of study in depth. The most useful are 'horizontal' and 'vertical' tastings. Horizontal tastings are wines from different châteaux or different districts but all of the same vintage; vertical tastings compare different vintages of the same wine, i.e. of the same château, or of the same type or district. I have successfully combined a horizontal and vertical tasting on several occasions, with the same vintage of six different châteaux and six different vintages of one of those châteaux. The point of all this is not to make the tasting impossibly complicated but, through the comparisons, to learn more.

How much wine?

For drinking one allows approximately six to eight glasses per bottle, depending on the size of the glasses. For *tasting*, the number of glasses per bottle doubles, even trebles.

Allowing 12–15 tasting measures per bottle, the next thing is to estimate the number one should allow per person. At a controlled lecture-tasting the answer is quite simple, one per person. At a *serious* tasting where there is a big range of wines on show one can plan for a fairly small consumption on the basis that most tasters will try and taste a little of most of the wines, but one should allow for the more popular types of wine and provide adequate supporting stock.

However large or small the range of wines on show, one thing can be banked on: the bigger the crowd, the more *per capita* will be consumed. The hour of the day and duration of the tasting will also have a bearing.

Summing up: with a large range of wines and a small number of tasters, allow one bottle to six or seven people; for a small range and large crowd, one bottle may serve only three or four people. If it is just a casual tasting party, allow at least half-a-bottle a head. But with a smallish number of people at a tutored tasting, one bottle will serve 15 or more tasters.

What time of day?

This short section deals with tastings that are business or social events, and not with internal staff tastings or visits to *chais*. The organizer has to bear in mind not only the appropriate times to taste, from the freshness of palate point of view, but the convenience of his guests. Indeed, the latter is usually of paramount importance. There are, in fact, just two practical alternatives: before lunch or early evening.*

Duration

The timing of an evening function will depend a great deal upon social conventions. The main thing to remember when planning the programme is to leave ample time for the tasting. Twenty minutes or half-an-hour is simply not enough. Half-an-hour may be sufficient if the 'tasting' merely consists of a glass of something prior to a meal, for it then merely comes into the '7 for 7.30' category of invitation.

The length of time allowed for the tasting must be pro portional to the number of wines on show and the number of guests invited. For 10–20 wines and 30–50 people the time allowed should be somewhere between one-and-a-half and two hours. The point is, that although one solid hour of tasting is more than enough for even the hardiest taster, sufficient allowance has to be made for late-comers, early leavers and social chit-chat.

A controlled lecture-tasting is probably best held in the evening. The length of time required will depend partly upon the speaker. Two hours just sitting, sipping and listening is the absolute maximum. On the other hand, it is surprising how long it can take to taste and talk about only half-a-dozen wines. One should aim at about one-and-a-quarter to one-and-a-half hours. Incidentally, it is most important that everyone arrives on time, so invitations should be explicit: 7 for 7.15 prompt, or words to this effect.

Big trade tastings are usually organized in suitable premises (in firms' cellars, even in the town hall) by experienced professionals, so we will confine our attentions to two moderate-sized types of tasting.

A FREE-RANGING TASTING
FOR 20–60 GUESTS

Space and flow

Ideally, the organizer removes everything that will interfere with his table layout and customer-flow. At all costs clutter

---

*I used to think that serious tastings could not take place during a meal, but I have been privileged to attend a quite remarkable series of dinner tastings organized by Joseph Berkmann, one of London's most knowledgeable and enterprising restaurateurs. It surprised me how effective as well as interesting tasting a large range (about 14 wines) at table could be.

must be avoided; there will be little enough room for his own assistants and impedimenta. Crowds bring their own problems and one of the first, too often overlooked, is hats, coats and bags. If there is not a cloakroom or spare room nearby, then set aside a large table for coats, etc.

The most important considerations after this are spatial: there must be enough room for tasters to circulate without obstruction; there must be enough space between the different wines to allow tasters adequate elbow room; and also enough space, preferably barred to tasters, for staff and assistants to service the tasting tables.

Table layout

The key to success is table layout. This will depend on the shape of the room, but basically there are two approaches: to have a series of tables round the room (continuous or spaced) with the tasters circulating in the middle, or to have a 'square' of tables in the centre, enclosing staff and stock. The virtues of the latter are that fewer assistants are needed to supervise the tasting – opening bottles, keeping them in order, removing empty bottles and used glasses – and that the service and stock areas are safely isolated (but bear in mind that assistants have to push through tasters to get to the central reservation).

If a large number of wines are on display it is probably better to arrange the tables around the perimeter of the room; they can be spaced better, and tasters can move from one area to another more easily. Do avoid corners, however, as these can become congested. Staff must be stationed at *each* table section, so at a big tasting this will mean one assistant per two- or three-metre section or per six wines.

Space requirements are often underestimated, particularly the space between different wines. Apart from the discomfort caused by nudgers, wines get mixed up and out of order if set out too closely. To avoid this, allow only four to six bottles to a three-metre trestle table, depending on the number of tasters expected. The more tasters, the wider the spacing.

Sequence

The wines should be laid out in the correct order of tasting and, most important and not always easy, incoming guests must be made aware of the sequence of wines and encouraged to taste in that order. This is where a clearly laid-out tasting sheet comes in handy: list order and table-layout should coincide. One very important point: do not place table number one too near the entrance as a queue of early tasters may form and impede the passage of other guests and assistants. If the room is small it is usually better to start the tasting on the far side to avoid congestion. If there are sweet or fortified wines in a mixed tasting place them at the end of the natural tasting sequence and traffic flow to discourage guests from tasting them first.

Side tables

Still on the subject of layout, and ignoring for the moment decoration and other incidentals, it is better to have quite separate tables for glasses, food and literature. Ideally, the table for glasses and tasting sheets should be placed somewhere between the entrance and the first wine to be tasted. Informative literature of the take-home variety should be handed out from a table by the exit. No purpose is served by burdening guests with supplementary reading matter at the start or part-way through the tasting: there is seldom time to read it during the tasting and the odds are that it will be discarded before the tasting is over.

Placing of spittoons

Spittoons are not easy to place. They should not be on the tasting tables but on the floor, either just in front of the tables (if the wines are well spaced and there is ample room for tasters' feet) *or* sufficiently away from the tables not to trip people up. They are probably best placed two or three metres from the tables, more if large crowds are expected, to allow an appropriate width of passage for circulation and to encourage tasters to retreat from the table with their tasting samples, permitting other tasters a chance to get to the tables. There is nothing more irritating at a tasting than a 'clinging vine' who stations himself semi-permanently by a bottle, helping himself, making notes (one hopes) and spitting, all without moving his feet. An out-of-reach spittoon helps to dislodge the blockers.

A 'TUTORED' TASTING

The room size required must be directly related to the numbers attending: each taster, as well as the lecturer, will need a chair and table space.

Tables essential

Make no mistake about it, tables are vital. It is impossible to conduct this sort of tasting session with tasting sheets, pencils, glasses and possibly maps and other literature on one's lap.

Either individual small tables or desks should be used, allocating one per taster. Larger tables may, of course, be shared. In any case, the spacing per person must be wider than a chair's width. Allow at least a metre per taster so that there is room on each section of table for several glasses in a row, and the tasting sheet.

It is much more comfortable for all tasters to face the lecturer, so only one side of the table should be used. If the tables are in continuous rows then there must be sufficient space between those rows for the assistants to pour or hand out glasses. It is a mistake to assume that fewer helpers are required for lecture-tastings, for although there may be just one lecturer, the timing of the service of the wines is very important and sufficient serving staff or willing volunteers must be available.

Wine service

There are two ways of serving the wine: either pouring into glasses already on the table, or pre-pouring and handing out glasses. I favour the latter. Assuming that a tasting quantity will range from about 10–15 glasses per bottle, it is desirable to have one assistant per bottle, i.e. per 10–15 tasters, otherwise the time taken pouring is apt to disturb the lecturer and fragment the session. It is difficult for tasters to concentrate whilst assistants are moving around with the wine, and if the service is protracted there is always the danger that those who get the wine first will be tempted to taste the wine 'solo' instead of waiting to be guided through the elements of colour, bouquet and taste by the lecturer. Frankly, I think the quickest and fairest way is to pour careful measures into glasses on trays in an adjacent room and hand them out at precisely the moment they are called for by the lecturer.

The problem of spittoons is even more acute with a seated audience. They should be behind the chairs, one between two tasters being ideal. Alternatively, small plastic cups can be placed on the table before each taster. But with a restricted number of wines no harm is done if the wine is swallowed.

DETAILS TO BEAR IN MIND

Tables

It may seem silly to say this, but the essential thing is that tables should be of normal dinner-table height, and firm. In other words, don't use tiny coffee tables or flimsy, unstable trestle tables. Nor should the tables used be too high or too wide, as they can be difficult to serve across.

Table coverings

There are several factors to consider: red wine stains; bottles can scratch; and a white background is essential to show off the colour of the wine. So, cover your table, whether it is plain deal or polished mahogany. If the latter, use a large white cloth with newspaper or some other lining underneath. If an ordinary trestle table is used, a white table cloth or rolls of plain white paper can be pinned to it.

Lighting

This is important, and yet often the least-considered factor. A natural north light is best; failing that, ordinary tungsten or warm-white fluorescent lighting. Ordinary blue fluorescent lighting is disastrous. It gives red wine an unhealthy dark, blue-black tinge and will make it appear far younger and less mature than it really is. Candles add appropriate glamour to the occasion but, truthfully, although a myriad of candles may look pretty, they really don't produce enough of the sort of light in which the colour of the wine can be effectively judged. Mind you, there is no reason why candles, either in proper candelabra or stuck in the top of empty bottles, shouldn't be used in conjunction with artificial light. One or two per table look attractive, and they are useful for observing the clarity of the wine. But do remember: candles consume oxygen and add to the heat of the room.

Service or self-service?

At an ordinary, largish tasting, is it better for the hosts to pour out the wine, or should guests be allowed to help themselves? In practice, whatever is decided, there is usually a bit of both. At a well-attended tasting, the staff will be busy doing several jobs at once and it is fairly certain that they won't be able to spend all their time helping the guests to wine, even if this is supposed to be their main job.

On the other hand, if tasters help themselves too liberally at a free-for-all tasting, then a bit of judicious and tactful pouring will be called for. This will prevent the host's stocks being depleted too rapidly and will encourage guests to taste a wider range more effectively.

Assistants and staff

Do not underestimate the number of people required to help, from supervisor to cloakroom attendant. Numbers and calibre of staff will, of course, depend on the nature of the event, its size and the place.

Small club tastings are usually no problem. Just make sure there are members prepared to lend a hand. Many small- and medium-sized trade tastings will be manned by members of the firm, usually principals and sales staff who know their subject and are identifiable by lapel badges bearing their name and/or that of their company.

When tastings are held in catering establishments – hotels, restaurants or clubs – staff will generally be employed. Even if supervised by a head waiter or 'captain', it should never be assumed that they will know exactly what is required. So a cardinal rule is to *brief all staff before the tasting commences*: where to station themselves, how many bottles to open, how much to pour; to clear glasses and avoid clutter, etc.

Insist on rigorous stock control, with a complete complement of bottles, full or empty, after the tasting, otherwise bottles simply disappear. Another tip is to provide a supply of inexpensive wine or beer for the staff to refresh themselves – preferably afterwards.

Let *one* person be in overall charge. Have enough 'front of house' personnel to host and advise; enough staff or assistants to serve. Don't forget to man the cloakroom and reception table. Make sure everyone knows precisely what he or she is to do.

Spittoons, bottles and funnels

Properly equipped tasting rooms have permanent spittoons of a basin, fountain or flushing variety. At the sort of tastings we have just been discussing, however, mobile spittoons are the order of the day and they run to three types: the pedestal-funnel variety, rather like a fat version of one of the nastier types of road-house ash-tray; the sawdust box or bucket; and the table-top bowl or cup.

Quite the simplest to prepare and satisfactory to use is the sawdust box. This type of spittoon is just a wooden wine case with the top removed and the inside two-thirds filled with sawdust. It is commodious and fairly absorbent; to be on the safe side, line it with oil cloth or polythene. The disadvantage is that it is easy to trip over a box in a crowded room.

If you can't find enough boxes, buckets of sand or sawdust will do. They present a smaller target, however, and knock over more easily. Never use glass tumblers as table-top spittoons: wine spittal looks horrible. Polystyrene or opaque plastic cups are best. Incidentally, empty bottles, with glass or plastic funnels stuck in the neck, seen on tables at many trade tastings, are *not* spittoons. They are receptacles for the taster to empty his glass in before moving to the next wine. Take care that they do not overflow: magnums are most suitable for this purpose. One often wonders about what happens to all the secondhand but almost virginal wine which is accumulated (staff perks? cooking wine? or re-corked as Château Grand-Mélange?).

Glasses

Clear, tulip-shaped, stemmed glasses are desirable. Naturally, at a large tasting, quantity and not quality of glassware must prevail. Standard goblets are perfectly adequate and can be hired at a reasonable price from any reputable catering firm. The 6-oz (170-ml) size tends to be too big for a tasting; 5-oz (140-ml) glasses are better, or even, at a pinch, large port glasses. Other suitable types are sherry *copitas* and 'dock' glasses. The ideal tasting glass is illustrated on p. 25.

The quantity of glasses required needs careful consideration. All depends on the number of different wines on show and people expected. It is rarely a practical proposition to provide one glass per person per wine. At a large tasting one glass is normally provided on arrival and the taster is expected to use it throughout the tasting, though a clean glass is usually obtainable if by chance the first is abandoned or if a fresh one is really required. If wines of contrasting colour and style are shown at the same tasting a change of glasses should be allowed for. Even if the basis is one glass per taster, allowance must be made for 'wastage': breakages, abandoned glasses, etc., so order double the quantity first thought of.

Nothing looks worse than a litter of partially filled glasses, particularly on tasting tables, so staff should continually remove them. If they are left on the tables they just get in the way and encourage other people to abandon theirs too.

If there are insufficient glasses, or if proper washing-up facilities are not available, it may be necessary to put rinsing bowls in the tasting room. They tend to look unsightly, however, and might be objected to on the grounds of hygiene. If assistants are expected to wash glasses on the spot, washing-up bowls should be either behind the table out of sight or on a rear service table.

How many bottles?

Even at a big and busy tasting it is better to have only *one* bottle of each wine open at a time. This is not just for the sake of economy; its main purpose is to avoid clutter and to prevent the bottles from getting out of order. It also discourages guests from picking up open bottles and wandering off with them, ostensibly to assist their friends. It usually stays with the group until it is consumed!

Nor should the entire tasting stock of bottles of each wine be put on the table in serried ranks. They may look impressive, but they soon get in the way of the serving staff. Bottles are picked up for a close look at the label, and usually put back in the wrong place, all of which adds to the disorganization and mess. However, it is not a bad idea to have one other bottle, opened but stoppered, alongside the tasting bottle. It acts as an immediate reserve and enables waiting tasters to look at the label and the general presentation of the bottle. The point is, it is difficult to see the label of a wine being poured; it is usually obscured by hand or napkin. Last, but not least, the number of wines open for tasting may be dictated by the heat of the room. A cold white wine can gain 5°C (10°F) in about ten minutes.*

Corks and capsules

The presentation of sample bottles is important. The capsules should be cut as for a dinner party, just below the top of the neck, and the top removed. Do not remove the entire capsule. Next wipe the top of neck and cork with a damp cloth and finally with a clean dry cloth.

After removing the cork, preferably in one piece – not so easy with older wines – it should be tied to the neck, wine-side

*An ideal solution is the use of Vinicool® transparent plastic open-topped vacuum flasks. The bottle must be at the correct cool temperature before being put into this receptacle but will retain its chill for the length of the tasting. These are used for white wine samples at Christie's pre-sale tastings.

up, with an india-rubber band. Lastly a wedge-shaped stopper cork is inserted until it is time to serve.

Older red wines should, of course, be decanted. Make sure the decanter is identified by name or number. The empty bottle is then placed alongside, with cork, for inspection.

Food?

Except at press receptions and the more social type of tasting, food should be kept to a minimum. It merely distracts and provides counter-flavours and smells. Nevertheless, it must be accepted that some people need something to cleanse their palates between wines. Cheese squares and dry biscuits are the conventional answer to this problem; dry bread and plain cold water are alternatives. (Iced water stuns the palate.)

It is perhaps important also to bear in mind that virtually all red wines and most whites have been devised by nature and man as an accompaniment for food. In fact, wine tastes different with food, and if to be pre-judged in a food context it is often easier to do so at a tasting with a nibble of something appropriate.

The old saying 'buy a wine over apples and sell it over cheese' has much more than a grain of truth in it. Cheese makes wine taste softer, mellower and sweeter. The riper and more 'smelly' cheeses are all right with rougher reds, but they tend to overpower delicate wines. An over-ripe brie will kill a mature burgundy stone dead. The other problems with richer and more exotic cheeses are that their smell will compete with the bouquet of the wine and can create in a warm tasting room a decidedly unpleasant atmosphere.

So, small squares of a mild cheese of the cheddar variety are safe and satisfactory: one generous plateful per table, with tooth-picks for those too delicate to use their fingers.

Reverting to apples for a moment, one English wine merchant, renowned for his port, used to clean his palate with a bite of apple between tasting samples of young vintage port. I confess I have not tried this though sorely tempted. There are few wines more palate-numbing than immature port.

No smoking – or strong scent

One would have thought that the 'no smoking' rule at tastings was sufficiently known and understood. But it seems that smokers are a law unto themselves; they do not even consider the spent matches and cigarette ends as litter, but unthinkingly discard them anywhere. A man who reaches automatically for his pipe and pouch at home or in the office will do so with equal unconcern when he has reached the contemplative end of a tasting.

So, beware. At a big public tasting put NO SMOKING signs up. Catch smokers politely at the door and advise all assistants to watch out for the tell-tale wreaths of blue smoke, particularly among the groups who are chatting in a relaxed fashion, their tasting completed.

Ladies should also refrain from using strong scent and powder. The delicate bouquet of wine simply cannot compete with a host of foreign smells; it is difficult enough as it is without one's nostrils being assaulted by smoke and perfume at the same time.

Tasting sheets

There is no surer way of wasting one's efforts than to invite guests to taste without providing some form of 'score-card' – a pre-printed list, folder or tasting sheet – for them to consult, make comments on, and take away afterwards.

There are three essential requirements:

- The sheet should contain the full name and vintage of each wine listed in tasting order, with prices if a trade tasting.
- There should be space for comments either alongside or underneath each wine, or on a blank page opposite. At least as much space should be allowed for notes as the name of the wine occupies. It is surprising how often no room is provided.
- It should be printed on card or stiff paper. Flimsy paper is hopeless to write on while standing up, and crumples easily when filed. Alternatively, provide clip-boards.

Embellishments such as wine maps and descriptions of wine districts, etc., can be included. Occasionally price list and tasting sheet are combined. The scope for variety is immense; but whatever form it takes, a tasting sheet is basically an *aide-mémoire*; for with wine, as with many other things, it is a matter of 'in at one ear and out of the other' unless specific action is taken to remedy the lazy human condition.

Licensing laws

Before concluding this chapter, a few words on licensing laws are in order. This section, of necessity, must confine itself to the British Isles, the licensing laws of which are complex enough without having to go further afield. Curiously enough, the English licensing laws are surprisingly inexplicit on the subject of tastings.

The moment that money changes hands or that licensed premises are used in connection with tastings, the laws of the land must be observed.

First of all, it is illegal for *any* person in an unlicensed situation (in the sense that although there are licence-*holders* it is *premises* that are licensed to sell wines, etc.) to sell wine by the bottle or glass. Strictly speaking, you cannot sell a bottle from your own private cellar to a friend without breaking the law. Bottles can only be sold from licensed premises, either fully licensed or 'off'-licensed. If an off-licence only is held, it is illegal for customers to pay for tasting samples, either by way of an entrance fee or per glass or per bottle if those samples are tasted on the premises.* Most wine merchants are in this position, but there is nothing wrong in their offering free samples for tasting, except in Scotland, where this is regarded, not illogically, as an inducement to make an eventual sale, something frowned upon by strong teetotal elements in certain licensing areas.

Only in 'on'-licensed premises (public houses, hotels and such-like – 'table' licences excluded) can tasting samples be sold by glass or bottle for consumption (which includes tasting and spitting out) there and then.

Tasters under the age of 18 are not permitted to consume wine on licensed premises, though there are no restrictions elsewhere.

Curiously enough, unlicensed amateurs are not so circumscribed. They can happily organize tastings at home, or in any other unlicensed premises, whether costs are shared on an *ad hoc* basis, or by subscription, or by the bottle-party method. What they must remember, however, is not to *sell* wine to each other or to non-members of a tasting group – even for

*Though I believe that a *bona-fide* tasting club can charge for these events.

charity. The organizers of big 'charity' tastings might be advised to clear their position beforehand with the police, H.M. Customs and Excise or local magistrate's court.

A wine merchant or his representative can also hold a tasting of his stock-in-trade on unlicensed premises too, so long as he makes no charge for entry or sale by the glass. He can also solicit orders at such a tasting so long as the orders are effected, i.e. the wines delivered, from 'off'-licensed premises.

To the organizers of private tastings my advice is, if in doubt say nothing; get on with it. A cautious official, not quite sure of laws of the land, may play safe at your expense. But if money changes hands, beware.

SUMMARY

Plan the tasting well in advance. Consider all the vital factors: date, time, place; number of guests and assistants; the type and number of wines. Do not leave important details until the last minute. The check list overleaf may come in handy.

CHECKLIST FOR TASTINGS

In advance	☐ Guest list
	☐ Room booking
	☐ Wine selection and stock reservation
Pre-tasting checks	☐ Cloakroom facilities
	☐ Tasting room layout
	☐ Tables – number, size, arrangement
	☐ Table cloths or rolls of white paper
	☐ Wine (delivered well in advance, to settle); temperature of wine and room
	☐ Two bottles of each wine at each tasting position; supporting stock
	☐ Corkscrews: one per assistant or one per table (there are never enough)
	☐ Stopper corks, wedge-shaped
	☐ Elastic bands for securing original corks to bottle necks
	☐ Lapel badges for hosts and assistants
Staff, assistants	☐ Brief all staff carefully before tasting commences
	☐ Allocate 'stands', tables, duties
After the tasting	☐ Separation of unopened, opened and empty bottles

- ☐ Printing: invitations, tasting sheets
- ☐ Order tables, cloths, glasses and other accessories
- ☐ Forewarn assistants; book staff

- ☐ Glasses: right quantity, shape and size (polished *and* clean-smelling)
- ☐ Lighting: correct intensity, type and position
- ☐ Spittoons, sawdust boxes or plastic cups
- ☐ Cloths or napkins for glasses and wiping bottle necks (one per assistant)
- ☐ Empty bottles (magnums) with funnels for dregs
- ☐ Candles, candelabra or empty bottles, and matches
- ☐ Rinsing bowls, if necessary
- ☐ Plain cheese cubes, and plates
- ☐ Dry biscuits or dry bread, and plates
- ☐ Jugs of water (without ice)
- ☐ Trays for removal of glasses
- ☐ Tasting sheets
- ☐ Price lists, supporting literature, hand-outs, press kits
- ☐ Sharpened pencils or ball-point pens
- ☐ Maps, posters, drawing pins and adhesive tape
- ☐ Visitors' book
- ☐ NO SMOKING signs (remove ash trays to discourage smokers)
- ☐ Lock-up room for storage of wine, particularly on strange premises

---

- ☐ Number of bottles to be opened, timing
- ☐ Keep tables uncluttered, remove empty glasses
- ☐ Boozers, free-loaders and smokers – refer to organizer

- ☐ Stock check

XII

THE USE OF WORDS

The first difficulty that tasters encounter is to find and to translate into precise and clear language the qualities and defects of a wine . . . **Pierre Bréjoux,** Revue du Vin de France, 1977

The problem

Put quite bluntly, most people simply do not know how and where to start describing a wine, and many are reluctant even to express an opinion. Some, knowing more, are less shy; but do they really mean what they say, or is a familiar-sounding wine word being used just because it *is* familiar sounding, perhaps impressive? The odds are that it will not convey the speaker's intention.

Renewed thoughts on the use of words in relation to wine were stimulated by an interesting paper by Adrienne Lehrer* which had been typically misquoted by a 'highbrow' Sunday newspaper and picked up, more accurately, by *Decanter* magazine. However, I was really shaken into action by contradictory statements about identical wines made by fellow Masters of Wine on a visit to the winelands of the Cape. It seemed to me that if experienced professionals, as well as untrained amateurs, could disagree on whether a wine was full, light or dry, or whatever, it was less likely to be a sensory problem than semantic: either carelessness in the use of words or alarming imprecision.

Clearly some guidance is needed.

Are words necessary?

It might justifiably be asked at this stage whether it is necessary to use words at all. Surely wine can be consumed, enjoyed and appreciated to the full without a word being said or written? There are several reasons for talking or writing about wine. Basically:

● to express a simple preference of one wine over another
● to communicate the style, quality, condition, etc., of a wine to someone else
● to increase the awareness of other tasters.

Terminology

Terminology is defined as the body of specialized words relating to a particular subject. The arts and sciences, gardening and snooker, have their own terminology often far more obscure than that used by winetasters, so why all the fuss, why the occasional snigger? It is extremely difficult to find words to describe taste, even more so bouquet, but one must try. One uses analogies and approximations. The most brilliant taster will be able to conjure up words which happen, at that moment, to fit, to illuminate the wine under scrutiny. The experienced taster harnesses his imagination to vinous terminology.

*Talking about Wine in the journal *Language*, Volume 51, Number 4 (1975) by Adrienne Lehrer, Committee of Linguistics, College of Liberal Arts, University of Arizona.

On what sort of occasion?

Tastings The context in which wine is tasted is all-important. In Chapter 2 I mentioned different circumstances in which wine can be tasted, from the cask to the table. On each of these occasions a written or mental note would be made, possibly after discussion with the cellar-master or merchant (or whomsoever).

At the sort of tastings described in Chapter 10 one would normally make notes, ranging from an abbreviated preferential tick or dismissive cross to more detailed descriptions.

Lecturing A lecturer on wine has several responsibilities:
- to stimulate interest and enthusiasm
- to 'open the eyes' of the audience by drawing attention to features they might not have noticed
- to select words which are evocative and meaningful
- to use words which can be clearly related to the wine being tasted by his audience
- in the case of lecturing wine-trade students, to guide them in the use of words, particularly those long-tried and conventional terms which, when written, will be understood by an examiner or, equally, by a customer.

Selling wine It is fairly common practice for wine merchants to annotate their lists, describing the qualities of different types of wine, of vintages, even of individual wines. Similar eulogies will be conveyed by the salesman to the potential customer. It is much less difficult to use words in a selling context, possibly because the descriptions are qualitative and general, not analytical: pleasure-invoking adjectives, and opinions regarding readiness to drink, rather than specific and analytical descriptions. Perhaps, in the case of white wines, merely whether sweet or dry; reds, whether full-bodied or light.

At dinner parties There are many reasons for giving, or attending, a dinner party. If it is mainly a social event, grand or less formal, the purpose will be to impress or to entertain: the occasion and the people will take precedence over the fare. The food and the wine are likely to be relegated to a supporting role. The choice of wine will depend on appropriateness and price. It is not provided as a subject for discussion. Even so, if you are keen on wine there is no harm in making a discreet note.

However, if it is a food-and-wine occasion, the host will expect comments, even a discussion, though the level and intensity will depend as much on the knowledge and enthusiasm of the people present as the quality of fare. The point is: whether wines are discussed considerably or not at all will depend on the type of dinner, the guests and the intention. To pontificate on wine in a non-wine context is tactless; *not* to comment intelligently on wine in a wine-orientated context is failure to rise to the occasion.

Great wine – for whom?

Arising out of my travels over the past few years it is abundantly clear that the vast majority of owners of fine and rare wines have a major concern; on what occasion, and for whom, shall their vinous treasures be opened? It is less a matter of expense than sheer waste, and the knowledge that once a cork is drawn, that's it. A fine picture can be looked at scores of times, and re-sold; a piece of silver can be admired for its beauty of craftsmanship, and still retain its intrinsic value. Apart from *haute-cuisine*, great wine is the only work of art which has to be consumed in order to be appreciated. Thereafter its only value is a treasured memory.

It seems sensible therefore to keep the finest wines for dinner parties (or tastings) which will be attended by people who really appreciate them, or at the very least are like-minded convivial souls. Having gathered together fine wine and appreciative palates, host and guests alike are unlikely to be satisfied with grunts, nods and mere smacking of lips.

Choice of words

Fine wine demands to be talked about. Words are needed. There is a wide spectrum of words, but they more or less boil down to two categories: factual and fanciful. There is, I believe, a place for both.

When it comes to wine, 'facts' very often turn out to be opinions. But let's not be put off by academic pedants. Better to fumble and stumble than not to try to express ourselves at all.

Basic words At the end of the chapter, just before the glossary, I have extracted a short list of words which, if carefully (I avoid the word 'correctly') used are meaningful to English tasters who have had a modicum of training and experience.

Fanciful words By all means let us indulge in flights of poetic expression, similes, flower analogies and so forth, but be careful about the context.

Unqualified and ambiguous words One taster will loosely describe a wine as 'full', another taster might disagree totally. The point here is that 'full', unqualified, can conjure up several meanings in other tasters' minds: full-coloured (deep), full-bodied (high alcohol and extract), full bouquet (i.e. well developed, very forthcoming), full-flavoured (positive, mouth-filling).

So adjectives like 'full' or 'light' should either be qualified or used in a distinctly recognizable context: colour, bouquet, weight in the mouth, style, flavour, etc. Words such as 'hot' and 'round' can have several meanings. A list of ambiguous words appears on p. 112.

Use of similes and analogies The French themselves, in writing and in speech, tend to be far more poetic than the English, their descriptions often roaming up a romantic path, associating wine with flowers, scents, exotic foods and the more delicate aspects of love-making. The English are generally more reticent, more terse and, let's be honest, often less imaginative. I find I cannot generalize about Americans. Their writing and talking depend on so many factors, from ethnic background to type of reader and audience. There *is* a tendency, in some quarters, to verbosity and polysyllables, many Americans preferring to use long words rather than clear simple expressions, but this is not confined to those who write, or speak, about wine. One could argue that likening a bouquet to violets or saying a taste is reminiscent of truffles is not very meaningful if the listener or reader is unfamiliar with the smell of one and the flavour of the other. Yet I believe it is quite defensible to do so; analogies add extra dimensions and help other tasters identify and memorize facets.

There are instances where, at a dinner party of like-minded individuals, the sheer compatibility of guests, food and wines will spark off conversation of a high order. The possibility that a profusion of abstract similes, analogies, evocations, richly enlightening at the time, would, if recorded, sound pretty flat the next morning is immaterial.

A fine example of evocative writing, neatly bridging the gap between the French and English approach to wine, is demonstrated by the late André Simon. In the first issue of the *Quarterly Journal of the Wine and Food Society* he recorded what was to be the first of a series of 'memorable meals'. It took place at the Hind's Head at Bray. At the end of the dinner the host, Barry Neame, asked André for his initial reaction to the wines. He answered that his 'first thoughts evoked memories of Berkshire'. A 1926 Chablis – this was in 1934 – reminded him of 'the grace of the silver willow', the 1919 Montrachet 'of the stateliness of the Italian poplar', the 1920 Cheval-blanc 'of the magnificence of the purple beech' and the 1870 Lafite 'of the majesty of the Royal Oak'. But as to the brandy (an 1842 Roullet et Delamain) 'there was no tree with its roots in common clay to be mentioned in the same breath . . .'!

The wine snob

Out of a lesser man's mouth, with inappropriate wines, without the touch of real poetry and, above all, without imagination and understanding, André Simon's words would represent the quintessence of wine snobbery. Frankly, 'snob' is a term I try to avoid. But, alas, it is only too frequently used, equally by the ignorant and by the academic. As I believe the snob's main armoury is language, it is appropriate to raise the subject at this point.

If there is such a thing as a wine snob, he or she will have all the attributes of any other sort of snob: affectation and pretentiousness covering up the lack of everything that makes a person worthy of serious attention. The aristocrat of the table, the nature's gentleman of the cellar, the true *amateur*, the deeply knowledgeable, is rarely, if ever, a snob.

Those who are modest, undogmatic, listen to others' views and are honest in their own opinions, should be safe from the brickbats of the envious and ignorant. Those who are knowledgeable about wine should merely be careful on what occasion and in whose company they air their opinions and display their scholarship.

The wine bore

People who say little or nothing are not 'bores', just boring. It is the man of words (woman equally) who is at risk. A great expert can be a bore, particularly if speaking out of context, being repetitive, pedantic, opinionated, never listening to others or merely intoning in a tedious, grinding, long-winded way.

The wine bore is the person who speaks about wine when no one is inclined to listen, or to the exclusion of all else. The answer is to try, which is not always easy, to talk about one's enthusiasm or business only in the presence of those who are interested, and, if possible, to anticipate the level of that interest.

Context of tasting

The trouble is, all those who talk about wine lay themselves wide open. If we talk of what we know not, to impress, we are wine snobs; if we talk of what we know, wine bores. Let us therefore forget these pejorative terms and concentrate on building up our knowledge, and on the correct use of words. 'Context' has cropped up many times in this chapter. It happens to be the crux of the problem. The *context* in which wine is tasted, and talked about, is of the greatest importance.

The occasion As stated earlier, tasting occasions, opportunities and settings, vary. The same wine may be viewed in a different light, and one's impressions and notes can differ.

Time and timing Tiredness, a rushed tasting, will affect one's judgment and reduce the value of the tasting notes.

Lighting and colour The effects of natural and artificial lighting were discussed in Chapter 5.*

Service of wine Wine served too warm or too cold, or tasted in too warm or too cold a room, will taste differently. Wines served in one order might taste slightly differently from the same wines in a different order (see Chapter 3).

Personal influences A dominant personality, or a dogmatic one, can make one's judgment waver. Try not to be swayed: rely on your own opinion.

One could go on. The point is that the senses, being delicate, are swayed by a multiplicity of outside factors. The impressions and the notes will reflect these; one must be conscious of influences and, if necessary, counter or allow for them. After all, we are only human!

Subjective or objective tasting

This brings me to a point which, I am sure, will be contentious. After 30 years of tasting and teaching I am convinced that to talk about, let alone claim, total objectivity – 'relating entirely to the external object' – in tasting is nonsense. Moreover, to be a subjective taster is nothing to be ashamed of. One can even argue that a subjective approach – 'arising out of the senses' – is the most enriching approach to *fine* wine. The problem is, as usual, to note or convey both subjective and objective impressions, using words which can be understood. The sole *object* of one's concentration should be the wine, but in the ultimate analysis 'I, the taster' am the final arbiter.

Judgment and taste thresholds

There are two areas in which judgment is required: at the commercial level and at the *amateur* (in the French sense). At the commercial level, a merchant, with or without formal training, will taste and use his judgment; will note and convey information about the wine to his customers. At wine festivals and shows, where wine is tasted competitively, the judges must work to a common approach and system of assessing wines. The more similar in quality and style the wines are, the more precisely the basis of judgment must be defined. When it comes to detecting small differences, particularly in wines of neutral character, the sensory thresholds (the level at which elements of smell and taste can be detected) of the judges are important. It would be sensible to test these; and it is possible to do so.†

Quantifying taste

I cannot subscribe to the dictum that, in effect, nothing is

---

*Professor Pusais (Directeur du Laboratoire Départemental et Régional d'Analyses et des Recherches, Tours) has conducted experiments leading him to conclude that certain wall colours will make a wine taste sweeter or more acid.

†Refer to the several Amerine and Roessler works listed in the Bibliography.

worth knowing unless it can be expressed numerically; indeed, in respect of fine wine I cannot help feeling that a preoccupation with numbers merely serves to divert the taster from the true appreciation of the manifold facets of quality and style.

Having said this I can see little harm in allocating marks to wines, so long as it is realized that a simple 'out-of-ten' (20 or a 100) score is only one taster's judgment of a given wine, in the context of a range of wines, in given company, on a particular day. It will merely serve to underline and summarize impressions and notes. Allocating a simple numerical rating also obliges one to reach a conclusion.

Averaging scores

Beware: to take the average of the scores or marks of a number of tasters, particularly if they are many and varied in experience and ability, can be highly misleading. It can reduce to a blurred middle-of-the-road sector both outstandingly good and below-average, even faulty, wines. An over-generous scorer will neutralize a highly critical one.

Statistical procedures

The French and American academics' partiality to algebra is altogether another thing. The object of the statistician is to reduce the chance element in tasting. In effect, one eliminates as far as possible all the conditions which induce the varying subjective impressions I have already referred to, and, after testing the tasters, analyses the results mathematically. I concede that with certain types of wine and in certain circumstances there is a case to be made, but it is generally beyond the level of knowledge and out of the area of interest of most wine lovers, in or out of the trade.

Summing up

Be honest with yourself. Try and express your own impressions and opinions but be particularly careful in your use of words if you need to note specific factors, convey them to a third person or recognize them again.

Frankly the sub-divisions are infinite. One can argue endlessly about what words should be used. What might be acceptable to, and perfectly understood by, one person, may sound fatuous to another. There are no hard-and-fast rules. Words will vary from person to person, group to group; they will depend on usage, on teaching. Some will come into favour, some will fall out of favour.

In a social context, with good wines and like-minded people, loosen up: don't be afraid to express an opinion or a preference; let your imagination roam. Evocative comments help open up new vistas for others, and aid the overall appreciation and mental 'digestion' of the wine. It is not so much precision that is required but a vital exchange of reactions and ideas, enabling so much more to be revealed, so much more to be gained.

In the final analysis, words should be used to illuminate and to enlighten; and they *must* be used as meaningfully as possible. If in doubt, refer to the following glossary. Check what *you* think you mean by what – let me be honest – *I* think I mean. You might not agree with all the definitions. At least they will provide food for thought. Lastly, try to use words in the correct context, and qualify them when necessary.

BASIC DESCRIPTIVE AND 'DANGER' WORDS

Below are listed basic descriptive words and expressions in the order of tasting any red or white wine. Refer to the Full Glossary of Tasting Terms for definitions.

Red Wines

Appearance

depth	very pale, pale, medium-pale, medium-deep, deep, very deep, opaque
colour/hue	purple, purple-rimmed, ruby, red, tile-red, brown-tinged, red-brown, mahogany
clarity	bright, dull, bitty, hazy, cloudy; light or heavy sediment

Nose or bouquet

condition	clean, unclean (sulphury, oxidized, etc.)
fruit	fruity, lacking fruit, vinous, varietal, named variety
development	dumb, immature, undeveloped, well developed, forthcoming, very mature, over-mature
quality	poor, ordinary, good, fine, great, magnificent

Palate

apparent dryness	(noticeably) dry; slightly or unusually sweet (for a red wine); tannic
body	very light (VL)*, light (L), medium-light (ML), medium (M), full-bodied (F), heavy
tannin	marked, noticeably drying, mellow
acid	soft, lacking acidity, refreshing, marked acidity, over-acid, tart, acetic
fruit, flavour	fruity, lacking fruit; vinous; very flavoury, lacking flavour (describe flavour – use analogies when appropriate)
development	well developed, very mature, mature, beginning to mature, undeveloped, 'green'
overall balance	well balanced, unbalanced
length and finish	long flavour, short; lingering, fine aftertaste

White Wines

Slight difference of emphasis, particularly regarding colour and sweetness:

Appearance

depth	colourless, very pale, medium, deep
colour/hue	green-tinged, yellow-green, yellow, straw, yellow-gold, gold, amber, deep gold, brown
clarity	star-bright, bright . . . dull, cloudy

Nose or bouquet

more or less as for red wines

Palate

dry/sweet	bone-dry, dry, medium-dry, medium-sweet, sweet, very sweet
body, acidity, fruit, development, balance, finish	more or less as for red wines. Tannin is not normally a factor in white wines; acidity is more important, balancing sugar content

*I use abbreviations in my own notes. The possible confusion between initials is avoided by tasting, and using words, in a regular order and under appropriate headings. For example, under 'Palate', 'D, MF' indicates 'dry, medium-full bodied'. Other abbreviations I use: fl. (flavour), bal. (balance), Y (young/youthful), V/A (volatile acidity), B/A (bottle-age), mat. (mature), ex. (excellent), t & a (tannin and acidity), etc.

WORDS USED IN THE DESCRIPTION
OF WINE, BY CATEGORY

For ease of reference, I have listed here those words in common use, those which need qualifying, those to use with care and additional qualitative adjectives. For a full list of tasting terms and their definitions, refer to the Full Glossary of Tasting Terms.

Words in common use

acid/acidity
aroma
balance/well-
balanced
bouquet
clean

dry/medium-
dry etc.
fruity
grapey
hard
harsh
poor

refreshing
soft
sweet
tannin, tannic
tough
vinegary
watery

Words in common use which
should be used in a qualified context

aftertaste
big
bland
body
bright
character
coarse
dull
fat
fine
finish

flat
full
heavy
light
little
long
mature/maturity
meaty
medium
neutral

ordinary
peppery
positive
rich
round
sour
strong
varietal
weak
youthful

Words to use precisely or with care

astringent
baked
bite
bitter
corked
dumb
earthy
extract
feminine
flabby
flinty

forthcoming
green
hot
iron
maderised
mouldy
nutty
oxidized
penetrating
piquant
pungent

robust
rough
sharp
smoky
stalky
tang/tangy
tart
vinous
woody
zesty/zestful

Additional qualitative descriptions

aromatic
breed, well bred
complex
distinguished
elegant
finesse
flowery
fragrant
insipid
luscious

mellow
metallic
musty
noble
perfumed
powerful
raw
ripe
scented
sensuous

silky
smooth
spicy
subtle
supple
unripe
velvety
vinosity
well developed
yeasty

XIII
FULL GLOSSARY
OF TASTING TERMS

The value of a winetaster does not depend only in his sensitivity as a receptive instrument, nor on his capacity to recognise odours, tastes and to appreciate their harmony; it also depends on his ability to describe his impressions **Emile Peynaud,** Le Goût du Vin

A

acetic vinegary smell; sharp, over-tart on the palate. A vinegary condition resulting from the action of acetobacter, harmful ferments that attack wine left open in bottle, or fermented at too high a temperature, or carelessly bottled. Ullaged wine, whether in cask or bottle, will usually be suspect. The latter is usually due to poor, wormy or dried-out corks, which let air in and wine out (weepers), the remaining wine often becoming acetic and undrinkable.

acetone a high-toned estery aroma connected with the ester ethyl acetate or with nail-varnish-like amyl acetate. Its presence, in moderation, adds to the fruity character of wine.

acid, acidity on the nose: mouth-watering, refreshing (tartaric), sometimes like raw cooking apples (malic); detectable on the tongue, giving wine essential crispness and zing. 'Volatile' acids are more pronounced on the nose, 'fixed' acids (tartaric, succinic and citric) less so. Esters of both acids make an important contribution to the overall bouquet of wine. There are several types and degrees of acidity commonly found in wine, some beneficial and some detrimental. The right sort of natural acidity is an essential component of a sound wine; it acts as a preservative, produces bouquet and provides the essential bite and finish. It also stimulates the gastric juices – one of the oft-forgotten main purposes of any table wine. Lack of acidity can be detected by a general flabbiness, lack of vitality and a weak watery finish; excess acidity by a sharp tart effect on the tongue. Youthful acidity tends to mellow with age. Some wines, such as vinho verde, champagne and wines from the Saar and Ruwer, have a deliberately and refreshingly high acid content. Fruity-acidity is perhaps the most desired characteristic of German wines (*see also* TARTARIC, MALIC and SORBIC ACIDS).

aftertaste 'the internal bouquet' that sometimes remains in the throat and back nasal passages after a wine has been drunk. Unpleasant if the wine is strong-flavoured and in poor condition; at its best, however, the hallmark of a great wine and usually part of what is more poetically referred to as a 'lingering farewell'.

aggressive more than lively on the palate, perhaps over-tannic.

alcohol an essential component, binding and preserving. In *pure* form the higher alcohols, amyl and butyl, have an unpleasant, throat-catching odour, phenethyl has an intense, rose-like smell and ethanol a burning sensation. However, diluted, as in wine, alcohol is scarcely detectable on the nose, though it can be assessed by its weight in the mouth, by a sort of burning taste and, cumulatively, by its well-known effects on the head of the imbiber. Although table wines may vary by only 3° (3% by volume), from light Mosels around 11° to Rhône and sauternes in the 13° to 14° bracket, the effect on the weight, character and strength of the wine is marked.

almonds, bitter the smell of almond kernels or bitter almonds emanates from a badly fined wine, possibly 'blue' fined. Probably drinkable but not sound.

apples a fresh, raw smell, indicative of an immature young wine (*see* MALIC ACID).

aroma that part of the smell of wine derived from the grape, whether distinctly varietal or merely vinous (oenologists also use the word in respect of odours resulting from fermentation) as opposed to 'bouquet', which is derived from the development of the wine itself in bottle.

aromatic fragrant, a richness of aroma and taste, spicy overtones, particularly from aromatic grape varieties, such as *muscat*.

asbestos odour imparted by new filter pads or old, dirty, over-used pads in bottling. Wine has flat, alkaline taste.

astringent a dry, mouth-puckering effect caused by a high tannin content (often accompanied by a high degree of acidity). Might well soften and mellow as the wine matures. Not bitter.

attenuated becoming thin on the palate, losing fruit and flesh, usually in respect of an old wine.

austere somewhat tough and severe; simple, uncomplex, possibly undeveloped.

B

backward retarded, undeveloped for its age/vintage.

baked a 'hot' rather earthy smell produced by burnt and shrivelled grapes due to excessive sunshine and lack of rainfall. A characteristic of red wine produced in hot vintages in the Rhône valley and in naturally hot wine-producing areas such as southern California, Australia and South Africa.

balance the combination and relationship of components (*see* WELL BALANCED).

banana overtone on the bouquet of wines made from frost-bitten grapes; also a specific smell of old wine in poor condition.

beefy substantial, muscular, well endowed with alcohol, tannic, extract.

beery an undesirable smell caused by secondary fermentation in bottle. The wine may be drinkable, just, but will be basically unsound, poor on finish.

beetroot, boiled reminiscent of, and recognition symbol for, the *pinot* grape aroma.

big manly wine, well-endowed with vital elements, not just high in alcohol.

bite inferring a substantial degree of acidity (plus tannin). A good factor in young wine. Generally mellows with age.

bitter, bitterness detected on the palate, on the back of the tongue and finish. Mainly unpleasant. A taste, not a tactile, sensation, though it can be a desirable quality in certain wines (usually an acquired taste) and vermouths. Bitterness is derived from either chemical salts or vegetable extracts. A certain bitterness can be imparted by colouring matter, though the depositing of this during maturation will normally reduce its pristine harshness. Polyphenols extracted from wooden casks, particularly when dirty and contaminated, will also, when oxidized, impart a bitter taste to wine. More rarely an unpleasant bitterness is due to *amertume*, a bacteriological disease.

bitters substances added to wine (for example, in the making of vermouth) that have a bitter taste and stimulate the appetite and digestion. They can be of vegetable origin, like gentian, or aromatic, containing volatile oil, like orange peel. Quinine has a similar effect, plus additional properties such as a remote action on the nervous system.

blackcurrants the nearest fruit-smell to the *cabernet-sauvignon* grape. Detectable in some degree wherever the grape is used but particularly marked on wines from Pauillac, and to a slightly lesser extent Margaux. Perhaps the first major clue to Bordeaux wine in a blind tasting.

bland not complimentary: mild, easy, characterless; not unpleasant.

body the weight of wine in the mouth due to its alcoholic content, extract and to its other physical components. These factors stem from the quality of the vintage and geographical origin, and in turn affect the style and quality of the wine. Wines from hotter climates tend to have more body than those from the north (compare the Rhône with the Mosel, for example).

botrytis short for *botrytis cinerea* known also as noble rot, *pourriture noble, edelfäule*: the phenomenal rot which is encouraged to develop on the skins of grapes in Sauternes and the best vineyards in Germany during the delayed autumn harvest. Botrytis shrivels the grapes, reduces the water content and concentrates the sugar content. The effect on nose and palate is akin to honey.

bottle-age extremely hard to describe but easily recognizable on the bouquet to an experienced taster and a vital factor in the judgment of a wine's age/maturity and development in bottle. On white dessert wines a mellow, honeyed quality; on reds a breaking down of raw edges to reveal forthcoming softness and mellowness.

bottle-sickness temporary oxidation after bottling, which wears off.

bouquet in the broadest and often-used sense, the pleasant and characteristic smell of wine. In the narrower sense, the odour created by the wine's own development: by the esters and aldehydes formed by the slow oxidation of fruit acids and alcohol (*see also* AROMA).

breed a distinctive and distinguished quality stemming from the combination of fine site, soil, *cépage* and the skill of the *vigneron*.

buttery self-descriptive smell and taste (not texture).

C

caramel a slightly burnt, toffee-like flavour which can have a literal origin in the case of certain spirits but can only be reminiscent in the case of wine. A characteristic flavour of madeira and marsala, for example.

carbon dioxide responsible for the sparkle of champagne and sparkling wines and the tingle of *spritzig* or slightly effervescent table wines.

cats the smell of cats or 'cats' piss', a strangely attractive and not unusual grape smell associated with certain young white wines, usually Moselle.

cedarwood characteristic scent of many fine clarets.

character a wine of any quality which has unmistakable and distinctive features.

characteristic having the style and character of the grape, district, vintage, etc. Often sweepingly used to avoid a detailed description.

chocolaty a chocolate-like smell and taste, rich, 'thick', slightly vanilla. Not bad, not unusual (some burgundies), but inelegant and possibly not the purest varietal characteristic.

cigarettes descriptive term. Some dry, lean, claret, Graves occasionally.

clean absence of foreign and unpleasant odours.

cloying a sweet and heavy wine which palls; lacking the acidity to make it crisp and interesting.

coarse rough texture; lacking breed and possibly indifferently made. Do not confuse coarseness with the rough rawness of a fine but completely immature wine.

common lacking breed, but none the less sound and drinkable.

complex many-faceted smell and taste. The hallmark of a developing fine wine.

cooked a heavy, sometimes sweet but not unpleasant smell from the use of sugar, concentrated grape juice or high temperature during vinification.

corked an 'off', oxidized and thoroughly obnoxious smell. A very over-used and misunderstood expression; the *sommelier's* nightmare.

corky having a distinct smell of cork, arising from a poor, soft or disintegrating cork, or one infected by weevil. A poor cork can, of course, let air in, in which case the wine may oxidize completely and become 'corked'. Indeed, the two expressions are frequently interchanged due to lack of agreement over definition.

creaming a light, slightly frothy *mousse*. Half-sparkling.

crisp a desirable feature in white wines; firm, refreshing, positive acidity.

D

deep an adjective that needs qualification: deep-coloured; deep bouquet, depth of flavour – opposite to superficial, indicating underlying richness, layers of flavour.

delicate charm and balance in a light wine of some quality.

depth richness, subtlety – seemingly 'layers' of flavour, all interlocked.

developed in relation to wine is a maturity stage: undeveloped, well developed (mature, balanced, rounded), over-developed (over-mature, cracking up).

distinguished marked and exceptional character and breed.

dry not sweet; absence of residual sugar; fully fermented.

dull appearance not bright; nose and palate lacking interest.

dumb undeveloped, but with inherent promise of quality.

Often the sign of an 'adolescent' stage.

dusty an evocative cellar-like smell; possibly high tannic content.

E

earthy characteristic overtone derived from certain soils.

eggs, bad (hydrogen sulphide) disagreeable, but harmless. Probably due to bad cellar treatment.

elegant stylish balance and refined quality.

estery high-toned, acetone smell. An ester results from the reaction of an organic acid and alcohol.

eucalyptus descriptive, analogous, spicy bouquet associated with certain top-quality *cabernet-sauvignons* notably Heitz Martha's Vineyard which is surrounded by eucalyptus trees which probably do affect the grapes, but also some of the finest ripest vintages of Château Latour.

extract soluble solids (strictly speaking excluding sugar) which add to a wine's body and substance.

F

farmyard a ripe, earthy, manure, sometimes pig-sty smell probably due to the presence of butyric acid, one of the several normal volatile acids which, in excess, creates the smell described. Not uncommon in classified red Bordeaux.

fat fullish body, high in glycerol and extract. If sweet, verging on unctuous.

feminine subjective and abstract term indicating a style of wine which is attractive, not heavy or severe, with charm – whatever delightful qualities all but a misogynist might conjure up!

filter-pads *see* ASBESTOS.

fine an all-embracing expression of superior quality. Perhaps the most overworked adjective in the vinous vocabulary.

finesse grace, delicacy, breed, distinction.

finish the end-taste. A wine cannot be considered well balanced without a good finish, by which is understood a firm, crisp and distinctive end. The opposite, a short or poor finish, will be watery, the flavour not sustained and tailing-off inconclusively. The correct degree of the right sort of acidity is a decisive factor.

firm implies a sound constitution and balance, positive in the mouth, as opposed to flabby.

flabby feeble, lacking crisp acidity, probably without finish. Either a poor wine or one that is cracking up.

flat dull, insipid, lacking acidity. Or merely a sparkling wine which has lost its sparkle.

flinty an evocative overtone. Certain white wine grapes grown on certain soils have a hint of gun-flint in the bouquet and flavour, e.g. Pouilly *blanc-fumé*.

flowery fragrant, flower-like. Certain Mosels in 'full bloom', for example.

forceful marked character, probably well endowed with tannin and acidity; assertive.

forward advanced in maturity for its age or weight of vintage.

foxy curious and distinctive earthy tang, flavour and finish of wine made from native American vine species. It does not imply an animal smell but relates to the wild or 'fox' grapes.

fragrant attractively and naturally scented.

fresh retaining natural youthful charm, vitality (and acidity).

fruity attractive, fleshy quality derived from good ripe grapes; but not necessarily a grapey aroma.

full (bodied) high in alcoholic content and extract. Filling the mouth. A table wine with an alcoholic content probably over 13° G.L. (i.e. percentage alcohol by volume). In the context of fortified wines a heavy sherry, port or madeira at the top of the alcohol and sugar scale.

G

gamey overripe, often on the verge of cracking up. As with game birds, very old burgundy and claret can be attractive if something of an acquired taste.

garlic, wild a faint reminiscent whiff denoting the presence of sorbic acid.

gentle mild, pleasant, unassertive.

geraniums not a complimentary flower simile: a geranium-like odour caused by the presence of an obscure micro-organism derived principally from esters formed during fermentation.

goaty a rich ripe animal-like flavour. For example, ripe fat Pfalz wines made from the *traminer* grape.

graceful abstract: elegant, unassertive, stylish.

grapey a rich *muscatelle*-like aroma produced by certain grape varieties, including *muscatelle* itself and crossings like *scheurebe* and *Müller-Thurgau*.

great almost as over-worked as fine. Should be confined to wines of the highest quality which, in practice, means top growths of good years: having depth, richness, character, style, complexity, fragrance, length and aftertaste.

green unripe, raw and young. Youthful, mouth-watering acidity produced by immature grapes, or the unsettled acidity of an immature wine.

grip a firm and emphatic combination of physical characteristics. A desirable quality in port, for example. The opposite to flabbiness and spinelessness.

gritty coarse-textured in the mouth.

H

hard severity due to the over-prominence of tannin and, to a lesser extent, acidity. Usually the product of a hot vintage or over-prolonged contact with skins and pips during fermentation. Time usually mellows.

harsh self-descriptive. Due to excess tannin and/or ethyl-acetate associated with acetic acid.

heady high in alcohol. Tipsy-making.

hearty robust, zestful, warm, alcoholic; generally in respect of red wine.

heavy more than just full-bodied; over-endowed with alcohol and extracts. Watch out for the context in which it is used. For example, a strapping Rhône wine will appear too heavy for a light summer luncheon but would be the right weight to accompany a steak and kidney pie in mid-winter. 'Heavy' is also an official definition: a fortified wine is subject to the higher rates of duty.

hedonistic a simple, subjective, personal rating, e.g. pleasant to the individual taster.

herbaceous between grasslike and flowery. Pleasant, open, fresh, appealing. Usually young white wines.

high-toned nose of assertive volatile character.

hollow a wine with a foretaste and some finish but without sustaining middle-flavour. A failing rather than a fault.

honest a somewhat condescending term for a decent, well-made but fairly ordinary wine.

honeyed characteristic fragrance of such fine mature wines as sauternes and *beerenauslesen*; indicative of bottle-age.

I

implicitly sweet apparent sweetness from sources other than sugar, e.g. glycerol, alcohol.

inky 'red ink': an unpleasant, tinny, metallic taste due to the presence of tannate of iron produced by the action of tannin on iron – a nail in a cask will have this effect. Tannate of iron is the chief constituent of ink.

insipid flat, somewhat tasteless. Lacking firmness, character.

iron a faintly metallic, earthy-iron taste derived from the soil. Noticeable in some St-Emilions and in these circumstances entirely natural, adding recognizable character.

L

lanolin a soft, sweet harmonious, possibly slightly oily smell like lanolin, associated with classic wines made from the *chenin blanc* and *semillon* grapes in good years.

legs the English term for globules which fall down the sides of the glass after the wine is swirled. Also known as 'tears'. Generally indicative of a rich wine (*see also* p. 30).

lemon lemon-like overtones. For example, noticeable on some fine but immature white Hermitage wines.

length the longer the flavour the finer the wine. The French use the word persistence and measure it in seconds.

light a low degree of alcohol (under 12° G.L.). Lack of body. A desirable characteristic of certain styles of wine like young beaujolais and Mosel-Saar-Ruwer wines. Rather confusingly, 'light' is an official term for a natural, unfortified table wine.

limpid clear (appearance).

limpidity colour appears to have extra sheen, outstanding brightness.

liquorice a flavour, like Spanish root, associated with certain mature vintage ports.

little scarcely any bouquet or aroma. Either a wine of no quality or character, or dumb.

lively fairly explicit. Usually in reference to a fresh, youthful wine; or an old wine with fresh and youthful characteristics.

long lingering flavour; a sign of quality.

luscious soft, sweet, fat, fruity and ripe. All these qualities in balance.

M

maceration carbonique a 'whole-fruit' modern method of wine-making involving the fermentation of the whole grape.

The results are, at best, a pleasant, very frail quaffable style of wine; at worst, tinny. The author's view is that this method reduces the individual character of wines, those of one district tasting much like another.

maderised the heavy flat smell of an over-mature, somewhat oxidized white wine (sometimes accompanied by brown-tinged colour and flat taste). *See also* OXIDIZED.

malic acid although without smell, its presence due to unripe 'green' grapes has mouth-watering, cooking-apple nose; mouth-puckering. A 'malolactic' fermentation in cask converts the raw malic acid into softer and more amenable lactic acid.

manly or masculine: positive, possibly assertive, even aggressive; a big wine, 'muscular'.

mature the maturity of a wine is one of its most crucial factors. Wines vary enormously in make-up and take anything from a matter of months to many years to reach full maturity, depending mainly on their tannin, acid and alcohol content. Maturity can be detected on nose and palate; the maturity of red wines is most easily and visibly measured by the brownness at the rim (*see* colour charts, pages 49–64). An immature wine has raw, unknit, component parts. A perfectly mature wine has all its constituent elements in harmony.

mawkish a trifle flat, drab-flavoured, sickly.

meaty heavy, rich almost 'chewable' quality.

medium (body) neither light nor heavy in alcohol and extract – probably between 12° and 13° G.L., depending on the style of wine.

medium-dry containing some residual sugar but dry enough to be drunk before or during a meal.

medium-sweet considerable natural sugar, but not really a dessert wine. Many German wines come into this category and are better drunk without food.

mellow soft, limpid, mature. No rough edges. A characteristic normally associated with maturity and age.

mercaptan a sour, unpleasant rubbery smell indicating the deterioration in some old hock, for example, due to the breakdown of sulphur dioxide, used as a preservative.

metallic not a pleasant quality. Usually due to some metallic contamination during wine making, storage in cask or bottling. If distinctly unpleasant and associated with a deepening of colour (of white wine) and a tawny deposit, it is usually due to copper contamination.

mouldy an undesirable flavour imparted by rotten grapes or stale, unclean casks, etc.

mousey smell and taste, flat yet acetic. Sign of bacteriological disease, *tourne*, usually affecting only wine in cask.

mulberry a more opulent, succulent type of fruitiness, softer than the blackcurrant of young *cabernet-sauvignon*, associated with exceptional ripe claret, often with a *merlot* dominating.

mushroomy specific smell of some very old wines.

musky a difficult term: spicy/dusty.

must unfermented grape juice.

musty due to poor casks or a cork fault. If the latter, allow the wine to stand after pouring and the smell may wear off after only a few minutes.

N

neutral without positive flavour marked physical characteristics. A common feature of very many blended wines, from quite respectable commercial burgundy to litre-bottled carafe wine.

noble indicates stature and breed; a wine of towering elegance.

nose the broadest term for the bouquet, aroma, the smell of a wine; the professional 'noses' a wine.

nuance having components reminiscent of specific smells, e.g. of almonds, of struck flint.

nutty a crisp rounded flavour associated with full-bodied dry white wines like Corton-Charlemagne, or good-quality amontillados. Fine old tawny port has a distinct smell of cobnuts.

O

oak an important factor, particularly in relation to fine wines. Oak casks impart an 'oaky' taste and smell, desirable in moderation, undesirable if over-apparent.

off-taste unclean, tainted or diseased wine; though not necessarily undrinkable.

old can be a factual statement or imply a state of bouquet and taste adversely affected by over-maturity.

olfactory to do with the sense of smell and its perception.

ordinary in wine terms is mildly derogatory: a wine of no pretensions or with no merit.

organoleptic the testing, by use of the senses, in an analytical context, of wine and food.

oxidized flat, stale off-taste due to exposure to air.

P

peach-like self-descriptive. Characteristic of the bouquet of certain German wines, notably ripe Mosels from the Ruwer district.

peardrops an undesirable overtone sometimes noticeable on poorly made white wines of lesser vintages. Wine probably unstable and in dubious condition, but may be drinkable.

penetrating powerful, with almost a physical effect on the nostrils. Almost certainly high in alcohol and volatile esters.

peppery a sort of raw harshness, rather hard to define, due to immature and unsettled components which have not had time to marry. Noticeable on young ruby and vintage port and many full young red wines. Probably higher alcohols.

perfume an agreeable scented quality of bouquet.

petrol analogous smell, slightly oily, petroleum overtone. Not necessarily bad.

piquant fresh and mouth-watering acidity. A desirable and customary feature of wines from the Mosel, Saar and Ruwer and from other districts, likc Sancerre. Less desirable but quite attractive in other youthful red and white table wines with a little more acidity than is usual.

plummy a colour indicating neither youth nor maturity, in between, somewhat ill-defined.

poor not 'off' or bad, but of no merit, character or quality.

positive marked and noticeable, as opposed to 'little' and 'dumb'.

powerful self-explanatory, but more appropriately used in the context of a big red wine rather than a light white wine; a Rhine wine with a full, flowery bouquet.

pricked an unpleasant sharpness due to excess volatile acidity. A pricked wine will not be pleasant to drink and will be beyond treatment. It may *just* be drinkable and will not have reached the final vinegary stage.

prickly indicates on nose, but particularly on the palate, a sharp-edged, raw, possibly almost effervescent quality. Only tolerable in certain circumstances: raw, young vinho verde and suchlike.

puckering, mouth- a tactile sensation induced by high tannin content.

pungent powerful, assertive, heavily scented or spicy, very often indicating a high degree of volatile acidity as in old madeira.

Q

quality three senses: quality wine, like fine wine, can be a vague and general term, often abused. In the EEC 'quality' wines are legally defined, with statutory minimum criteria. In the abstract sense, a wine exhibits quality by virtue of its correctness, refinement and clarity of colour; its pure varietal aroma with harmonious overtones of bouquet; with all its components well balanced, with rich and complex flavour, long finish and fragrant aftertaste.

R

racy an abstract term indicating zest, liveliness associated with breed.

raspberries a pleasant zestful and fairly common wine aroma, for example: a good Bourgeuil (red Loire), some young beaujolais.

refreshing pleasant, thirst-quenching acidity.

resinous literally imparted by the addition of resin, mainly to Greek table wines. An old practice but an acquired taste.

rich self-explanatory. Should not automatically imply sweetness, rather a full *ensemble* of fruit, flavour, alcohol and extract.

ripe wine in full bloom, having reached its maturity plateau. A mellowness prior to its decline. Ripe grapes give a wine a natural sweetness and richness.

robust full-bodied, tough yet rounded. A good strapping mouthful of wine. Could apply equally to a 13.5° Châteauneuf-du-Pape or Taylor '48.

rough a coarse, edgy sort of wine, usually of ordinary quality.

round a feature of a well-balanced, usually mature, wine. No raw immature edges.

rubbery probably presence of mercaptan, a disagreeable 'accident' of complex chemical background, often seen in old white wines due to the breakdown of sulphur.

rugged big, masculine, high in alcohol, probably tannic.

S

salty one of the so-called four primary tastes, but perhaps the least applicable to wine. A self-descriptive tang characteristic of good fresh manzanilla.

sap the little-used equivalent of a somewhat enigmatic French term implying the quality of inherent life that will develop a fine young wine.

savoury rich, spicy; mouth-smacking flavouriness.

scented positive, grapey-flowery, high-toned aroma.

sensuous rich, smooth, opulent flavour and texture.

severe hard, unyielding and probably immature.

sharp a degree of acidity between piquant and pricked. Implies a stage beyond that of being attractively refreshing. It could, however, become mollified with bottle-age.

short refers to the length of flavour on the palate, shortness, abruptness, indicating lack of quality.

sick diseased, out of condition.

silky a firm yet distinctly soft texture on the palate. A characteristic of most really fine dessert wines, also of good-quality Pomerols.

simple better than ordinary. Straightforward, un-complex.

sinewy lean yet muscular.

smoky a subtle overtone characteristic of some grapes in certain white wine districts, e.g. good *pinot-chardonnay*. *See also* FLINTY.

smooth soft, easy texture. No rough edges.

soft self-descriptive. Mellow; no rough edges; tannin and acidity fully married and absorbed.

solid full-bodied, four-square, packed with alcohol, tannin and acidity. Undeveloped.

sorbic acid not a natural grape acid but one sometimes added as a preservative. Its presence can be detected by a faint garlic-like odour.

sound the first thing a wine should be: appearance clear and bright; wholesome, clean bouquet and flavour. No faults.

sour a term to be used with care. To the English, sour has an off-taste, over-acid connotation. Others use the word as a synonym for acid.

sparkling a wine containing an induced degree of effervescence – the basis and whole point of a certain class of wine, such as champagne, the sparkle being obtained by the controlled release of carbon dioxide when the bottle is opened.

spicy a rich, herb-like aroma and flavour bestowed by certain grape varieties such as *gewürztraminer.*

spritz or *spritzig*, a slight prickle often noted visually by small beads or bubbles at the rim and on the tongue, indicating a touch of carbonic acid gas usually induced or, in a very young acid wine, left by the wine maker as a refreshing element in the wine. Examples abound: just a touch in some young moselles, blatant in vinho verde.

stalky reminiscent of the smell of damp twigs; a damp *chai*-like smell. This stalky or stemmy aroma is detectable in young wines and can arise from over-prolonged contact with grape stalks during wine making.

steely a firm, lean though not thin, white wine with a fair amount of acidity. For example, a good Chablis or Puligny-Montrachet.

stewed a somewhat ill-defined nose, not clearly varietal, not clear cut and not as good as it should be.

stimulus that which provokes a sensory response.

strange untypical, having a 'foreign' smell or taste.

stringy skinnier than sinewy, not very well constructed.

strong powerful, alcoholic.

sturdy fairly tough, substantial.

suave soft, supple and harmonious.

subtle veiled richness, unobvious complexity.

sugar grapes contain natural sugars which are converted through fermentation into alcohol. Traces of residual sugar in ripe wines are a major factor in the wine's evolution.

sugared/sugary several connotations: a sweet smell and blandness of a *chaptalized* wine; high sucrose content of a rich dessert wine.

sulphury sulphur, in its various forms, not only has a very pronounced volcanic smell but its presence can be detected physically by a prickly sensation in the nostrils and the back of the throat, like a whiff from a sulphur match or coke oven. It is commonly used as an antiseptic, for cleaning casks (by burning sulphur sticks) and bottles (using a mild sulphur dioxide solution) and if carelessly used or over-used its undesirable odour will be retained. The bouquet of many young wines is masked by a whiff of sulphur which is quite harmless and often wears off a short while after the wine has been poured out.

superficial without depth or follow-through.

supple easy to taste and sense, hard to define. A combination of sap, vigour and amenable texture.

sweaty saddle a rudely evocative smell characteristic of certain Australian red wines made from *shiraz* grapes.

sweet a wine with a high sugar content, natural or contrived. The essential characteristic of any dessert wine. There are two types of sweetness; that which is merely sweet and the other which is from the richness of fine, well-ripened grapes. The former kind will always remain sweet (e.g. Pedro Ximénez sherry), the latter will dry out as it ages. Fine Rhine wines and sauternes can be recognized by the smell emanating from *pourriture noble* but even dry wines can have a 'sweet', honeyed or grapey sweetness on the nose. The principal sweetening elements are fructose, sucrose, glucose; also, but less sweet, glycerol and alcohol.

syrupy usually used in connection with an excessively rich, ripe sauternes, *trockenbeerenauslese* or sweet sherry.

T

tactile that which provokes a response which can be physically felt (touched), e.g. sulphur, effervescence, velvety, creamy, burning (alcohol).

tang, tangy rich, high-toned, zestful bouquet and end-taste of an old madeira, old sherry, Tokay.

tannin an essential preservative derived from grape skins during fermentation. Part of the maturation process consists of the breaking down of the tannin content; it is precipitated over a period by the action of proteins and becomes, with colouring matter, part of the deposit or crust left in the bottle. The presence of tannin dries the roof of the mouth, grips the teeth and sometimes has a 'dusty cellar' smell. It is a particularly noticeable physical component of young red wine (Bordeaux in particular) which has a practical purpose: to 'cut' fatty foods and clean the palate. Tannin is less of a factor in white wines as grape skins – the main source – are removed prior to fermentation.

tart sharp and tongue-curling due to over-acidity, often with a touch too much tannin. This condition can be due to premature harvesting of grapes or a late bad harvest. The wine could recover and soften; it may, on the other hand, disintegrate. More pronounced than 'piquant'.

tartaric acid one of the good and essential acids in wine. Its chief virtue is the effervescent *spritzig* – cooling and refreshing – quality it provides (most marked in a good vinho verde, for example). Tartaric acid in the form of free acidity or acid tartrate of potassium is widely distributed in the vegetable kingdom but its chief source is the grape. Its presence gives wine its healthy, refreshing tang and contributes greatly to its quality and crisp finish. Occasionally it can be seen as light white flakes precipitated in white wine and sherry which have been subjected to an unusually low temperature.

taut somewhat severe, probably immature, firm, unyielding.

thin deficient in natural properties; watery, lacking body.

threshold level at which a given smell or taste can be perceived. Thresholds vary from person to person, from substance to substance. It is possible with practice to lower (improve) olfactory and gustatory thresholds.

tough a full-bodied wine of overpowering immaturity (not necessarily young) with an excess of tannin. May well turn out in time to be a great wine.

twiggy like stalky and stemmy, a 'reminiscent' smell; mildly derogatory and usually relating to somewhat coarse young wines.

U

unbalanced components ill-matched: over-tannic, over-acid, lacking fruit, etc.

unripe two senses: immature, raw; 'green'; malic acidity of wine made from grapes not fully ripened.

V

vanilla purely descriptive in one sense, though it can be detected in a more literal sense in the bouquet of some brandies; a tannic-like compound derived from oak giving certain cask-aged wines a distinctive aroma.

varietal a variety aroma is one with the distinctive smell of a particular grape variety such as *cabernet-sauvignon*, *gamay*, etc.

vegetal hard to define. A flavour and character more root-like than herbaceous or flowery. Related to plant growth.

velvety another textural connotation, related to silky and smooth, but implying more opulence.

vigorous lively, healthy, positive flavour associated with youthful development.

vinegar the smell of ethyl acetate, one of the simple esters, indicative of bacteriological infection. The wine will be unfit to drink, acetic and beyond redemption.

vinosity having firm, well-constituted, vinous character.

vinous a pleasant-enough and positive winey smell or taste.

viscous heavy oily wine, detected visually by its clinging meniscus and heavy bead or legs, and texture on the palate.

volatile acidity this is present to a greater or lesser extent in all wine, but an excess is undesirable and often indicates the first step in acetic deterioration (*see* VINEGAR).

W

watery lacking fruit, extract, low in alcohol and acidity.
weak low in alcohol, feeble fruit and character.
weight the heaviness or lightness depending mainly on the
  alcohol and extract and can vary enormously depending on
  the type of wine, grape, area of origin, climate, etc. Light
  wines tend to be made in the more northerly regions,
  heavier (table) wines in hot southerly areas. For example,
  the light and low in alcohol moselles and the heavier reds of
  the southern Rhône or the Cape; and contrast the light red,
  white and rosé wines of the Loire with fortified wines, a
  young ruby port being a typical heavy weight.
well balanced a satisfactory blend of physical components:
  fruit, acid, tannin, alcohol, etc., and, to a lesser extent, of
  the intangible elements: breed, character, finesse.
wishy-washy lacking crispness and distinctive flavour.
withered usually in reference to an old, dried-out wine, losing
  fruit and 'flesh' with age.
wood distinct and desirable odour derived from ageing in
  wooden casks (*see also* VANILLA).
woody an undesirable taste imparted by wine kept too long in
  cask.

Y

yeasty descriptive smell of ferments, live or dead. If detected
  in bottled wine, a sure indication of impending or recent
  secondary fermentation.
young, youthful a positive attractive feature: fresh, with
  youthful acidity; immature.

Z

zest, zestful a lively, crisply flavoured wine.
zing exciting, refreshing attribute.

FRENCH TASTING TERMS

acerbe acid; excessively sharp and bitter.
âcre harsh.
agressif raw, unripe, unharmonious.
aigre 'sour', vinegary, acetic acid taste.
aimable agreeable, nicely balanced.
amer, amertume bitter, disagreeable.
américain, goût fairly sweet (in relation to champagne). More vulgarly, implies a sugared-up blend of wine for the American market.
anglais, goût this depends on the district and context. In champagne, dry; in burgundy, big and smooth.
âpre rough, harsh; high tannin content.
arome aroma, relating to the perceived qualities arising from a particular grape variety, and so forth.
arrière-goût aftertaste.
asescence a bacteria-caused disease causing over-acidity, leading to vinegar.
astringent astringent, tannic, mouth-puckering.

bois, goût de woody taste, often the result of wine stored too long in a new cask.
bouchonné cork-tainted; smell of cork.
bouquet scent or perfume of a developing or mature wine.
bourru, vin new wine showing cloudiness prior to falling bright.
brut very dry (in relation to champagne, minimum liqueuring).

capiteux heady, high in alcohol.
casse showing cloudiness or darkening of colour usually due to metallic contamination.
charnu fleshy; full-bodied but with good acidity.
chaud 'warm', alcoholic.
chemise 'coating' – deposit on sides of bottle of old red wine.
chêne oaky character from the wood.
clairet light red, almost rosé.
classe wine of quality or potential.
complet balanced and harmonious.
corps body, robustness.
corsé full-bodied, well constituted. Satisfactory but probably not mature in that state.
coulant pleasant, easy to drink.
coupé 'cut', i.e. blended or diluted.
court short, lacking balance.
crémant 'creaming'; slight sparkle.
creux hollow; momentary thinness on palate.
cuit, goût de wine with a 'cooked' flavour, or with a natural flavour resulting from a hot summer, or very hot soil.
cuit, vin 'cooked' flavour derived from addition of concentrated must.

dégustation tasting – the subject of this book.
délicat delicate; light consistency, usually low in alcohol.
demi-sec 'half-dry' (in practice medium-sweet).
doux sweet.
dur hard; excess of tannin.

élégant elegant, stylish.
équilibré well balanced, harmonious.

étoffé well-marked qualities and well conserved.
évent, goût d' nasty, unclean smell and flat taste.
éventé wine which has been abruptly over-oxidized.

faible weak, thin.
ferme firm; the dumb unreadiness of a fine young wine.
ferment, goût de taste of a wine still fermenting; or in bottle
   having recently undergone a secondary fermentation;
   yeasty.
fin fine.
finesse grace, delicacy, breed, distinction.
fort strong.
frais fresh. In another context, cool.
franc natural, clean, sound.
français, goût sweet, particularly in relation to champagne.
fruité fruity.
fumet marked bouquet.
fusil, pierre à bouquet and/or taste reminiscent of gun flint.

garde, vin de good enough to lay down, or which *should* be
   laid down to mature.
généreux forthcoming; rich in body and extract.
goudron, goût de tarry taste.
goût taste. A term always qualified.
grain character; completeness.
graisse a diseased wine which is flat, faded and oily.
grossier big and coarse.

léger light in body and style.
liquoreux sweet and rich, implying a natural state.
long lingering flavour, intense and aromatic.
lourd heavy, dull, unbalanced.

mâché mashed: a disturbed, tired or unsettled wine.
maderisé maderised.
malgre meagre, thin and feeble.
mauvais goût bad taste; unfit to drink.
moelleux soft and rich, yet not necessarily sweet.
moisi, goût de musty taste.
mou flabby, flat, lacking in character.
mouillé watered.
mousse froth, foam, sparkle.
mousseux sparkling (fully, like champagne).
mout unfermented grape juice.
mûr balanced, in a mature not a youthful context.
muté muted; a must whose fermentation has been artificially
   arrested (leaving an unusually high unfermented sugar
   content).

nature, vin natural, unsugared wine.
nerveux firm, vigorous, vital; fine and well knit.

odeur smell, in the simple direct sense: smell of cork, smell of
   wine, of yeast.
oeil de perdrix 'partridge eye'; descriptive of the tawny-gold
   of certain types of wine.
onctueux full-bodied, fat and rich. Usually applies to sweet
   wines but not necessarily to the exclusion of red.

paille, goût de reminiscent of damp straw.
parfum perfume; fragrance. Term for grape aroma.

passé too old; going downhill (but may be drinkable, just).

pâteux thick, pasty consistency.

pauvre poor, small.

pelure d'oignon the colour of onion skin. May apply to certain *vin gris* and some rosé wines; occasionally to old and maderised white wines.

perlant slight sparkle more akin to a prickle (similar to the German term *spritzig*).

pétillant light natural sparkle.

petit a little wine, probably deficient in alcohol.

piquant sharp and acid; may be an attractive tartness or purely derogatory, depending on context.

piqué pricked. Dangerous degree of volatile acidity in a wine on its death-bed.

piqûre a disease which creates a grey film on the surface of the wine, decomposing the alcohol into vinegar.

plat flat and dull.

plein full. Not just body but character.

précoce precocious; early maturing.

race breed.

rancio, goût de smell characteristic of old *vin doux*. Usually involves a degree of oxidation and is something of an acquired taste.

riche generous.

robe colour; generally used in relation to that of a fine wine.

rond, rondeur round, harmonious.

rude astringent.

sauvage, goût taste imparted by native American vines and some hybrids.

saveur taste, in the mouth, in its broadest sense.

sec dry, fermented out.

séché dried out; harsh and flat. Withered after lying ullaged in bottle or too long in cask.

sève sap: a combination of vigour, firmness of body and aroma. The English have no equivalent term.

solide substantial, full-bodied but well balanced.

souple supple: no sharp edges; elegant balance, soft and pleasant to drink.

soyeux silky texture; supple, slightly plump.

spiritueux high in alcohol.

suave soft, supple, harmonious.

sucré a sweetness generally associated with arrested fermentation or some other less natural (i.e. added) degree of sugar.

taille, goût de raw, poor quality (after name for last pressing – the tail end).

tendre youthful delicacy. Charming: easy to drink; light and supple.

terne dull; lacking quality and interest.

terroir, goût de earthy smell and flavour derived from certain soils.

tourne a bacteriological disease that gives wine a dull appearance, a 'mousey' smell and makes it flat though acetic at the same time.

troublé 'troubled' (appearance): hazy, cloudy. Wine diseased, or temporarily out of condition.

tuilé of tile-red colour. A curious stage that a wine might reach having lost its youthful purple hue, showing a maturity which may not be long-lived.

usé worn out; past best and on decline.

velouté velvety texture.
vert 'green' – unripe.
vif fresh, young and lively.
vineux having vinosity; also high in alcohol.
vivace fresh and lively, implying youthful zing and possibly a
    certain tartness.

GERMAN TASTING TERMS

angereichert sugared.
ansprechend appealing; attractive.
art character.
artig smooth, rounded.

beerenton taste of (ripe) grapes.
bitter bitter.
bleichert rosé. Rare in Germany and mainly found in the Ahr
    Valley, and Schillerwein.
blume bouquet.
blumig flowery; good.
bukettreich rich bouquet.

charaktervoll characterful.

delikat delicate.
duft fragrance.

edel noble, fine.
edelwein very fine.
elegant elegant, stylish.
erdig earthy.

fade insipid.
faul mouldy.
fein, feine fine.
feinste finest.
fett fat.
feunig high in alcohol.
firn maderised.
flüchtig little to it.
frisch fresh.
fruchtig fruity.
fülle full, rich.

gefällig pleasing and harmonious.
gering poorish.
gewürz spice: spiciness – of bouquet or flavour.
gezuckert sugared.
glatt smooth.
grosse great, big.
grün green; unripe.
gut good.

hart hard and tart.
hefegeschmack yeasty taste.
herb bitter.
hochfeine very fine.
holzgeschmack woody taste.
honigartig honeyed.
hübsch handsome, pretty; nice, at least.

jung young.

kernig firm.
körper body.
körperarm lacking body.
kräftig robust.

lebendig racy.
leer weak in character.
lieblich pleasant.

mager thin; lacking body.
mandelbitter bitter-almond flavour.
matt flat.
milde pleasantly soft, middle of the road.

naturrein, naturwein pure, unsugared.
nervig full-bodied.

oelig of marked viscosity.

perle light natural sparkle.
pikant intriguing in tangy, spicy sense.

rafle stemmy: harsh and green.
rassig showing race; breeding.
rauh raw.
reif ripe.
rein pure.
reintönig harmonious; well balanced.
rot red.
rund round, harmonious.

saftig 'juicy'.
sauber pure; clean.
schal musty.
schaumwein sparkling wine.
schön lovely.
schwefel sulphur.
sehr fein very fine.
sekt sparkling wine.
spiel flexible, balanced.
spritzig with crisp natural prickle.
stahlig steely.
süffig not unlike *tendre* (French).
süss sweet.

trocken dry (in 'withered grape' sense).

ungezuckert unsugared; pure.

voll full.
vornehm exquisite, elegant, distinctive.

weinig vinous, displaying vinosity.
wuchtig potent.
würzig spicy.

zukunft for the future. A wine capable of development.

ITALIAN TASTING TERMS

abboccato with some sweetness.
acerbo taste of unripe apples.
aggressivo aggressive: raw, unripe, unharmonious.
allappante unpleasant, rough, ill-tempered.
amabile gentle, slightly sweet.
ammaccato disagreeable taste, between dry and musty.
ammandorlato blend of semi-sweet and almond-bitter tastes.
ampio ample: complete and generous.
aristocratico aristocratic; wine of fine pedigree: good soil,
    vines, vinification and vintage year.
armonico harmoniously blended and enhanced flavours.
asciutto dry: fermented out, clean.
aspro rough on the palate.
astringente astringent.
austero austere: a characteristic of big young wines.

carattere a wine with distinction and typical character.
caratteristico with characteristic individual traits.
carezzevole caressing: rich, flowing.
completo complete.
con retrogusto with aftertaste.
corpo body: rich in alcohol and extracts.
costituito well-constituted.

debole a wine with little character.
deciso with decisive qualities.
decrepito old and faded.
delicato fine and harmonious.
di corpo full-bodied; with high alcoholic degree.
duro hard, excess tannin.

elegante elegant, stylish.
equilibrato well balanced, harmonious.
erbaceo green, unripe, slightly piquant.

fiacco tired; lacking vigour.
franco blunt and straightforward. No subtleties.
fresco fresh in style, refreshing.
fruttato fruity.

generoso forthcoming; rich in body and extract.
grasso unctuous.

immaturo immature.

maderizzato, o marsalato maderised.
magro lean; lacking body.
marca of marked character (of grape, type, district).
morbido tender, gentle, soft and caressing in the mouth.

nerbo literally nerve. A wine of fibre and inner strength.
nervoso sensitive, delicate yet vivacious.
netto clean cut; basic taste particularly marked.
neutro neutral: of little character, lacking in acidity.

oleoso oily: probably spoiled.

passabile acceptable, inoffensive.
pieno full: with richness and body.
pronta beva a quickly maturing young wine.

rotondo round: full and mellow.
ruvido rough, raw-tasting.

salato salty character.
sapido similar to the French term *sève*.
secco dry: fermented out.
selvatico coarse, uncivilized character.
spogliato spoiled, through over-ageing.
stoffa applicable to great wines with mouth-filling many-
   faceted qualities.

tannico tannic.

vellutado velvety texture.
verde green, unripe.
vinoso vinous.
vuoto empty: superficial, short flavoured.

XIV

HOW TO RECORD
TASTING NOTES

. . . add a little to the literature of one of the three great joys in life. **George Saintsbury,** Notes on a Cellar-book

---

Why make notes?

Only two kinds of person can do without tasting notes: the rare and fortunate individual with a phenomenally freak memory, and the less rare type who chooses not to complicate matters by ever tasting more than the firm favourites he knows and likes. (There is, in fact, a third: the really experienced specialist who spends every day tasting wines in his own particular field. For example, the sherry, port or whisky blender. His highly developed palate for a comparatively limited range of smells and tastes may not require the support of the written word, save to record the names and proportions of the constituent parts selected for the blend.)

So, make notes. You will find them useful, and referring back to them enjoyable. Some methods follow overleaf.

Essential information

Frankly, any system is adequate that stores sufficient information for an individual's purpose in a speedy and accessible manner.

The following information is more or less essential:

- The date of tasting (too often omitted in the heat of the moment)
- The name of the wine (district, vineyard)
- The vintage year
- If in bottle, the name of the bottler (if estate-bottled the name of the estate. Château-bottlings merely require the qualifying initials C.B.). If from the cask, 'ex cask'
- The price (per bottle, per dozen or per cask or barrel, as appropriate)
- A description of the appearance of the wine: depth, hue or actual colour, clarity
- A description of its nose: aroma, bouquet
- A description of its taste: components, length, finish
- General conclusions: maturity, quality, value.

One important point should be made. Just because there are myriads of descriptive terms available it is not essential or desirable to overdo it; indeed, the experienced taster will tend to note only the outstanding and most meaningful characteristics, the faults and the exceptions.

All methods require time, patience and an orderly mind (or an obliging secretary with these attributes). Like piano-playing – many start, few continue – it is worth the effort in the long run, unless, of course, one is tone deaf!

A typical page of entries from my own tasting notebooks is given on pp. 150–151. I note the occasion, the host, the place and, if it is a special dinner, the food. I also index each wine by country and district, but frankly these details are very much up to the individual.

Card system

Of the various methods of collating tasting notes the card system has many virtues. A separate card for each wine is stored in district, vintage or alphabetical order. Appropriate sections can be extracted and taken to the tasting room thus saving considerable time as headings are already prepared. The main disadvantages are that it is a bulky system and individual cards can get misplaced or lost.

Tasting book

Notes are entered as the wines are tasted, in chronological order. The advantage of this system is that a series of pocket-sized books instead of boxes of cards can be used. The pages can be ruled up vertically to save re-writing main headings.

The disadvantages are the amount of work required (details of each wine have to be entered every time) and the need for an accurate and up-to-date index to make quick reference possible. Nevertheless, this is the type I use for my tasting 'daybooks'. This layout is the basis of the Tasting Notes section, pages 149–185.

Ring binders

Another system shown to me recently combines the virtues of card and book. It consists of ruled up or printed leaves, arranged horizontally and set into a ring or spiral binder. It is used like a book but leaves can be inserted as and where necessary. This, as a matter of interest, is the sort I use for the Bordeaux and port notes I extract from my day books and arrange in vintage order.

Loose-leaf

Like the card system, the wines can be kept in any order – district, vintage or alphabetical. (This combines the virtues of cards and books but tends to be bulky unless several wines can be written up on one page.)

Analytical score cards

Wines submitted to a panel of judges for comparative and competitive tasting have to be tasted methodically. Almost invariably a pre-printed tasting card is supplied, indicating the factors to be noted and assessed and giving each factor, or each group, a numerical value.

Points are awarded for positive features: negative points for faults. Maximum possible can be 7 points, more often 20, sometimes 100.

The points 'weighting' depends on the type and class of wine to be tasted, and the purpose of the tasting. For commercial entries judges might be allowed up to 4 points for colour, 6 for bouquet and 10 for taste; possibly 5, 5 and 10.

There are a variety of highly sophisticated and elaborate score cards used for equally varied types of tasting. But the vast majority are employed for either assessing and evaluating fairly closely related commercial wines, either at the academic level, producer or big trade buying levels, or at the various competitions which take place regularly in wine producing countries: for example in Mâcon, France, Orange County, California, and in the wine states of Australia. In addition, meticulous tastings along fairly rigid lines are conducted by professionals in their own regions, for example in the major German wine areas to award seals of quality.

When dealing with wines of a similar type, perhaps lacking the marked varietal characteristics and shades of colours, nose and taste of fine vintage wines, verbal descriptions tend to be inadequate and numerical ratings take their place. But just because some of these tastes and smells are so similar or hard to rate, and because all human beings are fallible – and most wine tasters impressionable – double checks are required. Hence the importance of statistical procedures, triangular tests and so forth, in strictly academic and commercial tastings. To accomplish this, the same wines are presented blind, in very clinical conditions, in varying orders. The object of these exercises is to eliminate bias and to establish, as objectively as possible, the validity of the tastings, the taste preferences and relative suitability of wines in a given context.

It is also important to test the tasters. One taster's susceptibility to sulphur dioxide, to volatile acidity, even to sweetness will be different to another's. The threshold, i.e. the level at which smells and tastes can be perceived by even experienced tasters, is not necessarily the same for tannins, the various types of acidity and sugars.

Members of professional tasting panels should be trained and those selected for competition judging must not only have proven ability but be given a clear idea of the parameters of such tastings: what to look for, what to take note of and, most important of all, on what basis should points be awarded. In Australia tasters begin as assistants to the state or area judging panel, arranging the tastings, helping out, studying the form. They then graduate to the tasting panel itself, the senior members of which eventually 'graduate' as national show judges.

Examples of numerical ratings

Systems abound, all awarding plus or minus points to facets of appearance, nose and taste. A brief summary of some of the better known follow.

The Davis Scorecard This was evolved at the famous Department of Enology at the University of California, Davis, whose graduates fill many, probably most, of the major technical positions at wineries throughout that state, and further afield.

The original Davis scorecard was as follows:

appearance	2 points
color	2 ,,
aroma and bouquet	4 ,,
volatile acidity	2 ,,
total acidity	2 ,,
sweetness	1 ,,
body	1 ,,
flavor	2 ,,
bitterness	2 ,,
general quality	2 ,,
a 'superior' wine would rate	17–20
standard	13–16
below standard	9–12
unacceptable or spoiled	1–8

It will quickly be noticed that a taster, however gifted, cannot be pulled off the street and be expected to rate a wine with even a superficially simple point system such as this without an explanation of both the terms and the weighting. In fact problems arose and a 'modified scorecard' was introduced:

appearance	2
color	2
aroma and bouquet	6
total acidity	2
sweetness	1
body	1
flavor	2
bitterness	1
astringency	1
general quality	2

An amateur would have difficulty in differentiating 'bitterness' and 'astringency'. Indeed, this sort of tasting rating is very much one for professionals who see eye to eye.

Another 20-point system roughly following the modified Davis scale seems simpler:

clarity	2
color	2
aroma	2
bouquet	2
acidity	1
balance	2
body	2
taste	3
finish	2
overall	2

Even so, each member of the panel has to have a clear idea of precisely what facet scores what. Finally, to test the significance of scores an elaborate series of statistical procedures have been devised at Davis. These are exhaustively dealt with by Amerine and Roessler (*see* Bibliography, p. 248).

My personal view is that these numerical scoring systems are doubtless valid and useful for the more humdrum wines but do not begin to aid the taster to form a meaningful assessment of fine wines.

The system used in Germany for their seals of quality is far more explicit. The following relates to German white wines:

1. Colour:	*colourless*	0
	onion skin	0
	pale	1
	typical	2
2. Clarity:	*cloudy*	0
	brilliant	2
3. Bouquet:	*faulty*	0
	mute	1
	clean	2
	fine	3
	fragrant and flavoury	4
4. Flavour:	*faulty*	0
	acceptable	1–3
	thin but characteristic	4–6
	balanced	7–9
	ripe and noble	10–12

The minimum points for an award are, respectively, 2, 2, 2 and 6 points. For Kabinett quality a minimum total of 13, for Auslese 15, Beerenauslese 16 and Trockenbeerenauslese 17.

The Italian 'National Order of Winetasters' uses the Buxbaum system which has a maximum of 20 positive points for the best, and for the worst, 'demerito', 10.

The French, as can be expected, have perhaps the most complete and sophisticated scoring systems and tasting cards. Distinguished academic tasters' names include Chabanon, Max L'Eglise, Emile Peynaud, Jacques Puisais, J. Ribereau-Gayon and A. Vedel.

The OIV (Office International de la Vigne et du Vin) has an ingenious and Gallically complicated scorecard which I first witnessed at an international wine competition in Budapest. Contrarily, the perfect score is zero, the judges noting defects which are then multiplied to arrive at the qualifying score. The card used for each wine is as follows:

Element	Weighting	Defects multiplied by				
		x 0	x 1	x 4	x 9	x 16
Appearance	1					
Colour	1					
Intensity of odour	1					
Quality of odour	2					
Intensity of taste	2					
Quality of taste	3					
Harmony/balance	2					

Outstanding features qualify for the 0 column, very good in column 1, good 4, acceptable 9 and unacceptable 16.

Once again, judges using such a score card must have explained to them precisely what is meant by the various terms and relative weightings.

Some tasters use a 10-point scale, some even 100 – though how a score of 85½ can be justified or remotely equalled on a subsequent occasion I do not know. Which brings me to my final point about scoring. The only virtue, as far as I can see, of a points system is in the context of a *range* of wines on one particular occasion, which wine was at that time considered best. And even then I regard a full description of each wine as more important, the total score being helpful to refer to at a later date when 'words fail' to convey precisely which, say, of two good wines one slightly preferred at the time.

If ever I resort to scoring, I use a simple 20 point rating:

Appearance *(depth, colour, clarity, viscosity)*	4
Nose *(grape aroma, bouquet, condition, development)*	5
Taste *(dryness, body, tannin, acidity, flavour, length)*	6
Overall Quality *(balance, finish, complexity, finesse)*	5

For the record, Hugh Johnson and I put our heads together to devise a tasting scorecard for the Sunday Times Wine Club. It is reproduced on page 140.

THE CHRISTIE'S–SUNDAY TIMES WINE CLUB TASTING CHART

		Comments
Name of Wine	Vintage	
District/type	Date purchased	
Merchant/bottler	Price	

SIGHT — Score (Maximum 4)

CLARITY cloudy, bitty, dull, clear, brilliant
DEPTH OF COLOUR watery, pale, medium, deep, dark
COLOUR (White wines) green tinge, pale yellow, yellow, gold, brown
(Red wines) purple, purple/red, red, red/brown
VISCOSITY slight sparkle, watery, normal, heavy, oily

starbright, tuilé, straw, amber, tawny, ruby, garnet, oeil de perdrix, hazy, opaque

SMELL — Score (Maximum 4)

GENERAL APPEAL neutral, clean, attractive, outstanding
off (eg, yeasty, acetic, oxidized, woody, etc.)
FRUIT AROMA none, slight, positive, identifiable eg. riesling
BOUQUET none, pleasant, complex, powerful

cedarwood, corky, woody, dumb, flowery, smoky, honeyed, lemony, spicy, mouldy, peardrops, sulphury

TASTE — Score (Maximum 9)

SWEETNESS (white wines) bone dry, medium dry, medium sweet, very sweet
TANNIN (red wines) astringent, hard, dry, soft
ACIDITY flat, refreshing, marked, tart
BODY very light and thin, light, medium, full bodied, heavy
LENGTH short, acceptable, extended, lingering
BALANCE unbalanced, good, very well balanced, perfect

appley, bitter, burning, blackcurrants, caramel, dumb, earthy, fat, flinty, green, heady, inky, flabby, mellow, metallic, mouldy, nutty, salty, sappy, silky, spicy, fleshy, woody, watery

OVERALL QUALITY — Score (Maximum 3)

Coarse, poor, acceptable, fine, outstanding

supple, finesse, breed, elegance, harmonious, rich, delicate

SCORING — Total Score (out of 20)

DATE OF TASTING

HOW TO USE THIS CHART
Wine appeals to three senses: sight, smell and taste. This card is a guide to analyzing its appeal and an aide-memoire on each wine you taste. Tick one word for each factor in the left-hand column and any of the descriptive terms which fit your impressions. Then award points according to the pleasure the wine gives you. Use the right-hand column for your comments.

Available from The Direct Sunday Times Wine Club

Compiled by Hugh Johnson and Michael Broadbent M.W. © 1975

Compiled by Hugh Johnson and Michael Broadbent M.W. © 1975

Descriptive rating cards

A variety of purely descriptive, as opposed to numerical, tasting cards have been published, but outstandingly the most interesting, again not surprisingly, is French. Steven Spurrier has kindly given me permission to reprint his English adaptation of the card devised by Castell and published by INAO. See *Academie du Vin Wine Course* (Century Publishing in association with Christie's).

The only problem with this elaborate card is that it is bulky and perhaps, for the advanced taster, somewhat inhibits the imagination and the development of one's own vocabulary.

I personally favour the written word, and the tasting sheets that end this chapter are based on the layout I myself have used for over 30 years.

The award of medals

Most professionals are wary of medals awarded at wine competitions, and, every so often, the organizers of such competitions have something of a purge, determining to give medals sparingly to avoid their devaluation and subsequent loss of credibility resulting from overmarketing.

By and large, competitions are organized in wine producing areas and open mainly to wine from those areas.

In Australia, where annual wine competitions not only thrive but are taken very seriously by the producers, high awards can lead to big sales. There, to qualify for a gold medal a wine has to score 18.5 or more out of 20; for a silver 17 to 18.4, and for a bronze 15.5 to 16.9. California has a number of similar events.

In France the highest award is generally the *Grande Médaille d'Or*, next comes the *Médaille d'Or*, then *Médaille d'Argent* followed by *2me Diplôme d'Honneur* and *3me Diplôme d'Honneur*. England has only one for local wine producers, the outright winner of which is presented with the Gore-Browne Trophy, given by a redoubtable lady wine-growing pioneer in memory of her husband. However, not to be outdone, England also boasts an international wine competition, the brain-child of Anton Massel and his Oenological Research Laboratory in which wines of different types and origins are judged in their respective classes. Medals are awarded annually, 'double-golds' being not uncommon.

There is no doubt that competition is healthy, and if the possibility of winning a medal will induce wine producers to strive for even better quality, so much the better for the eventual consumer.

Another benefit is the opportunity to compare; to see what one's rivals are up to and with what success. If the judges are fair and representative, the producer can perhaps gain a clearer idea of what style of wine has the greatest appeal. And of course the attendant publicity is good.

The one major snag is that some really top class wineries, such as Heitz in California, care not to enter their wine. They have an established reputation which does not need the endorsement of a medal. For Lafite or the Domaine de la Romanée-Conti, entering such competitions would be demeaning and any subsequent award superfluous. And there is always the nagging worry that they would not come top!

HOW TO TASTE –
A PRACTICAL RECAPITULATION

So far in this book I have given the reader a good deal of background detail; how the senses work, the elements which make up the tasting process, and characteristics of regions, grapes, etc. The organization of tastings and their use of words has also been dealt with. What I propose to do now is to precede the act of making actual tasting notes with a summary of how to approach the wine: what precisely to look for, how to sniff and taste effectively and what factors to bear in mind.

UNDER THE HEADING APPEARANCE

The two main elements are depth and the actual hue or colour. Secondary factors are clarity and viscosity. Here is how to set about spotting them.

Assuming we have the correct sort of tasting glass, a white topped table and suitable lighting, already described, the

Wine Type (White/Rosé/Red)			Appellation:
			Type:

Laboratory observations and conclusion   Date of Analysis

Specific Gravity		
Alcohol	Total Acidity	
Residual Sugar	Fixed Acidity	
Potential Alcohol	Volatile Acidity	
Total SO$_2$ pH	(corrected for sulphuric acid)	
Free SO$_2$ colour index P/x		
Index of permanganate		

Method of Vinification

Visual Examination	Surface of the liquid		*Brilliant – dull* *Clean – iridescent – oily*
	Colour	White Wine	*Pale with green or yellow tints – pale yellow – straw yellow – canary yellow – gold – amber*
		Rosé Wine	*Pale with violet or rose tints – grey – light rose – deep rose – partridge eye – onion skin*
		Red Wine	*Red with crimson or violet tints – cherry red – ruby – garnet red – red brown – tile red – mahogany – tawny*
		Colour Hue	*Frank – oxidized – cloudy*
	Aspect		*Crystalline – brilliant – limpid – hazy – cloudy – turgid – lead – grey/white – opaque, with or without deposit*
	Legs/Tears		*Quick or slow to form – non existent – slight – heavy*
Temperature of the Wine	**Any factor hindering the tasting**		

Olfactory Examination	First Impression		*Pleasant – ordinary – unpleasant*
	Aroma	*Intensity*	*Powerful – adequate – feeble – non-existent*
		Quality	*Very fine – racy – distinguished – fine – ordinary – common – not very pleasant – unpleasant*
		Character	*Primary – secondary – tertiary – floral – fruity – vegetal – spicy – animal – oxidized*
		Length	*Long – average – short*
	Abnormal odours		*CO$_2$ – SO$_2$ – H$_2$S – mercaptan – strongly oxidized – woody – lactic acid* *acescence – phenolic – corky* *flaw* { *temporary – permanent* / *slight – serious* }
	Details		

Any factor hindering or stopping the continuation of the tasting

Gustatory Examination	First Impression			
	Flavours and sensations	*Sweetness*	Sugar	*Heavy – very sweet – sweet – dry – brut*
			Glycerine and alcohol	*Soft – unctuous – velvety – smooth – rough – dried out*
		Acidity	Excessive	*Acid – green – tart – nervy – acidulous*
			Balanced	*Fresh – lively – supple – smooth*
			Insufficient	*Flat – flabby*
		Body	Alcoholic strength	*Light – sufficient – generous – heady – hot*
			Flesh	*Fat – round – full – thin – meagre*
			Tannin	*Rich – balanced – insufficient – astringent – bitter*
		Aromas in the mouth	Intensity	*Powerful – average – weak – long – short*
			Quality	*Very fine – elegant – pleasant – common – faded*
			Nature	*Floral – fruity – vegetable – spicy – wood – chemical – animal – other young – developed – complex*
	Inherent or Abnormal Flavours	*'Terroir'*		*Marked – noticeable – faint – non-existent*
		Sickness		*Grease – turned – aldehydes – sweet – sour – rancid – acetic acid – lactic acid*
		Accident		*Stagnant – mould – lees – woody – cork – metallic – H$_2$S – herbaceous – acrid*
	Final Impression	*Balance*		*Harmonious – bold – correct – unbalanced Xs acid, Xs sugar, Xs tannin, Xs alcohol*
		After taste		*Straightforward – unpleasant*
		Resistance of taste and aroma		*> 8 sec 5–7 sec 4–5 sec < 3 sec Very long long medium short*
Conclusions				
	Conformity to appellation or type			
	Score out of 20			
	Summary of tasting (character of wine – future, readiness for drinking)			

depth of colour is observed by leaving the glass on the table and looking down at an angle of 45° or from immediately above. The variations in the depth of white wine is slight and relatively unimportant. The depth of red wine *is* important and significant, a pale colour usually indicates lightness of body and extract (though some fine burgundies with fairly high alcohol content can be misleadingly pale), a deep colour foreshadows a fuller-bodied wine and a very deep, virtually opaque quality will be indicative of high alcohol content and extract and probably much tannin and fruit. The depth of colour can be controlled by vinification, but in classic districts like Bordeaux a deep colour generally indicates a good vintage, and conversely, a weak feeble colour a poor vintage. (Hot sun thickens the skins which provide this red pigment; warmth creates, through the leaves, the sugar content which converts into alcohol. So, in a good year, after a hot sunny summer and early autumn, the wine produced will have a deep, intense colour and high alcohol content: the hotter the sun the darker and more alcoholic the wine. Lack of both sun and warmth, usually associated with cloudy, cold and wet weather results in thin skins, low sugar converting to low alcohol, and pale colour.)

Colour or hue

Pick up the glass by the stem, tilt it over the white table top and, from above, observe the colour at the deepest part of the bowl and its gradation to the rim.

White wine Notice the hint of green in young dry whites, particularly from northerly wine districts like the Moselle and Sancerre; the more positive yellow pigment of a ripe *chardonnay* from Meursault or the Napa Valley; the already yellow-gold shades of young dessert wines and the deeper yellows, golds and ambers resulting from mature bottle age.

Red wine A bright purple rim indicates immaturity, a plummy red the transition stage and, before the red-brown of maturity, sets in, a no man's land which I describe as 'on the turn'. Note the rich mahogany rim of an old claret and watch out for the telltale drab brown of one which is too old and oxidized.

Colour, incidentally, is the most accurate measure of the maturity of red wine.

Clarity, brightness, limpidity

Pick up the glass by the stem and hold it up to a light.

A fine wine in a healthy condition seems to have that extra sheen, rather like the bloom on a perfect peach. A lack-lustre appearance will usually indicate a lack-lustre wine. Slight bittiness may be due to careless bottling and is usually of little importance, as are pieces of cork, the result of the corking machine or one's own careless cork pulling. Cloudiness, a slight milky, blue or orange hue indicates a fault.

Viscosity, legs and beads

Keep the base of the glass on the table and rotate it, swirling the wine up the sides of the glass. Observe the way the ring of liquid slips down and forms legs or tears. For their significance *see* p. 30.

At the same time see if there are any tell tale beads round the rim of the wine, tiny bubbles which, in a young white wine and some young reds indicate the presence of carbon dioxide which will give a *spritzig* prickle or *pétillance* in the mouth; in an old red wine it is more likely a sign of cracking up.

UNDER THE HEADING NOSE OR BOUQUET

Again, rotate the base of the glass to wash with wine the maximum inner surface area of the glass, arousing the wine and helping it release its volatile ethers.

The next movement is to pick up the glass by the stem and just waft it under the nose. It is essential to give one's fullest concentration to this in order not to miss the vital first impression. Just lightly inhale and note whether the wine is clean and fresh, has a distinctive varietal (grape) aroma, shows youthful acidity, or mellow age. By no means all that a wine has to reveal is yielded or conveyed by that first impression but it sometimes triggers off an immediate recognition. It is certainly the most evocative stage. And it is the first impression which, hopefully, will capture and encapsulate the fleeting volatile elements of the wine's make up. Emile Peynaud with refreshing simplicity describes volatile substances as 'those capable of escaping from the glass or disappearing in the mouth'. They are easy, superficially, to spot but very difficult to analyse; extremely important in relation to quality and, to quote Peynaud again, 'give the wine its personality'.

Next, give another gentle swirl, hold the wine to the nose and this time give it quite a few short, sharp sniffs. Whilst doing this try to sort out each element: the fruit, perhaps a noticeable grape variety, the acidity – mouth puckering malic, the cooking apple smell of unripe 'green' grapes; the pleasant mouthwatering tartaric acid; the high-toned faintly vinegary whiff of too high volatile acidity. Beware: if you sniff too protractedly over a short period of time the nose will become anaesthetized. The same applies to really deep long sniffs. The nett result in each case will be a diminution of smell.

Sometimes a very young red wine yields little on the nose. A leathery smell indicates the presence of considerable tannin, a pepperiness high alcohol content. Deeper sniffs will detect and draw out underlying latent richness and fruit.

A mature white wine of a good vintage will have a soft, fragrant, honey-like bouquet. A fine mature claret a well-knit mellow, warm brick smell which will develop in the glass to a rich, wholemeal-biscuity fragrance. But a magnificently opulent bouquet sometimes serves to disguise the structure of the wine itself which may be falling apart.

Young wines have raw component parts which can, in effect, be separated, i.e. individually detected. As wines mature, those components parts blend together, losing their individual identities, becoming a complete, homogeneous fragrance – but not by any means the same: burgundy and claret, Rheingau and Anjou, each will have its own character, weight, style.

UNDER THE HEADING PALATE OR TASTE

For the experienced taster, the wine in the mouth will largely confirm what the eye has seen and judged and the nose smelled and assessed.

Take a sip, a reasonable mouthful. Notice the entry: here any sweetness of the wine will be detected. Draw in air as the wine crosses the tongue. This will help the aromatic elements of taste fill the mouth. If at a tasting, spit out, otherwise swallow, noting various facets as it crosses the palate, its length and finish.

Note the taste elements in a logical order.

Sweetness

Perhaps the most important feature of a white wine, and certainly the first to be noticed. Is it dry, i.e. totally lacking sweetness, slightly sweet or very sweet?

Virtually all red wines are fully fermented out, leaving little or no residual sugar. So the dryness/sweetness factor is not important: red wines are basically dry. Having said this, a certain softness and slight sweetness is noted when a red wine has been made from fully ripe grapes, of a particularly good vintage in Bordeaux or Burgundy, or from a hot sunny wine area. This is partly due to a minute amount of left-over sugar but mainly, I believe, from the unusually high level of ethyl-alcohol, which gives an impression of sweetness.

Sweetness should be judged on entry not at the back of the mouth as the acid content of the wine can have a masking effect or, conversely, may exaggerate the 'dryness'. Wines with naturally high acidity, like madeira and some German dessert wines, need sweetness to be palatable, as strawberries need sugar.

Acidity

Acidity makes one cluck one's tongue. An agreeable degree of tartaric acid will give the wine a pleasant, refreshing quality. To me, acidity is the nervous system of a wine, for apart from its effect in the mouth it is one of the essential elements, a corner stone, without which the wine will not keep, without which the wine will be flat and dull. Acidity gives the wine finish. It also acts as a balancing partner with the natural sugar content of sweet wines.

Too much acidity, raw unripe acidity, upsets the balance, tastes tart, draws in the cheeks. There are various sorts of acidity listed in my Full Glossary of Tasting Terms and many words used to describe degrees and effects of acidity – such as acetic, sharp, tart, green, sour – are defined on page 112.

Body, weight, alcohol

Is the wine light and insubstantial in the mouth or is it heavy, massive, mouth filling? The dominating factor is alcohol. 11° G.L. (the Gay Lussac measure) or 11% by weight or volume, more or less the same, feels light, is light: for example moselles. Medium weight will probably be in the 12% area, say a moderately good claret of a moderately good vintage. Full-bodied is 13% or more: a red Corton or classic Châteauneuf-du-Pape. But alcohol does not travel alone. A full-bodied young red wine will also be loaded with tannin; it will have fruit, extract, in short, substance. But alcohol is the wine's backbone.

Tannin

As this is derived from skins and pips during fermentation, also from long storage in small oak casks, tannin is a major element in the structure of red wines (white wines are fermented without skins and pips and sometimes spend little or no time in wooden casks).

Tannin dries the mouth. In young wines it is also bitter, but this ameliorates with age. It is essential to have high alcoholic content to balance, with its sweetness and warmth, the astringency of a substantial tannic content. Where the alcoholic content and extract is comparatively low, as with young Beaujolais, the tannin is exposed and often leaves a bitter, tinny taste in the mouth.

Fruit, wood and other flavours

Sugars, acids, alcohols and tannins are perhaps the basic structural elements. Happily the flavour of wine is supplemented by a myriad of other trace elements, volatile, fixed, derived from the fruit itself, from the minerals taken from the soil, from the process of fermentation, the yeasts, from the wood, even from the air.

A lot of spicy and aromatic flavours (and smells, for they are linked) are directly attributable to a particular cause. For example, vanilla is from ethylvanilline, the principal odour of oak wood; leather, tannin. But by far the most smells and tastes are described by analogy, the closest resemblance to the wine in the mouth. Yet all there for a particular physical or chemical reason.

This is why the taster should first of all try hard to recognize smells and tastes such as tobacco, pine or petroleum, caramel, crusty bread, liquorice, pepper, cinnamon, and note the wine, its origin, age, grape variety, so that one can link a smell and a place, a soil, a method of wine making, a hot year. The combination of these smells and tastes often results in something indefinable. Add an element, try to take it away, and the whole ensemble crumbles. This is the mystery, and the challenge of wine.

The taster should not be afraid to try and put into words the immediate impact of the smell and taste of a wine no matter how fanciful these may sound. Let the wine do the speaking, you do the translating.

Balance, finesse – the facets of quality

By balance we mean that the interwoven component parts are in equilibrium: not just that the acidity balances the tannin, that the alcohol is sufficient to support both, but that the subtler, volatile and often evasive elements add to the sum total, not detract, add character without being intrusive.

A young wine can be balanced despite its lack of development, but only a fully mature wine will have the softness, yet firmness, delicacy with strength, length without attenuation, unfolding and revealing the more one noses and tastes.

Length is a measure of quality; the time the flavour takes to cross the mouth; fragrant intensity, filling the mouth with flavour; the aftertaste, the persistence of flavour and fragrance after the wine has been swallowed.

A poor wine might well have a raw, coarse texture, lack of positive flavour and a grubby, unclean end taste. An ordinary wine comes into the mouth with no particular impact, has a neutral, faintly winey flavour which disappears into a short insipid end. A good wine will have a positive entry, positive flavour – a beginning, middle and end. A fine wine has length, possibly a silky texture, mouth filling yet delicate flavour, good length, crisp finish and a lingering after taste. A great wine is a fine wine with extra dimensions and, like a kaleidoscope, presents the taster's nose and palate with extraordinary changing patterns.

Making your own tasting notes

Try different ways of expressing in words the qualities of the same wine, first noting the basic elements: *deep purple/low-keyed nose/dry, full, tannic, unready.* Then expand, for example: *deep, opaque at the centre, immature purple rim/ bouquet undeveloped but underlying aroma, merlot dominating. Will develop/hint of ripeness on entry but overall dry with*

147

substantial tannin and acidity. Full-bodied, high alcoholic content, rich extract, good length. Drinkable in five years, possibly fully-developed in 10, sound mature lifespan up to 20 years from the date of tasting. And what about a numerical rating, say 17/20 for intrinsic quality and future promise. If all this is too much, then at the very least: *'deep, young, will be good.'*

A last word of advice: try and gear your notes to match the type and quality of wine. It is fatuous to dream up an elaborate description of a wine whose sole virtue is a bargain price allied to modest drinkability. Conversely it is a tragic waste not to notice, and note, the beautiful appearance, fragrant nose and lovely taste of something really special.

TASTING NOTES

Date	Name of wine	Vintage	Source/price	Tasting notes	Rating †
(1984) April 4	Dow Oporto bottled	1960	at pre-sale tasting (Sold £110 per doz.)	fairly deep plummy colour; rich, singed nose, raisiny and spirity, not yet fully knit; sweet, fullish body, very flavoury, good tannin & acidity. Long life.	xx(xx)
April 9	'Claret' (Ac Bordeaux)	—	Peter Dominic £2.39 per bottle	Medium, cherry red; fresh, youthful, some fruit; overall quite pleasant and good value	x
April 17	Chas. Heidsieck (half-bottle)	1966	old stock	ominously look corky. Old straw colour; little life; nose to match; drab, oxidised, beery end-taste. Ugh!	
April 18	Tignanello Antinori	1979	at Wine & Food Society tasting, Montreal	fairly deep but looking mature (for its age; Vitaclli) pleasant brambly-fruit nose; slightly sweet on entry, dry tannin finish. Agreeable flavour, weight, style impressive depth and richness; 'legs' like Gothic arches; bouquet meets the nose half way; rich, well-developed, elegant, fragrant, fruit — prune?	xx(x)‡ x
	Gran Coronas Torres	1976	''	raspberry fruit? Positive on palate, fairly full-bodied, alcoholic, good supporting tannin & acidity. Lovely	xxx x(x)
April 21	Ch. La Tonnelle (Blaye)	1976	Bottled by Berry Bros. £3.95	Medium colour; pleasant nose, touch of sweetness on entry; n/a, soft, pleasing now — ready	xx

Date	Wine	Vintage	Source	Notes	Rating
April 22	Hochheimer Victoria Berg Königin Riesling Estate bottled: Tabishaum	1981	Deinhard's 1983 Trade price £33.16p per case + VAT	With Rosemary & Michael Ward at CL. Pale; light, fragrant, slightly grapey; medium-dry, lightish, pleasant flavour. Just enough acidity. Fresher & better last summer?	) x
April 26	Vougeot 1er cru Georges Clerget	1976	Delamotte's	At Delamotte's — lunch. Deep colour; sweet soft fragrant 'beetroot' nose but, curiously showing a touch of old age. Flavour to match. Characteristic firm '76 Burgundy backbone	xx(x +?)
April 27	Ch. Palmer from an impériale	1962	— (donated by a member)	At Sainsbury Club dinner. Deep impressive colour; intense, still maturing; fabulous forthcoming bouquet; harmonious, elegant; medium-dry entry leading to a very dry, slightly acidic finish. Touch of bitterness on finish but wore off with time, air & food. Zestful, flavoury.	xxxx

Footnote: unless at a comparative tasting, when I work to a 20-point scale, I generally stick to a broad 5-star classification or rating; no star = poor, * fair, average, xx quite good, xxx very good, xxxx outstanding
† xxx(x) = good to drink now but very good when fully mature

151

Date	Name of wine	Vintage	Source/price	Tasting notes	Rating

Date	Name of wine	Vintage	Source/price	Tasting notes	Rating

Date	Name of wine	Vintage	Source/price	Tasting notes	Rating

Date	Name of wine	Vintage	Source/price	Tasting notes	Rating

Date	Name of wine	Vintage	Source/price	Tasting notes	Rating

Date	Name of wine	Vintage	Source/price	Tasting notes	Rating

Date	Name of wine	Vintage	Source/price	Tasting notes	Rating

Date	Name of wine	Vintage	Source/price	Tasting notes	Rating

Date	Name of wine	Vintage	Source/price	Tasting notes	Rating

Date	Name of wine	Vintage	Source/price	Tasting notes	Rating

Date	Name of wine	Vintage	Source/price	Tasting notes	Rating

Date	Name of wine	Vintage	Source/price	Tasting notes	Rating

Date	Name of wine	Vintage	Source/price	Tasting notes	Rating

Date	Name of wine	Vintage	Source/price	Tasting notes	Rating

Date	Name of wine	Vintage	Source/price	Tasting notes	Rating

Date	Name of wine	Vintage	Source/price	Tasting notes	Rating

Date	Name of wine	Vintage	Source/price	Tasting notes	Rating

=== XV ===
FROM CELLAR
TO TABLE

O for a draught of vintage! that hath been
Cool'd a long age in the deep-delvèd earth. **Keats**

Ideal wine storage

There is no doubt about it, the traditional cold and slightly damp cellar beneath the ground floor of the English and Scottish country mansion was, and still is, ideal for the storage of wine of all types: red, white, sparkling, fortified, young or old.

But I, as an old-fashioned romantic, readily accede that an above-ground, temperature and humidity controlled, wine 'cellar' will protect and preserve wine in the most demanding of climates. My frequent travels in the United States have demonstrated the efficacy of air-conditioning, the only problems being the possible exposure to heat *en route* from supplier to final destination, and failure of the electricity supply.

Before defining the ideal conditions and alternative layouts of the cellar, a word about transport might be timely.

Safe transport of wine from producer to consumer

It is significant that only recently have the overall problems of wine transportation been the subject of concentrated thought. The first International Symposium on Wine Transportation took place in Montreal in April 1984. Jointly organized by the Quebec Liquor Authority and *L'Union Internationale des Oenologues*, every aspect of transport and the condition of wine was discussed by world experts.

But there is nothing new about the problem. It was the practical difficulty of transporting wine to the frontier provinces which encouraged the Romans to carry vine stocks rather than wine, to grow grapes and make wine on the spot.

In England, in the Middle Ages, there was an immense trade in wine. We are reminded by wine historians that for 300 years, following the marriage of Eleanor of Aquitaine to Henry II, Bordeaux and its wine hinterlands came under the English crown. What is less well known is the sheer scale of the wine trade during this period. At its peak, during the reign of Edward III, not only was claret as common a tipple as ale but wine, from the Rhine as well as Bordeaux, was the third biggest business in England. Wine shippers abounded and were highly experienced. Every spring huge convoys of wine-laden ships would set sail down the Gironde bound for London, Bristol and the other traditional wine ports. Spring was chosen not just because there was a taste for 'new wine' but to avoid the rigours of winter and the danger of summer heat spoilage.

The stability of wines made in and shipped from areas farther south and hotter than Bordeaux presented additional problems. The solution was to dose the wine with brandy. This was probably done to stabilize red Douro wines as early as the 17th century and became the norm in 18th century for port, for sherry shipped from Cadiz, and even farther to the south, from Madeira. Indeed, such was the effectiveness of fortification that madeira, far from deteriorating actually benefited from long sea voyages to hot climates. It was the wine, *par excellence*, suited to the steamy climate of the American colonies, well before the advent of air-conditioning.

Until very recent times, wines tended to be shipped to England from classic European vineyard areas only in the spring and autumn. Certainly the traditions of the trade and our temperate climate reduced the risk of deterioration to the absolute minimum during shipment, handling, bottling and final delivery. However, it is my belief that the economies of continuous overland container transport and the necessity to keep expensive bottling lines in operation has lulled us into carelessly or deliberately ignoring both the weather and the wine's readiness for bottling. Perhaps it is as well that most fine wine is now bottled by the producer, for the importing trade and merchants have, by and large, dissipated both their experience and skilled staff. The sort of wines which are shipped for bottling in England are fairly insensitive commercial blends.

Across the seas, it is another matter. It is alas not uncommon for wine to be frozen aboard ships in the St. Lawrence river bound for the American Midwest; for wine to be overheated, almost boiled, on the dockside at Galveston in the oppressive heat of August before being trucked to cities in Texas; for the corks of first-growths to be popped in the cargo hold of a transcontinental jet liner. The shipper still has a great responsibility to see that his wine, which has been made with such care arrives at its destination in good condition, despite all the risks and vagaries of the weather.

Cellars and 'cellars'

I must assume that every responsible wine merchant knows perfectly well how to store wine. My advice is directed towards the amateur.

Temperature Assuming that one has a single storage unit and wants to set the air-conditioning unit at a steady year round temperature I would suggest 55°F (13°C). This, in my experience, is the average temperature of the traditional country house cellar. I say average advisedly, for I have found it to vary from a fairly rare, unvarying, 48°F (8°C) – this was in the famous cellar at Fasque, a house in Scotland belonging to the Gladstone family: the whole house was cold; the cellar, a smallish, roughly seven metres square, three-section cellar with stone floor, walls and ceiling, beneath the centre rear of the house – to temperatures well above 60°F (16°C) and even worse, those near to recently installed boilers or with central heating pipes traversing the cellar.

By and large, the best traditional cellars have been beneath the ground floor but with air bricks or vents just above the outside ground level. Ventilation is important, and a slight current of air is considered essential to prevent stale air and muggy conditions which encourage the formation of mould and rot.

I will just mention one remarkable modern cellar. Built in California with three sections, the main area, in which cases of youngish vintage wine are stacked, is kept at a steady 55°F (13°C). Beyond it, through double glass doors is the old-wine section where pre-phylloxera claret, ancient sauternes, hock and other rarities are binned in metal racks at a temperature of 50°F (10°C). The outer cellar area, with the steps leading down is held at 60°F (16°C) or perhaps even a little warmer. Here are stored the very young vintage ports, to encourage their development, and wines for everyday drinking.

Humidity This is rarely a problem in country house cellars but is important to control in artificially maintained modern cellars. The ideal appears to be around 60°%. Without adequate humidity there is the risk of corks drying out and shrinking.

The other extreme, damp, will not harm the wine but, if excessive, will soon cause labels to disintegrate, cartons to collapse and the base of wooden cases to rot. 'Bin-soiled' labels are not really worrying but become a problem when the labels become unreadable. The longer bottles are stored in a damp cellar the more the labels are likely to deteriorate, which is why vintage port was traditionally binned away unlabelled, identification being by means of bin labels, bottles having wax seals embossed with the vintage year and either the bottlers name or that of the shipper or his brand name. As the final line of defence, the long port corks are branded with the name of the port and its vintage.

The effect of a damp cellar can sometimes be catastrophic. I recently came across one in which a stack of cardboard wine cartons had collapsed and the contents, claret and burgundy of different châteaux, domaines and vintages, were very hard to sort out. Not only were the labels badly damaged but, to make matters worse, the weight of the collapsed boxes resulted in quite a few breakages which, in turn, stained the remaining labels.

Temperature and humidity For the unsophisticated I can define the ideal, which is based on Lord Rosebery's cellar at Dalmeny House, his Scottish seat. When entering the cellar there is a distinct chill: one needs warm clothing. And as for humidity, a gummed label will start to curl in seconds after it is put on a flat surface.

Shelves and bins Without becoming too technical or complicated, for we are straying a little beyond the subject, the type of shelves or bins will depend partly on the space available and partly on the needs of the owner. Assuming that storage is to be as versatile as possible I recommend:

For long term storage:
- an open space for stacking red Bordeaux and any other wines in original wooden cases
- sturdy shelves one or two cases deep, one to three cases high, for storing cases and cartons. (One end of a box or carton usually bears the name of the wine. Keep this to the outer side)
- rectangular 'bins' or shelves two to four bottles deep, about 75 cm high and 90 cm wide, the bottles being stacked in rows on wooden laths. This is the traditional method and, for large quantities, is far and away the most economical use of space
- in diamond-shaped wooden wall bins, each side measuring roughly one metre. This is convenient for smallish quantities.

For everyday use and small quantities:
- small bins or shelves, one bottle deep
- diamond-shaped bins as mentioned above
- traditional metal and wood single-bottle racks.
  These are ideal for a collection of odd and old bottles but uneconomic in space for large runs of one wine.

Decanting table It is handy to have a small table for making notes whilst binning, for decanting and for minor cellar equipment. I will not presume to enumerate such minutiae;

save to say that many cellars I have been in, and not just in the United States, are incredibly elaborate with fancy lights, wall maps and a decoration of vinous miscellany. Each to his own . . . (I have a bicycle in my London cellar!)

Bringing wine up from the cellar

This is not meant to be superfluous waffle but practical advice. It is given in answer to questions I am frequently asked about how far in advance one brings up, or pulls out, wine for a dinner party, its temperature and how, in general, to handle it.

The need for looking ahead does not of course apply to ordinary everyday wines, nor for most white wines. The following remarks apply to most good quality red wine, claret in particular.

My practice is to bring the wine from the cellar at least 24 hours before the meal in question, standing the bottle upright on a sideboard in the dining room to give it reasonable time for the sediment to settle, also to allow the wine to lose its cellar chill and gradually attain room temperature. Never heat the bottle, either by standing it in front of a fire or in hot water.

Most restaurants have a dispensing area where a range of red wine is kept at drinking temperature. The selection is usually based on the more usually asked for wines, the rarer, more expensive bottles being stored at cellar temperature. So if you are planning a dinner party in a top class restaurant with really good wine it is sensible to order the wines at least a day before to avoid the problem of having the red wine brought to the table too cold or, worse, 'just warmed a little sir'.

When to draw the cork?

How far in advance should one open a bottle? This is a most frequently asked question, particularly in relation to fine and/or old wines, and one to which there is, paradoxically, no firm and sure answer. (The question does not arise in the context of most white wines, rosés and the youngest and cheapest reds: just pull the cork and serve.)

If your vintage wine is old enough to have thrown a deposit then I recommend drawing the cork a couple of hours before decanting. The reason for this is that if there is a stubborn or difficult cork and one jolts the bottle and disturbs the sediment, the wine is given time to settle down again before decanting and serving. Leave the bottle upright after the cork is drawn and either balance the cork on the top or re-insert it fractionally.

Removing the cork

This might not be deemed worthy of mention in a book on tasting but a great deal of ingenious thought, from the 18th century until the present day, has been given to this essential operation.

The object of the exercise is to remove the cork cleanly, without it breaking or dropping bits into the wine, and without shaking the bottle and disturbing the sediment. Most corks give little trouble, and most corkscrews work, after a fashion.

However, some corkscrews are decidedly better than others. The best have added refinements such as ease of insertion and maximum pull for minimum effort. The early-to-mid-19th century patent continuous-action and ratchet types were undoubtedly the best* and the highly effective modern version is the Screwpull which for ease and ultimate refinement is outstandingly the most efficient, its only slight drawback being the time taken to remove the cork from the thread of the screw when drawn. As an added bonus, not thought of by the inventor, its base can be used as a candle holder. On occasion, the long corks of very old claret and of mature vintage port are best tackled with a long-shanked, broad-bladed corkscrew. Old claret corks can be crumbly and a broad-flanged corkscrew will give greater support, minimizing the bits of cork and cork powder dropping on to the surface of the wine. My old friend Alexander (Sandy) McNally uses compressed air cork removers at the Heublein pre-sale tastings. The cushion of air probably does not disturb the wine, but I have never liked the implement.

Vintage port poses a different problem. In addition to the length and strength of the cork, the traditional port bottle is slightly bulbous between the top of the shoulder and upper neck, the lower half of the cork swelling to form a very efficient air-excluding wedge which makes it difficult to extract the cork in one piece. In older bottles the applied top has an internal ridge which forms an obstruction. In face of these difficulties I normally partially insert the corkscrew and remove just the upper half of the cork, pushing the lower part back into the bottle. I find this is better than thrusting the corkscrew the full length of the cork and only pulling out bits.

On those rare occasions when the precise name and age of the port is unknown I break the bottle after decanting to retrieve the lower half of the cork and, matching it with the upper part previously removed, hope that branding will reveal the shipper's name and vintage year, an impossibility if a difficult cork has been removed in little pieces by just digging away with the corkscrew.

Cracking a bottle of port

To 'crack a bottle' is an old colloquialism for opening/sharing a bottle. But if the bottle happens to be of old vintage port, the 'cracking' can be literal. One way is to use the back of a heavy knife, the other with port tongs. Both methods have as prime aim the literal cracking of the upper part of the neck in order to remove it cleanly, with the cork still in place. The top removed, one decants the port in the normal way. If necessary, one can then break the glass of the severed neck to remove the branded cork in one piece. I frequently do this to identify otherwise anonymous old bottles. It is sensible to wrap the neck in newspaper or an old cloth to stop fragments of glass flying around. I use a hammer, but with just sufficient force to crack the glass, not to damage the cork.

Now for the heavy blade and port tong techniques.

Perhaps I can best describe the first method by recalling a superb performance by an old friend, a retired colonel with an excellent cellar, who – quite unselfconsciously – at a great wine dinner held a bottle of old port in his left hand and, over the fireplace, with his right hand briskly swept the back of a sword upwards, more or less parallel with its neck. Catching

---

*Those who would like to delve into this fascinating sideline are recommended to read the authoritative and well illustrated book on the subject, *Corkscrews for Collectors* by Bernard M. Watney and Homer D. Babbidge (Sotheby Parke Bernet, London and New York, 1981)

the underside of the lip of the bottle he removed it, and the top of the neck, at one stroke. The bottle itself received a bit of a jolt but the crust was firmly formed and there was no problem decanting. Two words of advice: the back of a light modern bread knife will not do, an old fashioned carving knife is better – unless one has a cutlass handy. Also modern – say post 1960 – machine-made port bottles do not have a sharply jutting ledge just below the top of the neck like the bottles of old, which make it difficult to hit it fair and square.

Port tongs are as traditional but, happily, in the right hands, more effective. The object is to introduce a sudden change of temperature which will crack the glass.

Take a pair of cast-iron port tongs (they can be bought from enterprising merchants of vinous artifacts) and stick the pincer end into the fire or on to a really hot stove until they are just about red hot. Clamp the tongs round the upper part of the neck of the bottle, hold them there for a few seconds to heat the glass then touch the neck with a cloth soaked in cold water. The neck will crack. Remove the whole of the top carefully so as not to disturb any shards of glass, and decant. The advantage of this method is that it works even with modern bottles.

Decanting

More fatuous argument has been stimulated by this side issue than almost any other.

The reasons for decanting are quite elementary, and the procedure is not difficult.

The principal reason for decanting is to be in a position to serve wine clear and bright, leaving any bits of sediment in the bottom of the bottle instead of pouring it into the glasses. Does it matter? Well yes, it does. It is not only unsightly to have a hazy or bitty wine in the glass but the sediment, mainly dead colouring matter in red wine, will affect the taste.

The second, in my opinion far less important, reason for decanting is to aerate the wine. It is in this area that there is a great deal of muddled thinking so let me deal with this first.

Aerating wine or 'breathing time'

By general consensus, young wines can take, possibly need, plenty of breathing time, older wines less. Very old wines scarcely any time at all: just extract the cork and decant carefully.

If it was only as simple as that.

Once again I must preface my remarks by saying that the vast majority of the world's wines can be treated in an offhand way: just open and pour. Virtually all commercial reds, rosés and quite a few better quality whites do not change with exposure to air in normal serving and drinking conditions. However *all* will oxidize and 'flatten' in taste if left open or ullaged for any length of time, by which I mean several days.

So we are talking here about better class vintage wines, principally red.

The important thing to bear in mind is that once exposed to air, fine red wines will change. The main problem is to anticipate how much and how quickly.

The longer I deal with fine wines the more firmly convinced I am that if the wine is good – from a good vineyard, well made in a fine vintage year – when it is put into the bottle, then, as long as the storage conditions have been sound and the cork has not deteriorated, the wine will also be good, stable and drinkable when the cork is drawn, no matter what its age. A good sound wine – 5, 10, 25 or 50 years old – is unlikely to crack up shortly after the cork is extracted and the wine decanted; indeed quite the opposite, a century-old wine will catch its second breath, as it were, unfolding its bouquet, expanding and developing over a period of two or three hours, sometimes longer.

If the wine is of a poorish vintage and lacked body and balance when young, or if the storage has been poor, perhaps too warm, allowing the cork to shrink, then the wine is likely to break down very soon after it is poured out, in perhaps, a matter of minutes.

Claret of a sturdy young vintage, say a 1979 or a '75, even one of the tougher '70s, will be so full of tannin and extract, so closed up, that decanting early afternoon for drinking around 8.30pm will encourage it to 'relax' and soften a little. How many times has one been told, and occasionally discovered accidentally, that a young red wine seems softer and better on the palate the next day? The same can occasionally happen to very old wine of the finest quality, though it is a brave or singularly curious man who will risk this.

It is my considered opinion that no noticeable oxidation occurs for a very considerable period after the cork is drawn, and, surprisingly, little change occurs in the decanter. The main development takes place in the glass. The greater the wine, the more revealing and complex the bouquet and the longer it and the flavour will last. To give an example: at a recent Bordeaux Club dinner my reds opened with a (my only) bottle of Lafite 1961. The problem was how to present this wine at its very best. I took the wine from my London cellar to Christie's cellar two weeks in advance. The day before the dinner I brought it carefully up to my office, leaving it standing upright. The afternoon of the dinner, I dusted the bottle gently, removed the capsule and wiped the top, first with a damp cloth then with clean dry kitchen paper. The cork was drawn about 5pm and stood loose on the top, less to prevent air than dust from getting in. The wine was decanted at 6.45pm into a rather wide-mouthed carafe, without a stopper, and carried at 7.30, just before the first guest arrived, to the boardroom where we were to have dinner. It was actually served at 8.30pm. By 9pm the bouquet had blossomed nicely and by 9.45 it had developed fully, with a nice warm, spicy, biscuity fragrance. I kept a little in my glass and two hours after it had first been poured it still smelled incredibly delicious. As a matter of interest, the last of four red wines I served was an 1875 Château Desmirail. The bottle had an excellent provenance. It came from the private cellar in Paris of a noted connoisseur, had been recorked, probably in the mid 1930s, and its level was still good. In the middle of the dinner I returned to my office to draw the cork and decant the wine which was then served right away. To describe this remarkable pre-phylloxera claret would need another chapter. Suffice to say that there was not a trace of decay on nose or palate. It seemed fatter and rounder after 15 minutes and even an hour later, the scent in the emptied glass was exquisite.

My final advice on 'air' is: be bold, and try decanting well in advance. Above all, with a really fine wine (and this applies as much to a top-class white burgundy as to claret) give the wine a chance to blossom in the glass: sip it, make it last, revel in its marvellous development.

How to decant

Before recommending the best method of decanting let me again mention those wines which rarely, if ever, need decanting. Basically, they are all wines without a sediment: very young red wines, ordinary commercial red table wines, young white wines, including sherry, also rosés, champagne, ruby and tawny wood ports and less expensive madeira.

White wines that benefit from decanting are old ones, whether sweet or dry, which quite frequently have a slight powdery sediment, sometimes younger whites which, through a sudden change of temperature, have thrown a tartrate deposit – perfectly harmless and tasteless white crystals – and some rare old sherries and old solera and vintage madeiras. The latter, with their glowing amber colours, and old sauternes, usually a beautiful warm yellow-orange, shot with gold highlights, look particularly beautiful in clear glass or cut glass decanters.

Prime candidates for decanting are mature claret and vintage port. Even young claret, which has had little time to throw a sediment, might as well be decanted. It does give the wine a little air which has a slight softening effect and, in any case, the colour always looks so attractive.

When it comes to red burgundy, there are two schools of thought. In Burgundy itself, the wine is rarely decanted. I am not at all sure of the reason for this, but I *am* sure that great care must be taken when pouring from the bottle and ample time given for the sediment to settle. You need a steady hand or an old-fashioned decanting cradle with a cranking handle and smooth action. In the latter instance, the glasses are brought to the decanting cradle, not cradle to glasses. If this contraption is not used, for most of us do not possess one, then I recommend that the glasses are all lined up by the bottle, the wine being poured steadily from glass to glass. In either case, it is essential for the pouring to stop before the sediment reaches the upper neck. (I recently witnessed a magnum of beautiful burgundy being spoiled by my host, a noted connoisseur, who poured steadily into eight large glasses, continuing round to the bitter end, giving everyone's glass a final *coup de grâce* of sediment!) I personally consider that all red burgundy should be decanted. It is far safer.

Now for the method.

The bottle must have been left resting, preferably upright, undisturbed for an hour or two, better still, for a day, before decanting so that the sediment has had time to settle. This is, of course, particularly vital if, as I recommend, the bottle has been moved from cellar or store to the dining room, or wherever one wishes to decant. The only exceptions are, perhaps, old sauternes which are intended to be served cold and can be decanted in the cellar, and vintage port which can be lifted carefully from the bin and decanted (*see* p. 195) on the spot.

So, assuming that the bottle of claret or burgundy has been standing upright, capsule removed and cork extracted, the following should be ready at hand:

Decanter Clean, dry, sweet smelling and also at room temperature. (It is amazing how little thought is given to the temperature of the decanter(s) and glasses. There is no point in having nursed the wine to room temperature and putting it into decanters and glasses which have been brought at the last minute from a cold cupboard.) Incidentally, if the stopper has been left in a decanter for any length of time the air within can smell stale, particularly if the decanter had not been properly rinsed out and left upside down to dry before it was put away.

Candle For me, the ideal is a four to six inch candle in a table top candle holder. The base of a Screwpull corkscrew works admirably. A tall tapering candle in an equally tall candle stick is impossible to decant over unless it is on a low table or stool.

The alternative to a candle, and as effective, is an electric light bulb or torch placed on the table top and shining upwards.

Funnel A plain glass funnel is best. A plastic funnel looks nasty and I always worry about its cleanliness. Silver funnels look splendid, but when and with what, were they last cleaned? Traces of metal polish, Duraglit and so forth, might taint the wine.

There is just one wine for which I personally use a rather handsome antique silver funnel and sieve, and that is for vintage port. A Victorian or modern equivalent (we use very plain metal ones at Christie's) will of course do. The reason for this is that the sediment of vintage port, known as the crust, is heavy and flaky. The wine pours bright and one merely catches the crust in the sieve.

Decanting procedure

Place the cradle holder on the edge of a table top, the decanter to the left, the bottle to the right – unless you happen to be left-handed.

Make sure that the neck, shoulder and upper half, at least, of the bottle is free of cellar dust or grime which will otherwise obscure the view through the glass.

If you have a funnel, put it into the neck of the decanter. If not, and a funnel is not absolutely essential, one just has to pour carefully.

Now either leave the decanter where it is or pick it up by the neck with the left hand – all depends on you, and the height of the candle, the flame of which should be about four inches below the level of the top of the funnel.

Place the right hand over the lower half of the bottle, not at the upper or shoulder end, pick it up and tip it gently over the rim of the funnel or the lip of the decanter. Start pouring slowly but steadily. Once the wine has started flowing then manoeuvre the bottle gently towards the lighted candle so that the eye, the underside of the shoulder of the bottle and the candle are in a straight line. Do not line up vertically, i.e. with the bottle directly above the candle, as the flame from the candle will smoke up the glass and obscure one's view of the wine. A slight angle is better. Do not stop pouring whilst this manoeuvring is going on otherwise the sediment might be disturbed. Practice makes perfect.

By the time you have reached the right position a little over half the contents will have been poured and the wine should be showing clear and bright as it passes over the shoulder into the neck. Continuing pouring steadily, watching carefully for the first traces of light powdery sediment which will be easing up the underside of the bottle. I personally let the very light sediment move up, and if a fair amount of wine is still in the bottle, continue until the main swirl of heavier sediment appears. Let this slide across the shoulder of the bottle but do *not* let it enter the neck. This is the moment to stop. By now the base of the bottle will be higher than the neck: to stop decanting, quickly but smoothly swing the base down. It is more effective than pulling the bottle away horizontally from the funnel as this movement results in the remaining wine welling over to the left, risking sediment spilling into the decanter.

This procedure is used for all wines except vintage port.

The amount and type of sediment will vary to some extent, depending on the style and age of the wine, but the method described above should cope with all situations. Burgundy bottles have more gently sloping shoulders and one has to be a little more careful than with Bordeaux or Bordeaux-style bottles which have conveniently rounded corners to delay the sediment.

Vintage port The bottles used traditionally by English merchants to bottle port were of extremely dark glass, often so dark that the level of the wine cannot be seen even if the bottle is held against a high-powered spotlight.

The sediment or crust is also different. This forms along the lower side of the bottle. It is a continuous process. The sooner a vintage port is laid down (binned) after bottling and the longer it is left undisturbed the more steadily and firmly the crust will form, and, as a result, the easier it will be to decant when it is fully mature.

With an old (say 25 years or older) vintage port no candle is needed when decanting. Traditionally port used to be decanted in the cellar, the bottle would be lifted gently from the bin, put into a wooden cradle (not a flimsy basketwork version), the cork extracted and the wine poured steadily into the decanter via a funnel with a sieve. The wine would inevitably be bright, its black, flaky, filmy crust being caught by the sieve.

Muslin and filter papers The use of a strainer is very tempting. It appeals to the timid, the palsied handed and, dare I say it, the mean-minded amongst us.

Frankly, if the wine has been handled properly, cellared for a decent length of time, brought from cellar to sideboard to settle and uncorked properly there should be no need to use a filter.

On the other hand, even the most farsighted and careful will, on occasion, find themselves with a rush job or have disturbed the bottle, giving the wine insufficient time to settle down. This is perhaps the only good excuse for using a piece of fine clean muslin or linen cloth over the funnel to act as a filter. Filter pads – those most frequently used are for coffee – are a fairly untenable last resort. My own experience is that muslin rarely does a proper job and filter pads can give the wine a slightly powdery taste, even on occasion taking the stuffing out of a wine.

As for extracting the last ounce of liquid from a bottle by filtering the remnants, sediment and all, this, in my opinion, is shortsighted. The dregs, however well strained, do not taste good, and if tipped into the decanter slightly spoil the rest of the otherwise bright and sound wine.

Cloudy wine One occasionally comes across a bottle of wine which has a suspended haze of very fine particles which will not settle. If it has been recently purchased from a regular supplier take it back. If it is a very old wine there is little one can do. It is probably worth trying a filter pad but the wine might not be up to much anyway.

Glasses Another word on this subject of glasses. The 'ideal' tasting glass is illustrated on page 25. As it happens this is a most excellent size and shape for virtually all white and red wines. However, a table setting looks more interesting if the glasses for the different types of wine are varied and I personally like a slightly smaller tulip-shaped glass for my white wine and matching but larger glasses for reds. Having for years scorned 'gold-fish bowls' I must confess a liking for fairly large rounded glasses for burgundy: the perfume seems to arise more exotically from them. But do remember that large glasses use up a lot of wine and, a minor phenomenon, the larger the glasses the more one's guests drink (if you do not believe this, do a little experimenting).

Dessert wines and vintage ports are often confined to small glasses, which is a mistake. A medium-size tulip or thistle glass is better than a copita, ghastly 'schooner' or thimble.

In addition to shops specializing in glasses, many wine merchants now carry a range, sometimes uniquely their own.

The temperature of wines at table

It may be comforting, or irritating, to be told that there is no such thing as a precise temperature at which a specific wine should be served. The season of the year and the temperature of the dining room itself have a bearing. One thing is certain, extremes are undesirable. Having said this, the temperature of wine *is* important and lack of consideration will result in a wine 'performing' less well than it should.

Red wines

It is said that red wines should be served at room temperature. This is a broad generality, for not only are some dining rooms too cold and some too hot, but the age and weight of red wines require different serving temperatures.

● Young red bordeaux tends to have a high level of tannin and a certain raw austerity. The bigger the wine and the younger the vintage, the warmer it should be served: say 65°F (18°C), even up to 68°F (20°C) in a warm room or on a warm day

● Mature red bordeaux: about 65°F (18°C). On a hot June day in 1970 I well remember a fine claret (it was a 15 year old Domaine de Chevalier) being served at a Master of Wine lunch: the temperature seemed perfect. To my surprise, when tested with a thermometer it turned out to be 70°F (22°C)

● Old red bordeaux (of the vintage 1959 and older) should not be served too warm. It seems to take the stuffing out of the wine. Possibly a maximum of 63°F (17°C) depending on the room temperature.

● Red burgundy. A good burgundy should definitely be served cooler than claret. Very often in Burgundy itself it is brought straight from the cellar.

Burgundy is less tannic, very often more alcoholic and usually sweeter. It tastes livelier if served around 60°F (16°C)

● Rhône and other full-bodied reds: about 60°F (16°C) or, if very tannic, up to 68°F (20°C)

● Beaujolais and red wines from the Loire. Serve cool, say between 54°–58°F (12°–15°C)

White wines

It is well-known and generally true to say that white wines should be served cold. But how cold? In my experience, far more care is needed to get the temperature right for white than for red.

I shall just deal with recommended temperatures, then with

the methods of achieving and holding those levels.

- Light dry acidic wines: Muscadet and the range of light, refreshing wines made with the *Sauvignon Blanc* grape such as Sancerre should be served cold, between 45°–50°F (7°–10°C)
- Fine white burgundy: I single this out for special treatment for though it is always dry, the alcoholic content can be surprisingly high, in the 12.8% to 14% range. It is therefore a big mistake to serve, say, a Bâtard-Montrachet too cold. From experience I would suggest just half an hour in the refrigerator or ice box (stand the bottle with the milk) and let it rise almost to room temperature in the glass. The bouquet will develop miraculously
- Medium-dry German wines and others with a light fruity-acid balance: about 48°–50°F (8°–10°C)
- Sweet white wines: the finer the wine the less cold it should be served. A minor sauternes-type wine and any sweet wine low in acidity should be served very cold, near to 45°F (7°C). A top class mature Sauternes no less than 50°F (10°C).

The late Otto Loelb drank Trockenbeerenauslesen poured at room temperature into ice-cold glasses. I tried this recently. It seemed to work but the glasses did not stay cold long.

Rosés

Pink wine from whatever source. Serve cold: 45°–50°F (7°–10°C).

Champagne

Cheap non-vintage champagne and sparkling wines serve very cold. However, the bouquet and flavour of fine vintage champagne, like great white burgundy, is muted and wasted if served too cold. Serve cool enough to be refreshing but not so cold that the glasses become frosted.

Sherry

Serve cheaper sherry and sherry-type wines cold. Fine finos and manzanillas are more refreshing slightly chilled, say around 48°F (8°C). Serve fine old amontillados and olorosos at room temperature. It is sometimes suggested that 'cream' sherry should be served on the rocks: so be it!

Madeira

Temperature depends on the grape style:
- Sercial, the lightest and driest, serve cool, say 48°–50°F (8°–10°C)
- Verdelho, roughly medium dry, also cool but not too cold
- Bual, richer and fuller bodied, I suggest around 55°F (13°C) or, if old and fine, over 60°F (16°C)
- Malmsey, the sweetest and richest, at room temperature

Port

A surprising variation of temperatures is recommended
- White port is generally dry or medium dry so serve very cold
- Ordinary ruby or tawny is generally drunk at room or 'pub' temperature
- Fine old tawny. This is the favourite drink of the port shippers in Oporto where they serve it cool
- Vintage port at room temperature

Time needed to chill white wine In an average refrigerator set at say 42°F (5°C) a standard-size bottle of wine takes roughly 30 minutes to reach 59°F (15°C), and 1 hour to achieve 55°F (13°C). In 2 hours it will have dropped below 50°F (10°C).

Keeping the wine at serving temperature The problem with white wine is keeping it at the prescribed serving temperatures.

Old fashioned ice buckets are, in my opinion, unsatisfactory. In them wine tends to become over chilled. Moreover, they are messy to use and labels come off. So I should recommend using ice buckets only for light dry white or sparkling wines which can endure maximum chilling. A practical tip: do not use chips or cubes of ice alone; instead part fill the bucket with water so that the bottle can be put back into the bucket easily. A generous sprinkling of salt keeps the temperature down.

The ideal way to keep white wine at an even serving temperature is to stand the bottle in an open-topped vacuum flask. A fellow Master of Wine has invented one which is marketed under the name Vinicool®★. The principle is simple: hot air rises, cold air falls. The already cold bottle is stood in the Vinicool® and cools the air round its sides, the warmer outside temperature being kept at bay by the vacuum-sealed double sides. The bottle will hold its temperature for the entire time needed for serving and drinking. Vinicool® vacuum flasks are used regularly at pre-sale tastings at Christie's: they have the added advantage of being transparent so one can see the labels on the bottles and are not messy like ice buckets, dripping water everywhere.

Glasses for white wines are, conventionally, smaller than for red. The reason for this is largely ignored, or taken for granted: there is a smaller surface area of wine and glass to transmit the warmth of the room. My last tip is to pour only a half-glass of white wine at a time, topping up frequently from the cool bottle.

★Obtainable from some wine merchants and speciality stores.

CELLAR
NOTES

CELLAR NOTES INTRODUCTION

> *'There is no money among that which I have spent since I began to earn my living, the expenditure of which I am less ashamed, or which gave me better value in return, than the price of the liquids chronicled in my Cellarbook.'* **George Saintsbury**, Notes on a Cellarbook

Just as you can drink and enjoy wine without the fag of making notes, so can you acquire and dispose of the bottles themselves without recourse to a cellar book.

Tasting notes are a somewhat whimsical option open to any keen-enough amateur but, perhaps, more of a vital chore for the professional: but a cellar book is a vehicle for the physical accounting for wine bought and consumed which has for generations appealed to the neat-minded householder. For a large establishment it is a prudent aid to management and for merchants, in computerized form, an essential tool of the trade, accounting for stock purchases and sales.

As I am addressing myself principally to the wine buff let me blow away all mystery and mystique. The elements are simple: one merely enters the number of bottles acquired and, on the same bit of paper, notes the depletions. For fuller information one can record details of each wine, its vintage, the château, domaine, estate or merchant/bottler, the date of purchase, source and price paid. In addition, one can note not only the date and number of bottles taken from the cellar but also the occasion, perhaps the dinner menu, and the guests. Although all this might seem humdrum, it is surprising how quickly time passes and how fascinating it is to look back on what one has actually possessed, consumed and with whom – and how little the wine cost compared with current prices.

Later in this chapter we include a straightforward, very practical cellar book. For those who would like to have some background information, read on.

Cellar books past and present

Historically, cellar books record the tastes of the time: a sort of Pepys' diary glimpse at life styles, relative affluence and the politics and economics of wine. To the best of my knowledge no cellar books of the Middle Ages have survived although there are plenty of records of what wines were shipped to England. The household accounts of John Hervey, the first Earl of Bristol, detail wine purchases from 1720 to 1739 and, by inference, consumption, but I suspect that it was not until the 19th century, the era of the full-blown traditional wine merchant that aristocratic and prosperous middle-class customers started to keep the sort of cellar book which we now regard as classic. The most complete and elaborate I have seen are those of the Dukes of Wellington at Apsley House and of the Earls of Strathmore at Glamis Castle. The latter are large leather-bound volumes recording the name of wine, vintage, date of purchase, price paid, bin number and subsequent withdrawals. These were immaculately maintained by generations of butlers and stewards. Their accuracy is important for auctioneers of rare wines who occasionally have to rely solely on the bin numbers recorded in the book to identify the wines in the cellar.

Some cellar books are of considerable social interest. Christie's sold both the wines and the cellar books of the late

Sir Gerald Kelly, a past president of the Royal Academy of Arts and a noted connoisseur. In addition to the cellar book itself he indexed the names of all his guests, with the date of the luncheon or dinner and details of the wines consumed.

The most famous of all is surely George Saintsbury's cellar book. It inspired the crotchety old professor to write his 'Notes' which were of peculiar appeal, and an instant publishing success: a seminal work which has inspired subsequent generations of wine writers. His actual cellar book, which I examined prior to its sale at Christie's, was the most ordinary of notebooks, with a roughly drawn plan of the professor's cellar and almost indecipherable hand-written entries. So there is hope for us all.

The cellar book

The following cellar book note sheets have been designed to be simple and practical. I do not claim great originality, for more or less the same information and variations on the theme are common to all household cellar stock books. Apart from recording purchases and consumption (for posterity or to inspire the ultimate book on the subject) it will provide the foundation for future purchases based on average entertaining/consumption per annum. Unless one buys 'futures' solely for re-sale, laying-down young vintages must be planned with a drinking timescale, and for this a properly maintained cellar book is more or less essential.

Date	Name of Wine	Vintage	Purchased from	Price	Quantity
Dec.12 1974	Ch. Trotanoy (Pomerol) (Pomerol)	1971	Corney & Barrow	£72 per dozen	3 dozen
Date	Occasion/guests	Fare	Comments	No. used	Balance
July 13 1975	Dinner at Gloucester Street. June & Michael Hague	Cold roast beef etc.	Lovely deep fruity wine but unready	1 bottle	2 . 11
Nov. 18 1978	Dinner at G.St. Len Evans, Peter Fox & wives	Rack of lamb	Quite good as the opening claret. Softening. Shows great quality & potential	2 bottles	2 . 9
Sept. 3 1980	At Christie's. Janie & Jack Davis (Sothusbury) Bella & Barney Rhodes (Napa)	Crown of lamb	Seems to be increasing in length and depth. Developing well	2 bottles	2 . 7
June 19 1981	25th. Wedding anniversary lunch. Just Daphne & J	Culham ham & pink chops in aspic	Approaching its 10th. anniversary, the wine has come of age. Lovely	1 bottle	2 . 6

Autumn 1983	I notice the wine auction prices is up to £40c per dozen. Decide to sell 1 dozen + replace it with 2 dozen of late 1981 vintage @ £140 (see folio 12) (3 bottles missing on taking stock. Emma again?)		1 dozen 3 bottles	1.6 1.3
April 14 1984	Bordeaux Club dinner Messrs. Waugh, Behrens, Ld. Walston, Jack Plumb + Neil MacEndoe	Navarin of Lamb (brought by Michael Rouse)	Sensationally rich, fully developed Pomerol silkiness (see Tasting Notes Vol. 56 p. 14)	2 bottles 1.1

Date	Name of Wine	Vintage	Purchased from	Price	Quantity
Date	Occasion/guests	Fare	Comments	No. used	Balance

Date	Name of Wine	Vintage	Purchased from	Price	Quantity

Date	Occasion/guests	Fare	Comments	No. used	Balance

Date	Name of Wine	Vintage	Purchased from	Price	Quantity
Date	*Occasion/guests*	*Fare*	*Comments*	*No. used*	*Balance*

CELLAR NOTES

209

CELLAR NOTES

Date	Name of Wine	Vintage	Purchased from	Price	Quantity
Date	Occasion/guests	Fare	Comments	No. used	Balance

210

Date	Name of Wine	Vintage	Purchased from	Price	Quantity
Date	Occasion/guests	Fare	Comments	No. used	Balance

Date	Name of Wine	Vintage	Purchased from	Price	Quantity
Date	Occasion/guests	Fare	Comments	No. used	Balance

Date	Name of Wine	Vintage	Purchased from	Price	Quantity
Date	Occasion/guests	Fare	Comments	No. used	Balance

Date	Name of Wine	Vintage	Purchased from	Price	Quantity
Date	Occasion/guests	Fare	Comments	No. used	Balance

Date	Name of Wine	Vintage	Purchased from	Price	Quantity
Date	*Occasion/guests*	*Fare*	*Comments*	*No. used*	*Balance*

Date	Name of Wine	Vintage	Purchased from	Price	Quantity
Date	Occasion/guests	Fare	Comments	No. used	Balance

Date	Name of Wine	Vintage	Purchased from	Price	Quantity
Date	Occasion/guests	Fare	Comments	No. used	Balance

Date	Name of Wine	Vintage	Purchased from	Price	Quantity
Date	Occasion/guests	Fare	Comments	No. used	Balance

Date	Name of Wine	Vintage	Purchased from	Price	Quantity
Date	Occasion/guests	Fare	Comments	No. used	Balance

Date	Name of Wine	Vintage	Purchased from	Price	Quantity
Date	Occasion/guests	Fare	Comments	No. used	Balance

Date	Name of Wine	Vintage	Purchased from	Price	Quantity
Date	Occasion/guests	Fare	Comments	No. used	Balance

Date	Name of Wine	Vintage	Purchased from	Price	Quantity
Date	Occasion/guests	Fare	Comments	No. used	Balance

═══ XVI ═══
BUYER'S GUIDE

Choosing wine

In this all too brief chapter I will unashamedly be like the strip-tease artist who, in the end, does not reveal all.

One of the tremendous attractions of the wine market nowadays is its great diversity. The choice of wines is virtually limitless; and as a result choosing is increasingly more complicated. To do justice to the subject this section of the book would have to be a world gazetteer, and it would be out of date and misleading the minute it was published.

Bearing in mind what has been stressed more than once, I shall give the broadest advice which is necessarily based on my own experience and therefore very subjective.

Wine for keeping

Whether you have in mind future drinking or investment, the wines selected must have more than just an ability to age, they must be able to improve with keeping. The two major factors are the vineyard/winery and the vintage. The château, domaine, estate and wine maker should have a proven track record. The weather conditions during the vine growing year and grape harvest must be beneficial, with sun and rain in correct proportions.

It may come as a surprise to learn that of all the world's wines relatively few will benefit from keeping. This is not to say that decently made wines will not keep, just that they are really best drunk young. By and large, only the top wines from major districts will improve with age in bottle, indeed need to be kept to achieve full maturity. A list of those districts and wines follow:

Red Bordeaux

Claret from leading châteaux and of the better vintages heads the list. Although the wines of scores of châteaux will keep, only 100 or so will develop interestingly over a 10 to 20 year period and only 20 to 30 châteaux have a universal reputation and are worthy of investment.

The following are the best vintages currently for laying down: 1982, 1978 and, still, 1975. Good vintages for mid-term drinking: 1981, 1979 and 1976. The 1983 looks interesting but, at the time of writing, it is too early to classify it either as a *vin de garde* or for early drinking; although from what I have tasted so far they fall neatly, and inconveniently, in between.

My personal list of the 20 best châteaux for future drinking and investment are, in alphabetical order:

Ausone (since the 1978 vintage)
Beychevelle (elegant, stylish)
Cheval-Blanc (top of its class)
Cos d'Estournel (making better and better wine)
Ducru-Beaucaillou (as decent and reliable as the Borie family owners)
Figeac (some genius here, and pricey to prove it)
Gruaud-Larose (deep fruity style)
Haut-Brion (unique. Suave, elegant yet earthy)
Lafite (quintessence of delicacy and finesse)
Lagune, La (the burgundy of Bordeaux. Rich, stylish)

Latour (massive, solid, long lasting, high quality)
Léoville-Barton (often understated, the gentleman's claret)
Léoville-Las-Cases (suave, subtle, length. The best of the 2mes crus)
Margaux (famed for elegance and scent. The Queen of Bordeaux)
Mission Haut-Brion, La (masculine, assertive, earthy)
Montrose (slow developer, long lasting, dependable)
Mouton-Rothschild (con brio. Brilliant, intense, great flair)
Palmer (fleshy, almost voluptuous in a great year)
Pétrus (tiny production, high price. Concentrated velvet)
Pichon-Lalande (firm, elegant, stylish)
  And a personal list of Bordeaux châteaux for future drinking without a thought of return on capital:
Angludet, d' (soil laden with semi-precious stones. Great character, good value)
Batailley (plummy, fruity, foursquare, consistent)
Beauséjour-Bécot (stylish and at best a brilliant St. Emilion)
Branaire-Ducru (underrated, elegant, flavoury)
Calon-Ségur (slightly variable. St. Estèphe firmness, fruit)
Canon (totally dependable. Fine fleshy St. Emilion)
Cardonne, La (vivacious, flavoury)
Chevalier, Domaine de (an outstanding red Graves)
Cissac (dependable, stylish, reasonably priced)
Conseillante, La (a magnificent Pomerol which amply deserves the recognition – and price – its owner demands)
Coufran (soft, fleshy bourgeois claret at its best)
Evangile, L' (elegant, too little known)
Fleur-Pétrus, La (firm flesh, dependable style)
Gazin (at best a fine deep Pomerol)
Giscours (dry, lively, crisp, keeps well)
Gloria (well made, ready to be upgraded)
Grand-Puy-Lacoste (uncompromising classic Pauillac, firm, stylish)
Haut-Bailly (a firm, fleshy red Graves, high quality)
Haut-Batailley (elegant, leaner and more supple than Batailley)
Latour-Pomerol (high quality, broad, meaty)
Léoville-Poyferré (at best stylish, high quality)
Lynch-Bages (crisp, *cabernet* aroma and flavour. Zestful)
Magdelaine (deep, melodious, too little known)
Mouton, Baronne Philippe (light style, crisp, feminine)
Pape-Clément (the firmest and most Médoc-like of the great Graves)
Pavie (usually a dry, masculine St. Emilion. Excellent in '82 and '83)
Pichon Baron (more variable, less fashionable than Lalande, but can be excellent)
Pointe, La (lighter style Pomerol. Usually reasonably priced)
Prieuré-Lichine (stylish, flavoury, usually excellent value)
Sales, de (often soft, gentle, an easy sort of Pomerol)
Siran (firm, some elegance)
Talbot (the vigorous, drier 'young brother' of Gruaud)
Tour-de-Mons, La (stylish and totally dependable)

Red Burgundy

Although burgundies made in the 1920s can still be quite delicious, often showing better than the equivalent quality and age of red Bordeaux, it is hard to foresee how well some latter-day burgundies will keep.
  Burgundies have always been quicker to develop than

clarets as they are less hard and tannic when young, but the great growths are not only capable of development but positively need bottle age, the wines of the Domaine de la Romanée-Conti being a case in point: they positively gain in depth and complexity, also, curiously, in colour.

The best vintages for laying down are undoubtedly 1983, 1978 and, still, 1971. For mid-term drinking vintages: 1981 and 1979. 1976 is hard and difficult to generalize.

The wines of the Côte du Nuits and Corton from the Côte de Beaune are probably most suitable for long keeping (see pages 67–68) and it is best to stick to the top growths of domaines such as de Vogüé, Henri Gouges, Rousseau, Drouhin-Laroze and the individual domaines, not bought-in wines, owned by leading Burgundy houses: Bouchard Père, J. Drouhin, Jadot and Louis Latour. (For fuller burgundy information see Bibliography on page 252.)

Vintage Port

Supremely appropriate, indeed a necessity, to lay down. Ideally port should be bought when the new vintage is first put on the market, and stored, preferably without being disturbed in one cellar, for at least the first five years of its life to allow the 'crust' to form. Of all wines, port is just about the most stable and reliable, rarely presenting any problems. Vintages are simpler, too, as the leading port shippers only 'declare' as vintages their top wines of the best years.

For laying down: 1977, 1975 and, still, 1970.

The top names:

Cockburn (stylish, great name, though not always my favourite)

Croft (firm yet lissome. Good fruit)

Dow (possibly the driest, flavoury, 'high-toned')

Fonseca (marvellous flesh and fruit. One of my favourites)

Graham (generally the sweetest, a fine, fleshy, fruity wine. High quality. My top wine)

Noval (an individual *quinta* wine, nowadays one of the lightest and most feminine)

Taylor (the most massive, with characteristic firm tannin backbone. Needs plenty of time. Long lasting)

Warre (elegant, stylish, very reliable quality. A 'copybook' vintage port)

For good maturing qualities, but lacking some of the investment glamour are Delaforce, Gould Campbell, Martinez, Offley, Rebello Valente and Sandeman.

Other reds

Most good, well constituted, red wines will keep, but only the most outstanding are capable of development. Some of the world's other top-quality reds follow, by country:

Italy

This vast wine-producing country deserves special study, but as far as keeping qualities are concerned three reds only need be considered: the top Chianti Classicos, Barolo and Brunello di Montalcino. The latter two are massive, tannic wines which take years to come round. Two excellent new books on Italian wines are referred to on page 251.

California

Cabernet Sauvignon and Zinfandel, particularly from the Napa Valley. Top California 'premium' wineries include

Beaulieu Vineyard, Clos du Val, Heitz, Stag's Leap Wine Cellars, Robert Mondavi, Freemark Abbey, Louis Martini, Phelps, Ridge, Jordan, Trefethen and Mayacamas.*

Californian wine makers are now, at long last, having success with Pinot Noir, notably Chalone and Acacia.

Australia

The wine scene is vibrant, with excellent reds being made in the now classic Coonawarra district and elsewhere. However, the blending of wine of different grapes and different districts by a multiplicity of wineries makes it very hard for an outsider to follow. New releases are tasted and reviewed by major Australian wine journals (see page 254). If I was to pick just one new winery making outstanding reds for keeping, it would be Toltarni.

White wines

Virtually all white wines are made to be drunk whilst young and fresh. Of the dry whites, only the greatest like the classic white burgundies will benefit from bottle age, also Graves, particularly Haut-Brion Blanc and Laville Haut-Brion, both of which positively need bottle age.

There are, however, several semi-sweet and sweet white wines which not only will improve but need age to reach their zenith. For example, the top growths of sauternes, notably Château d'Yquem, and others such as Suduiraut, Climens, Coutet, Guiraud, Rieussec and La Tour Blanche. Also the small-production Rhine and Moselle wines of Beerenauslese and Trockenbeerenauslese qualities from leading estates such as von Buhl, Bürklin Wolf, Bassermann-Jordan, Stumpf-Fitz in the Palatinate; the Schlosses Vollrads and Rheinhartshausen, the estates of von Schönborn, Groenesteyn, von Simmern, Senfter, Dr. Weil and the State Domaine in the Rheingau; Franz Karl Schmitt, G.H. Schmitt, and Guntrum in Rheinhessen; Anheuser, von Plettenberg, Herf in the Nahe; and J.J. Prüm, Thanisch, Deinhard, von Schubert, the Bischofliches Konvikt and Priesterseminar, in the Moselle.

In the Loire, top quality Vouvray (leading growers Foreau and Brédif) and Coteaux du Layon of particularly favourable vintages will keep, also the outstanding *vendange tardive* rieslings and tokays of Alsace, notably Hugel's.

Magnums and large-size bottles

It is fairly common knowledge that wine keeps better, and takes longer to develop, in large – what the French call *grands formats* – bottles, and vice versa: they develop more quickly in half-bottles, and quarter bottles of champagne, for example, are notoriously unreliable given any age. The reason is superficially simple: the greater the volume of wine in relation to cork/surface area and ullage (the gap between the wine and the underside of the cork) the slower the oxidation and maturation process.

In practical terms the magnum or two-bottle size is probably

---

*Of the cabernet-sauvignons Heitz Martha's Vineyard is probably the most famed – and expensive; Beaulieu Vineyard's George de Latour Private Reserve has, for the past 35 years, represented the finest classic Napa tradition; Stag's Leap mirrors the unassuming brilliance of Winiarski the owner/wine maker; and Louis Martini, in a quiet old-fashioned way, great style, longevity and good value.

best. Larger sizes like double-magnum and jeroboam* are impressive but because of their utility value (one needs to have a fairly big dinner party to open these large bottles, and they are not the easiest of things to handle) their production tends to be small. As for the even grander sounding 'impériale' (an eight-bottle bottle) this is more for trading, I feel, than drinking.

In Burgundy one rarely comes across sizes larger than magnum and in Champagne, beware, jeroboams and larger bottles tend to be filled to order, i.e. the wine has not spent its developing life in those bottles. They should be drunk quickly, not kept.

Wine for current drinking

It is my theory – indeed my experience – that a soundly made wine will keep for years if stored in suitable conditions (see page 186). However comforting this might appear, not only is most of the world's wine made for quick consumption but even the sound wines which can keep will not actually benefit much, if at all, from keeping. Happily, in this hand to mouth range one is spoiled for choice.

There are people, right across the social spectrum, for whom quantity and, above all, price is all-important – the cheaper and more copious the better. However, 'cheaper' in a wine context usually turns out to be 'worse'. Indeed, I am rather tempted to avoid any further comments on wines at the lowest commercial end of the spectrum on the basis that the people who drink them will not be readers of this book. In any case, those who want to learn more about wine, and about the pleasures of positive tasting, are wasting their time and money on the sort of wine which is sold in litre and larger containers (I am not of course referring to classic magnums and jeroboams referred to above), and virtually anything under £2.50 (say $4.00) a bottle. This is not to say that bag-in-box wines ('jug' wines in the USA, 'cask' wines in Australia) and other commercial blends are necessarily unpleasant to drink: it is just that, even at best, they do not add to the sum of human knowledge. To be realistic (and crude), they are bought to be swigged, not pontificated upon.

Mind you, I do not support the other extreme: the sort of person – and I met one recently, an American – who does not drink wine as part of his normal daily life but merely toys with fine and rare wines at the occasional tasting he organizes. Knowing my passion for tasting and note taking, this gentleman expressed surprise when he was told that I and my family drink wine with every meal.

As I am frequently asked *what* I drink every day at home, my answer is that though I would prefer to stick to decent claret, as the most wholesome of beverages, I range quite widely, first of all because I feel it is part of my job to keep my horizons broad, and second because the cost of a family bottle or two a day mounts up, and good red Bordeaux is not cheap. Incidentally I rarely drink white wines with a simple meal at home, unless it happens to be fish.

---

*Jeroboam, a marvellous-sounding name and impressive looking bottle, tends to be a 'movable feast': in Bordeaux it is generally taken to mean a six-bottle bottle, but the old hand- and mould-blown bottles were significantly variable, from the equivalent of about five to six and a half bottles. In Burgundy and Champagne a double-magnum (four-bottle bottle) is usually termed a jeroboam.

In fact, I practice what I preach. I go to tastings and buy what I like best, particularly German wines for summer drinking and young claret. I also select from merchants' lists mixed cases to try, and, from time to time, I ask my wife to select mixed half-dozens in local supermarkets. In each instance, when I come across a wine I particularly like, I hurry back to buy one, two or three cases. (Never delay: they might run out of stock or have a new consignment of a younger, less good, blend.) Whilst still on a personal note I must admit that from time to time I am brought, usually by visiting American friends, bottles of interesting Californian wines. However, though an established, if part-time, wine writer, I am not, as might be supposed, endlessly showered with bottles to taste and to comment upon.

My recommendations for everyday dinners at home:

Portuguese reds Dão is foursquare and reliable, Periquita has more shape and style, the '71 having almost a mature bordeaux elegance. But younger vintages are also pleasant.

Spanish reds Riojas vary enormously from the oaky and tannic bordeaux style to the whole-fruit light burgundy types. I prefer the more old-fashioned Riojas like Riscal. Also top of the league for price and quality are the Torres range, of which the Gran Coronas is outstanding (really in the 'for keeping' category) and the excellent Coronas of lighter weight and style.

Chile produces excellent wines. Harvey's of Bristol pioneered Chilean reds in the early 1950s. Of the, admittedly few, wines tasted recently I have been particularly struck by those of Concha y Toro.

Italy I confess I do not drink much Italian wine – except in Italy. Being brought up with the classic bordeaux taste I find many, even of the grandest, Italian wines strange in smell and taste, sometimes slightly oxidized, many too bitter (I am referring to reds). I prefer northern Italian wines made from familiar Bordeaux vine varieties: *merlot* and *cabernet-sauvignon*. Antinori's wines are excellent as they have a long-established understanding of the international market, Tignanello being particularly attractive; also their Vila Antinori Chianti Classico – both incidentally keep well. Carema, though not in the inexpensive price bracket, is also excellent. And amongst the whites, a delightfully refreshing range is produced in the Alto Adige or South Tyrol, the latter producing firm *chardonnays*, a variety of German-grape styles and a crisply fragrant, good-value *goldmuscat*.

French I like many of the less expensive clarets, which generally means 'bourgeois' and young, i.e. the less-grand growths of the Médoc like the Châteaux Coufran and Cissac, some of the châteaux of Bourg and Blaye, and, even better, those of Fronsac. The happiest hunting ground, usually easier to drink when young, is St. Emilion, though perhaps my favourite district of all is Pomerol. In Bordeaux one is spoilt for choice. The 1979 is a particularly good and still not over-priced vintage, and 1981, 1982 and 1983 provide quality and variety.

Amongst other reds, the Rhône can still provide style and quality at a fair price, though the top estates and the excellent Jaboulet Aîné wines are no longer cheap.

Alsace provides perhaps the purest and best-value dry whites. Indeed I have rarely come across a bad wine from Alsace. The worst I would merely describe as dull. Consistently good growers/merchants are Hugel, an old-established family firm with some of the best vineyards, and Trimbach, making a crisper lighter style.

Particular favourites of mine are those from the mid-Loire – Anjou, Vouvray, Savennières – the most attractive and summery dry and medium-dry whites.

Australia and the United States The citizens of these countries are perhaps the most favoured of all. They pay little or no basic tax on wine, and everyday wines, even 'jug' and 'cask' wines, are very sound, can be most attractive and are incredibly cheap.

My final advice in a hopelessly too-wide subject is, particularly for everyday and middling price wines, read the pundits. In England the *Which? Wine Guide* and *Decanter* magazine, not to mention Sunday supplements and other organs of the press, provide endless panel tastings which do the experimenting for you. Try their recommendations. Wine journals in other parts of the world (see page 254) do the same, the Americans being particularly fortunate in their outspoken critical newsletters, notably Finigan's and Parker's (see Bibliography, pages 254–255).

Where to buy wine

With the exception of frustrated wine lovers who happen to live in the 'dry' states of America or under the yoke of state monopolies, the majority of us have a surprising range of outlets with an unprecedented range of wine at our beck and call. At least, this is the theory. Finding just what one wants is another thing.

Historically and economically, world wine production generally exceeds demand; and the present time is no exception. The result for the producer is downward pressure on prices forced by the distributive trades – shippers, wholesalers, retailers – who themselves suffer from intense competition. Again, in theory the consumer should benefit. In practice, pressure on prices and ruthless competition tends to downgrade quality, so the buyer on price alone can find himself landed with some pretty nasty wines.

The cellar door

The chain of distribution starts with the producer. Cellar door sales, with the exception of some of the more prestigious Bordeaux châteaux, are not only normal but an ever growing practice. The advent of the autoroute has made Burgundy a relatively speedy drive from Paris and the increase of direct sales has seriously reduced the availability of stocks to the traditional merchants of Beaune. The 'cellar door' is wide open to casual and regular buyers throughout the wine districts of Germany, Austria, Italy and elsewhere in Europe – including the several hundred English vineyards. In the new world quite a few Australian and Californian wineries would have financial problems were it not for the cash flow provided by weekend visitors.

It is fun buying at the cellar door, and the wine, one assumes, is pristine, genuine and unadulterated. But of course choice is limited to what the owners produce. The wines tend to be very young or at best 'new releases', and prices are not as advantageous as one might expect. However, whereas in Bordeaux and Burgundy the vineyard owner will tend to make just one wine whose quality and style will depend on two variables, the vintage weather and the age of the wine*, estates in Germany produce different qualities and styles depending on the sort of grape used, the date of picking and the particular vineyard – all, admittedly, variations on a white wine theme.

In California the spectrum is wider, with individual wineries in the Napa Valley, such as Mondavi, producing quite a variety of reds and whites in a surprisingly wide price and quality range: for example the classic Chardonnay and Cabernet Sauvignon in ordinary and 'reserve' qualities, German-style Johannisberg Riesling†, the ruby red Zinfandel, crisp dry Loire-like Fumé Blanc, and so forth.

In Australia, winery portfolios can be almost ridiculously elaborate. I remember visiting one quite small winery south of Adelaide where cellar-door buyers could stock up with red and white wines, sweet and dry, port- and sherry-style wines, 'champagne' and even vermouth.

Négociant or shipper

This is the traditional middleman merchant exemplified by the *négociants-éléveurs*, formerly the 'merchant princes' of Bordeaux and the worthy burghers of Beaune and Nuits-St-Georges. By and large these firms do not sell to casual callers though many have direct-mail customers (as have many Bordeaux châteaux).

At one time major buyers from the grower, blenders of generic wines and big stockholders of classed growths, many négociants now carry only comparatively limited stocks and work instead as large-scale brokers, acting as go-betweens for the vineyards and overseas importers.

Shippers and importers

Every major importing country used to have shipping houses which were the counterpart of the négociant. A distinguished calling, these firms, based in London, New York and other major cities, usually had a wide portfolio of wines/suppliers and sold exclusively to the trade, often as sole importing agents.

The demise of the traditional wine merchant in the United Kingdom and the vertical integration of large brewers and liquor conglomerates has reduced the importance of the shipper though not eliminated him: many good firms survive. The man in the street was scarcely aware of this strata of middleman for rarely was he allowed to buy from him direct. Nowadays shippers act as more or less exclusive agents of individual merchants and growers, the more prosperous firms on both sides of the Atlantic having built up the large distribution of brands such as Liebfraumilch Blue Nun.

Wholesaler

Every country has its wholesaler. In England, where, as in so many fields, traditions arose and became accepted practices,

---

*The effects of vintage weather and ageing are dealt with in detail in *The Great Vintage Wine Book*, with supporting tasting notes to illustrate their effect on a wide range of individual wines.

†Only 10 years ago the Johannisberg Riesling was one of the non-successes of the Napa. Now, not only is the general standard far higher but certain growers and wine makers are picking early for extra fresh acidity (Phelps notably), some later for extra ripeness, some are even picked with *pourriture* to make the equivalent of a TBA (Freemark Abbey, for example).

the wholesaler was the stockholder between the shipper/ importer and the smaller retail outlet. Sometimes known as 'market house' its function was to provide a speedy service of a wide range of wines to restaurants and corner shops. They never sold direct to the consumer. Always an ill-defined area of trade, the wholesaler is still around to provide a service to retailers, though almost everywhere his function is changing. Wholesaling is a bit nebulous.

As traditional markets open up and the old trade barriers crumble, the wholesaler has to be nimble to stay in business. The former rigid licensing laws in England have loosened up considerably, to the extent that absolutely anyone can trade as a wholesaler, with no restriction on sales except for a minimum case-lot quantity. Many are, in effect, retailers and their keen prices are proving a boon to consumers.

Retailers

It is at the retail level that the vast majority of us have contact with the trade. This is the consumer end of the business, and it still remains the most licensed and regulated: indeed, I know of no part of the world where the retail wine merchant is not hemmed in by laws and restrictions.

Restaurants too are considered retailers and they tend to be a law unto themselves, each having its own approach to the range of wine served and but one thing in common: a high mark-up. It is small consolation for the reader to know that the price of wine in restaurants has been continually criticized, ever since eating out in such places began after the French revolution; nor are voluble criticisms confined to French and English establishments.

But let me confine my review of the retail trade by concentrating on the different types of shop, for these are crucial to the consumer.

Surprisingly, although individual wine outlets vary enormously in size and scope, most of the civilized countries in the world have a wide variety of retail outlets and, even more surprisingly, they often have much in common.

The traditional English wine merchant

As long as wine has been produced, and this goes back to Asia Minor and millenniums BC, there have been wine merchants. In the Middle East and Greece it was considered a high calling. The wine merchants of the Middle Ages were a solidly prosperous coterie (wine was the third most important item of commerce in the time of Edward III), but what we regard as the traditional English wine merchant grew out of the coffee shops of the 17th and 18th centuries and took final form in the 19th century. Berry Bros. and Rudd in St. James's Street epitomize precisely this growth and development. Happily they still survive, but London and the county towns of England, Scotland and Wales, once well endowed with wine merchants, have become denuded. Alas, there are as few real wine merchants in the United Kingdom today as there are decent bookshops, bespoke tailors, saddlers and the like. Their disappearance has been, in historical terms, quite sudden. It all started with shortage of capital and death duty problems in the 1950s. Many family wine merchants sold out to brewers. Then, when resale price maintenance was abolished, the early 1960s witnessed intense competition. Now supermarket chains handle an ever-increasing proportion of the British trade in wine.

Happily, quite a few traditional wine merchants have survived, with parlours and desks and scarcely a bottle in sight; where young gentlemen, or gentlemen's gentlemen, proffer advice and take orders. Some, it would seem, exist more to provide a respectable front for a brand-owning conglomerate than to make money. Some manage to do both. Others achieve neither. But young firms and partnerships not only exist but, phoenix-like, rise to fill the gap left by the departed traditionalists and the aching void created by limited-range off-licences and supermarkets.

Wine merchants and retail outlets in Europe

Much of what I have just said applies equally to similar consumer countries of Europe, such as Holland, Germany, Denmark and Switzerland. France, Italy and Spain being large wine-producing countries have always had a different approach to retailing, though excellent wide-ranging wine shops exist in Paris, Turin and elsewhere. Norway, Finland and Sweden are burdened with wine monopolies, though, following a recent visit to Stockholm, it is apparent that a more liberal attitude is being stimulated by a groundswell of intense interest in wine.

The North American scene

Apart from the so-called 'dry' states of America and the provincial monopolies in Canada, all of which run contrary to the interests of the consumer, there has been a miraculous growth of interest in wine over the last 15 years and, at long last, a remarkable number of top-class retail shops to satisfy this demand.

Unfortunately prohibition between the two world wars was not only an unmitigated disaster socially, but it fostered a breed of trader as far removed from the civilized British tradition as it is possible to be. Bootleggers, post prohibition, became 'wine merchants', and it has taken decades for this taint to wear off – indeed, in many American cities it is still evident. However, thanks to the switch in emphasis from hard liquor to more civilized wines, and to the growing influence of wine writers, the man in the street has no excuse: the world of wine is within easy reach.

The difference, as far as I can see, between the good American wine merchant and his English counterpart is that the former has a far wider range of wines, often extremely attractively presented, but without depth of stock. Basically, what you see is what they have got. The traditional British merchant might have a smaller range, but he will certainly have a back-up stock which will support the printing, twice a year, of a quite elaborate price list.

A summary of consumer outlets, the pros and cons

As this is a consumer guide, perhaps I might be allowed to encapsulate the pros and cons of the wide variety of outlets at which wine can be purchased.

The traditional wine merchant One expects above all a good range of sound to excellent wines (and spirits) and service. Most encourage regular account customers and give credit. They know their own stock and their regular clientele and are usually fully qualified to advise. A delivery service is expected, so is immediate redress if a wine is less good than it should be.

Service has to be paid for but competition tends to keep

prices at a reasonable level. And a merchant will usually give
a discount for quantity and for cash. Traditionally, this has
been a man's domaine.

Although no one owes a wine merchant a living I, for one,
certainly think they should be supported, for without them
the sale of fine wine would wither and so would some of the
quality of life.

At a more mundane level, it is short-sighted to imagine that
buying from a wine merchant is more expensive than, for
example, from a supermarket. If value for money, rather than
just a low price, is the main consideration, then most proper
wine merchants are hard to beat.

Merchants specializing in certain types of wine A totally new
development – something unknown prior to the 1960s and, as
far as I can ascertain, peculiar to England – has been the rise
of merchants, usually small partnerships, specializing in the
wines of specific countries or areas. There are several
specializing in Italian wine, a few in Spanish, particularly the
excellent Riojas, and one in those complementary French
districts, the Rhône and Loire.

If you are interested in these wines I am certain that this sort
of firm can offer the best range and advice. They mainly
operate from single premises, usually in the country, and for
this reason are mainly mail-order. Most of them advertise in
wine journals, *Decanter* in particular.

The wine department of a big store Known as speciality stores
and department stores in England, many have specialized
wine departments. To cite two prominent examples, Harrods
in London and the 'Tastemaker' shops of Sakowitz in
Houston. The best have a range of wines and services equal to
any wine merchant. Offering the convenience of 'one stop
shopping', this type of outlet is usually pretty high class.

The big retailer This I think of as the nearest American
equivalent to the traditional British wine merchant. As said
before, the range is usually very wide and appealing and the
presentation almost invariably more vivid and forceful.
Whether one can obtain wine on credit, or deliveries, or good
advice, depends on individual areas and shops; whether one
can rely on keen prices, availability and continuity of stock,
is another matter.

The 'off-licence' This is a retail outlet peculiar to the United
Kingdom. Originally a separate section of a public house in
which wine could be purchased for consumption off the
premises, necessitating an additional licence, these developed
into off-sales areas attached to the public house premises but
with their own entrances, and later still into quite separate
brewery-owned off-licence shops. Despite their numerical
strength, many of these chains of 'off-licence' depend for
their existence on casual round-the-corner sales of beer,
spirits, cigarettes and the most ordinary of wines. Competition from supermarkets is intense. With the exception of a
few enlightened firms, range is poor, quality modest and
service minimal.

Grocers selling wine Since the 1860s, when Gladstone reduced the duty on light wines, the grocery 'off-licence' has
been of some importance. After all, it is natural to associate
wine with the sale of food. But few grocers in England seem
to have taken advantage of the situation, rarely rising to wine
merchant status, despite offering credit and deliveries. Most
are now swamped by the supermarkets. Nevertheless many
grocers sell wine, the W.H. Cullen group being notable for its

enterprising selection. Undoubtedly the flagship is Fortnum & Mason, though this is almost a fully-fledged 'department' store.

Generally speaking, however, at the licenced grocers' one can expect credit and delivery but only a limited range and no advice.

In the United States, the emphasis seems to be on fine wines, delicatessen and top-class food specialities, but the situation varies from state to state, city to city. New York wine retailers are currently fighting to prevent food shops from selling wine.

Supermarkets As with food, the retailing of wine by super-market chains has transformed the market.

Alas, it is not possible to generalize. Some supermarkets carry an excellent range, others a miserable selection. All, of course, are highly competitive. Although most have concentrated on fast-moving cheap wines, some are noticably trading up.

The advantages, curiously, are few; mainly convenience, for those who buy wine, with food, on a hand-to-mouth basis. Credit is generally unavailable, there is no one personally to advise and one is expected to cart heavy bottles home oneself. Top-class wines are to be seen in the bigger and better French supermarkets but rarely elsewhere. In any case, is a super-market shelf the best place to present – standing or tilting – fine wine?

As for prices, these can of course be keen, as the buying power of the large supermarket chain is considerable. Their aim is to keep stock moving. The combination of advantageous purchases and speedy turnover enables them to sell cheaply. But do not forget that the object of any business is maximum profitability and the margin on wine will rarely be as slender as that on food.

Cash-and-carry wine warehouses What began as a cost-cutting wholesaler's food operation has recently spilled into the field of wine. Known as 'wine warehouses' most are just that: off-centre of town with, ideally, good car parking facilities and a reasonably enticing range of wines at very enticing prices.

For any serious, i.e. regular, wine drinker the minimum case lot stipulation is no deterrent. As the title implies, no credit and no deliveries. But credit, in the old-fashioned sense, is no longer important as credit cards have taken their place. Unlike supermarkets, specialist cash-and-carry wine ware-houses often have staff on hand who at least know their own wines. As with supermarkets, the aim is to have fast-moving lines to keep the cash flowing, which enables them to work on a small margin of profit.

Wine auctions There is nothing new about auctioning wine. In England it began in the coffee houses 'by the candle', and auctioneers, like Lloyd's insurance underwriters, moved to their own premises in the 18th century. Also from time immemorial wine has been auctioned as part of the contents of houses, giving rise to the expression 'sold lock, stock and barrel'. But leaving aside these spasmodic one-off sales (which *can* be happy hunting grounds), charity sales (which *rarely* are) and the occasional wine auctions which take place as far afield as Sydney and Paris, there are only two auction houses in the world with specialist wine departments and full-time wine expert staff: Christies' and Sotheby's.

Christies' have been selling works of art and wine longest.

Wine – claret and madeira – featured in James Christie's first sale in December 1766 and, except for a break following World War II when public auctions of wine were not permitted (trade only), have sold wine ever since. A completely new specialist department was set up in 1966 and in the same year Christies' acquired the century-old firm of City wine auctioneers W & T Restell.

Sotheby's began life in the 18th century as book dealers, entering the fine art field later. Their wine department was established in 1970.

Together Christies' and Sotheby's dominate the wine auction scene and have made London the international centre of the fine and rare wine trade.

The main attraction for the sophisticated buyer is the unmatched range of wines and vintages which flows through the saleroom. Christies' alone organizes 40 wine auctions a year, 32 of which take place in London, the rest in Geneva, Amsterdam and Chicago.

Lot sizes depend on the scarcity and value of the wine on offer and lot values tend to be high. An average lot value at a major Christies' specialized claret sale being over £300, though bargain prices and far lower lot values obtain at their South Kensington premises. Payment is due within seven days and wines are not released until paid for. This is because the auctioneer acts as agent for the vendor. Contrary to some ill-informed opinions, auctioneers do not carry stock or sell wines on their own behalf. They act as totally objective middlemen to establish a 'fair and just' price.

As for *caveat emptor* (buyer beware), although the drinkability of very old wine cannot be guaranteed, experienced staff can usually pinpoint its condition with accuracy and totally objective advice is always given, when required; moreover, pre-sale tastings enable potential buyers to assess the condition and value of samples representing the cellars on offer.

The pros and cons for buyers at wine auctions: the unmatched range of wines and vintages at the top end of the market, and undoubted bargains at the lower end, particularly in the trade surplus sales. However, continuity cannot be guaranteed: the same wines do not usually appear in sale after sale. The contents of a catalogue will depend on what vendors happen to be selling. Payment on receipt of invoice. Wines can be collected or delivered. (Overseas buyers have to employ a specialist shipping agent.) If wines are not available for tasting, totally reliable and objective advice can be relied on as it is the duty of the auctioneer to satisfy the buyer as well as the seller. But once in the buyer's ownership, unless immediate action is taken, that's that.

Summing up, I firmly believe that at the present moment, for sheer range and availability, for quality and price, the consumer has, to use Prime Minister Macmillan's phrase, 'never had it so good'.

Happy drinking. But don't forget to taste first!

Wine chart — body (horizontal) vs. sweetness (vertical):

	VERY LIGHT	LIGHT	MEDIUM LIGHT
VERY DRY		*Muscadet*	*Chablis* · *Sancerre* · *Pouilly-Blanc Fumé* · Bourgeuil · Chinon · ***Manzanilla*** · *Champagne* · *Savennières*
DRY	*Saar-Ruwer* · Beaujolais · *Vinho Verde*	Saumur-Champigny · *Saumur* · *Mâcon blanc* · Santenay · Gigondas · *Vouvray* · Lirac · Côtes de Ventoux	***Fino*** · *Steinwein (Würzburg)* · *Puligny-Montrachet* · Valpolicella · *Nahe* · *Chevalier-Montrachet* · *Chassagne-Montrachet* · *Nahe Spätlese* · Montagny · Listrac · Moulis · Mâcon rouge · Provence rosé · *Riesling (Alsace)* · Rully · Mercurey · *Steen (S. Africa)* · *Fumé-blanc (USA)* · *Tokay d'Alsace* · *Beaujolais blanc* · *Pinot d'Alsace* · Tavel rosé · *Muscat d'Alsace* · Pomerol · *Meursault* · *Rheingau Kabinett and Spätlesen*
MEDIUM DRY		*Mid-Mosel* · *Mosel Spätlese* · Anjou rosé	*Rheinhessen Spätlese* · *Austrian whites* · *Rheingau Auslese*
MEDIUM SWEET		*Mosel Auslese* · *Moscato d'Asti* · *Bonnézeaux*	*Rheinhessen Auslese* · *Champagne demi-sec* · *Vouvray demi-sec*
SWEET			*Coteaux du Layon* · *Mosel Beerenauslese* · *Mosel Trockenbeerenauslese*
VERY SWEET			

KEY TO TYPE FACES: Red wine, *White wine*, **Red fortified wine**, ***White fortified*** and *liqueur wine*

MEDIUM MEDIUM FULL FULL BODIED

VERY DRY

Château-Chalon St. Estèphe

Vin Jaune Brunello **DRY**

Provence (White)
Volnay
Bourg
Zinfandel
Pauillac
Hermitage blanc
Blaye Chianti Barolo
Dão Beaune
Bâtard-Montrachet
St. Julien Hermitage rouge
Aloxe-Corton Pomerol *Côte-Rôtie*
Tokay Szamorodni Le Corton
Chambolle-Musigny Cabernet Sauvignon (USA) .)
Colares Pommard Cahors
Semillon (Australia) Morey St. Denis Richebourg
Chardonnay (USA) Le Chambertin
Margaux Echézeaux Vougeot
Graves *Corton-Charlemagne*
Rioja Nuits St. Georges
Palo Cortado Vosne-Romanée
Graves (Red) *Le Montrachet*
Sylvaner d'Alsace St. Emilion
Pinot (USA)
Shiraz (Australia) Chateauneuf-du-Pape
Dão

Château Grillet **Amontillado** Pinotage (S Africa) **MEDIUM DRY**
Gewürztraminer **Sercial**
Johannisberg riesling (USA)
Palatinate Spätlese **White Port**
Châteauneuf blanc
Verdelho

Tokay 2 putts **MEDIUM SWEET**

Palatinate Auslese
Vintage Port

Tokay 3 putts **Bual** **SWEET**
Rheingau Beerenauslese Barsac **Oloroso**
Lunel **Ruby Port**
Beaumes de Venise **Muscat (Australia)**
Muscat de Frontignan **Marsala**
Rheinhessen Beerenauslese **Tawny Port**
Moscatel de Setubal *Tokay 4 putts* **Brown Sherry**
Palatinate Beerenauslese
Cream Sherry

Rheingau Trockenbeerenauslese *Sauternes* **VERY SWEET**
Rheinhessen Trockenbeerenauslese **Malmsey**
Palatinate Trockenbeerenauslese **Pedro Ximenez**
Tokay Essence

BIBLIOGRAPHY

Wine writing

Books should add to one's knowledge *and* understanding of wine. There is a place for the discursive as well as the strictly factual book though the former is only tolerable if written with scholarship and style, and the latter only if accurate and unbiased.

The older breed of writers seem to me more literary, more broadly civilized; the more recent tend to be more mundane purveyors of general information (and all too frequently secondhand opinions). There is no denying that there has been a veritable spate of books on wine over the past few years, some outstanding, few original, and many repetitive – for what new fact can a writer expose or what opinion can be expressed that is not already in print?

There would seem scarcely enough fresh material to fill a new chapter; yet books continue to appear, willing authors being encouraged by publishers anxious to feed a seemingly inexhaustibly ravenous market. Not even the duplication of title seems to worry the bookseller, two 'Entertaining with Wine' appearing – in the UK and USA – within weeks of each other; two 'Wines of the World' within months.

Of latter-day authors, Hugh Johnson towers above the rest in his singular ability to master and assimilate facts and present them in a concise form, neatly wrapped and highly informative. Cyril Ray is one of the few remaining stylists: he understands and enjoys words. He composes and polishes. Now I come to think of it, he is also one of the few witty writers on wine. Being a simpleton myself, I find that some academic writers write for fellow intellectuals and seem to be either incapable of making themselves clear to the layman or fearful of doing so lest their status is diminished.

Selection

I am not a book collector though, quite naturally, I have amassed quite a few volumes over the past 30 years. I used to read, from cover to cover, every book and every wine article I could lay my hands on, force-feeding myself as it were. Even though many were repetitive I was, and still am, grateful for a new insight or new perspective. I am less avid now, mainly because there are not enough hours in the day.

So the following list represents a very personal selection. It opens up with all the books that I have come across dealing directly with the subject of tasting, whether or not I agree with the techniques or opinions expressed; next come books that add to one's knowledge of wine, and those which fill out one's understanding – but the sub-headings speak for themselves. I have also included one or two libraries, specialized wine booksellers, wine magazines and major trade journals.

Layout

The title of the book and author(s) come first. The publisher and date of original publication appear in brackets, the second date being that of the latest edition, if applicable. The availability of a cheap or paperback edition is indicated with a †. Finally, I have added a brief critique: after all, anyone who has the temerity to commit himself in writing is laying himself open to criticism, even if, like tasting, it tends to be subjective. But that is life! I am equally vulnerable.

Scientific approach to tasting

Modern Sensory Methods of Evaluating Wines by M. A. Amerine, E. B. Roessler and F. Filipello (Hilgardia, University of California, June 1959). A scholarly pamphlet dealing with the senses, chemical components, statistical tasting techniques and mathematical scoring systems. One of the first modern treatises on the organoleptic examination of wine. Not for the amateur, even if he managed to obtain a copy.

Sensory Evaluation of Wines by M. A. Amerine and E. B. Roessler (Wine Institute, San Francisco, 1964). A follow-up of *Modern Sensory Methods* but still concerned with the academic approach to product-testing.

Wines, Their Sensory Evaluation by Maynard A. Amerine and Edward B. Roessler (W.H. Freeman & Company, New York and Oxford, 1976; revised and enlarged 1983.) Putting 'Wines' first, introducing the Christian names of the authors and including an odd *New Yorker* cartoon or two is a clear indication of intent: to present his two distinguished professors in assimilable form. However, whereas at least half the book is still too complex for non-academics, the remainder is a must. Though some curious prejudices are exhibited, it is scholarly, informative and impressive.

On the senses

Odour Description and Odour Classification by R. Harper, E. C. Bate-Smith and D. G. Land (J. and A. Churchill, London, 1968). Very scientific review of systems and classifications.

The Human Senses in Action by Roland Harper (Churchill Livingstone, Edinburgh and London, 1972). The structure of sense organs, nature of stimuli, methods of measuring perception; with an exhaustive bibliography. Dr Harper, of Reading University, writes for fellow scientists; but really keen wine students might well find the book fascinating, as I did.

For keen wine buffs

How to Test and Improve Your Wine Judging Ability by Irving H. Marcus (Wine Publications, Berkeley, California, 1972†). A small paperback by the former owner-editor of *Wines and Vines*. The first part compact and helpful, the second a potted version of the Amerine–Roessler evaluation tests.

The Flavour of Wine by Dr Max Lake (Jacaranda Press Pty. Ltd., Sydney, 1969†). An attractive, original and sometimes complex little book by an erudite Australian surgeon-cum-winery-owner.

For beginners

Masterglass by Jancis Robinson (Pan Books, 1983†). A sensible, 'jolly hockey-sticks' approach with unnecessarily complicated layout. Effective and recommended.

Wine Taster's Secrets by Andrew Sharp (Horizon, Toronto, 1981†). An unoriginal 'consumer's guide to wine tasting'.

In French

Essai sur la Dégustation des Vins by A. Vedel, G. Charle, P. Charnay and Journeau (S.E.I.V., Mâcon, 1972†). A detailed and, for the lay-reader, complicated tabulated treatise full of

Gallic logic and thoroughness. Doubtless this impressive team was jolted into action by the appearance of an English author on *their* subject in a French wine journal!

Précis d'Initiation à la Dégustation by Jacques Puisais and R. L. Chabanon (Institut Technique du Vin, 1969†). A detailed work by two distinguished French wine oenologs.

Une Initiation à la Dégustation des Grands Vins by Max Léglise (Defense et Illustration des Vins d'Origine, Lausanne, 1976†). A scholarly, somewhat schoolmasterly, work by the Directeur de la Station Oenologique de Bourgogne à Beaune.

Le Goût du Vin by Emile Peynaud (Dunod, Paris, 1980). A magnificent book, beautifully and deceptively designed to cover the most comprehensive work on the subject based on 30 years of teaching by a great oenologist.

La Dégustation des Vins by Norbert Got (published privately through SODIEP, Beziers, 1955). A little-known but thorough work dealing with the theory and practice of tasting with a description of the wines of the French districts, major and minor.

Translated for Americans

Initiation into the Art of Wine Tasting by J. A. Vaccaro (Interpublish Inc, Madison, Wisconsin, 1974†). A rather laboured version of the *Précis* . . . by Puisais and Chabanon (above), well illustrated and interesting, but including the original irrelevant apple and cream-cracker score sheets and information about French hotel school courses.

Books with tasting a major feature

Académie du Vin Wine Course by Steven Spurrier and Michel Dovaz (Century Publishing in association with Christie's, London, 1983). The complete study course in wine appreciation of the Académie du Vin, Paris. Recommended.

The Physiology of Taste by Brillat-Savarin (Peter Davies, London, 1925†). A famous classic: discursive, civilized. Translated from the French *Physiologie du Goût*, 1825.

Notes on a Cellar-book by George Saintsbury (Macmillan, London, 1920). Detailed reminiscent jottings, which had a seminal influence on wine writing and connoisseurship (with Yoxall preface, 1979).

The Great Vintage Wine Book by Michael Broadbent (Mitchell Beazley, London, and A. Knopf, New York, 1980). A complete record of vintages of all the major classic districts, good, bad and indifferent, and the reasons why, illustrated by 5000 tasting notes.

A Matter of Taste, Wine and Wine Tasting by Jack Durac (André Deutsch, London, 1975). A New York book reviewer incorrectly credited Mr Durac, a research scientist at London University, with being 'the first' to make 'a systematic attempt at explaining how a wine should be tasted . . .' etc. Appalling maps, stodgy production, some curious approaches, but full of earnest guidance.

The Taste of Wine by Pamela Vandyke-Price (Macdonald and Jane's, London, 1975). Sixty pages of somewhat idiosyncratic taste classifications flanked by less original general matter: wine making, maps and so forth. This book outlines the tasting approach of one professional writer. But there are other methods if this approach is not for you. Nevertheless, this one book contains a broad spectrum of information and is very good value.

Harry Waugh's Wine Diaries (Christie's Wine Publications). A series of travel journals and notes on tastings that started with *Bacchus on the Wing*, *The Changing Face of Wine* and *The Pick of the Bunch* (all by Wine and Spirit Publications, London, 1966, 1968 and 1970); *Diary of a Wine Taster* and *Winetaster's Choice* (both Quadrangle, New York, 1972 and 1973) and *Harry Waugh's Wine Diary Volumes Six, Seven, Eight* and *Nine* (Christie's Wine Publications, 1975, 1976, 1978 and 1981†). Personal, full of warmth, charm, enthusiasm and honestly expressed opinions on wines and vintages.

Gorman on Californian Premium Wines by Robert Gorman (Ten Speed Press, Berkeley, California, 1975†). Thoughtful approach to tasting, with model notes.

Essential works of reference

The World Atlas of Wine by Hugh Johnson (Mitchell Beazley, 1971/1981). Comprehensive, exhaustive; invaluable to have at one's side whilst reading about or visiting wine districts. An astonishing wealth of information, inimitably presented. This is the book I would take to a desert island.

Encyclopaedia of Wines and Spirits by Alexis Lichine (Cassell/Christie's, 1979). The other book to have at one's side. It is the encyclopaedia I like and use most.

Encyclopedia of Wine by Frank Schoonmaker (Hastings House, New York, 1964/1977).

Wine primers and all-rounders

The Signet Book of Wine by Alexis Bespaloff (New American Library, 1971†). Deservedly a best-seller in the USA. Nice direct style of writing and accurate information.

Wine by Hugh Johnson (Nelson, 1966/Mitchell Beazley, 1982†). His first major book, in which he demonstrated his art of succinct 'distillation' and lucid presentation.

Teach yourself Wine by Robin Don, M. W. (The English Universities Press, 1968/1977). Concise, informative.

Wines of the World by John Morrell (John Bartholomew, 1975).

Hugh Johnson's Wine Companion (Mitchell Beazley, 1983). A cross between a gazetteer and encyclopedia. Packed with erudition.

Books on the wines of countries

Guide to the Wines and Vineyards of France by Alexis Lichine (Weidenfeld and Nicolson, 1980). I like writers who express opinions, even if one does not always agree with them. Lichine's first book.

A Book of French Wines by Morton Shand (1928) revised by Cyril Ray (Penguin, 1964†)

German Wines by Frank Schoonmaker. New edition updated by Peter M. F. Sichel (New York, 1980).

Catalogo dei Vini d'Italia by Luigi Veronelli (Bolaffi, Milan, 1972). So well illustrated and presented that it is useful for non-Italians to refer to.

Vino by Burton Anderson (Atlantic-Little, Brown, 1980). An outstanding new book on Italian wines.

The Wines of Central and South-Eastern Europe by R. H. E. Gunyon (Duckworth, London, 1971). About the only book on this area, by a former English wine shipper.

The Wines of America by Leon D. Adams (Houghton Mifflin, 1973). Comprehensive, erudite, readable, by the dean of American wine writers.

Australian and New Zealand Complete Book of Wines by Len Evans (Hamlyn, 1973/1976). A fully comprehensive compilation by the outstanding wine personality of Australia.
The Classic Wines of Australia by Max Lake (Jacaranda Press, Australia, 1966/7).
Estate Wines of South Africa by Graham Knox (David Philip, Claremont, Cape Province, 1976). Beautiful and comprehensive.

About particular wine areas

The Wines of Bordeaux by Edmund Penning-Rowsell (Allen Lane, revised 1979†). Definitive and exhaustive, by England's soundest and most respected commentator on claret and the wine market in general.
Bordeaux et Ses Vins (known, after the publishers, as 'Cocks et Feret', Bordeaux, 1982). The 'bible' of Bordeaux, listing all the châteaux, great and small, by district. Vast index of vineyards and their owners.
The Great Châteaux of Bordeaux by Hubrecht Duijker (Mitchell Beazley, 1982). Original, comprehensive notes by Holland's leading wine writer. A beautifully illustrated book.
Bordeaux by David Peppercorn (Faber & Faber, 1982).
Burgundy by Anthony Hanson (Faber and Faber, 1982). Controversial and honest in opinion.
Les Vins de Bourgogne by P. Poupon and P. Forgeot (Beaune, 1969†). A small, authoritative classic.
The Wines of Burgundy by H. W. Yoxall (Michael Joseph, 1968†). Wise and civilized, by a past-chairman of the Wine and Food Society.
Burgundy, Vines and Wines by John Arlott and Christopher Fielden (David Poynter, London, 1976). Two Englishmen, one a leading journalist, the other a former sales director of a major burgundy house in Beaune, combine to produce a lively, informative treatise.
Burgundy by Anthony Hanson (Faber & Faber, 1982).
Alsace and its Wine Gardens by S. F. Hallgarten (Wine and Spirit Publications, 1969).
Champagne by Patrick Forbes (Gollancz, 1967/1977). Definitive.
Italian Wine by Victor Hazan (Alfred A. Knopf, New York, 1982).
Vino by Burton Anderson (Little, Brown and Company, 1980).
Sherry by Julian Jeffs (Faber and Faber, 1961/1982).
The Story of Port by Sarah Bradford (Christie's Wine Publications, 1983). A new and revised edition of *The Englishman's Wine* (1969). An absorbing historical account, beautifully written, with vintage notes.
Port by George Robertson (Faber and Faber, 1982).
Port by Wyndham Fletcher (Philip Wilson, 1978).
Madeira by Noel Cossart (Christie's, 1984).

Monographs

Mouton-Rothschild by Cyril Ray (Christie's Wine Publications, 1974/7†). By the master of the pen portrait, the 'elder-tasteman' of English wine writing.
Lafite by Cyril Ray (Peter Davies, 1971; new and revised edition, Christie's Wine Publications, 1984†).
Château Margaux by Nicholas Faith (Christie's Wine Publications, 1980).

Historical and classical

Wines of the Ancients by Sir Edward Barry (London, 1775).
A History of Ancient and Modern Wines by Alexander Henderson (London, 1825).
A History and Description of Modern Wines by Cyrus Redding (London, 1833).
Wine, the Vine and the Cellar by T. G. Shaw (Longmans Green, 1863/4). Frankly my favourite. The wine travels of an energetic character with a lively and enquiring mind. We still have the same problems he encountered! Nothing changes.
Vintagewise by André L. Simon (Michael Joseph, 1945). A civilized, erudite follow-up to Saintsbury's *Notes on a Cellar-book*.
Dionysius, A Social History of Wine by Edward Hyams (Thames and Hudson, 1965). A monumental work.
A History of Wine by H. Warner Allen (Faber and Faber, 1961). Learned and literary: a style of writing no longer encountered.
Gods, Men and Wine by William Younger (Michael Joseph, 1966). For those with time on their hands.

Discursive semi-classics

Viniana by Charles Walter Berry (Constable, 1929) and *In Search of Wine* by C. W. Berry (Constable, 1935). Not a travel book: the travels and jottings of a London wine merchant of the old school.
Stay Me with Flagons by Maurice Healy (Michael Joseph, 1940). Lusty, articulate, anecdotal. No one writes like this now, more's the pity.
Wayward Tendrils of the Vine by Ian Maxwell Campbell (Chapman and Hall, 1948). The reminiscences of a most eminent wine shipper.
French Wines by Paul de Cassagnac, translated by Guy Knowles (Chatto and Windus, 1930). The approach of the true French *amateur* – civilized and wise. Collector's piece, worth seeking out.

Wine libraries

The Guildhall Library, in the City of London, houses the Library of the Institute of Masters of Wine, which in turn incorporates the old Wine Trade Club Library, founded and amassed by André Simon (Reference library open to the public).
The Jack Harvey Memorial Library, forming part of the Harvey Wine Museum in Bristol (well worth a *détour*, but by appointment only).
The Fresno State College Wine Library, California, incorporating the extensive library collected by Roy Brady, a former editor of *Wine World*.
The A. J. Winkler Library in the department of Viticulture and Enology, University of California, Davis.
Public Libraries: most public libraries in the United Kingdom have a food and wine section, and titles not stocked can usually be obtained, on request, through the scheme of inter-library loans.

Specialist wine-book sellers

The Wine Book Club (Woodlands, Hazel Grove, Hindhead, Surrey, GU26 6BJ). Comprehensive lists, titles old and new.
The Wine and Food Library (Jan Longone, 1207 West Madison, Ann Arbor, Michigan 48103, USA).

Janet Clarke, Antiquarian Books (3 Woodside Cottages, Freshford, Bath, BA3 6EJ).
Mrs Marian L. Gore (Box 433, San Gabriel, California 91775, USA).

Wine magazines

Decanter (St. John's Chambers, 2–10 St. John's Road, London SW11 1PN). The best English monthly.
The Wine Spectator (Opera Plaza, Suite 2040, 601 Van Ness Avenue, San Francisco, Ca. 94102, USA). The only consumer and trade twice-monthly wine newspaper.
Wine World (Wine World Publications Inc., Suite 115, 6308 Woodman Avenue, Van Nuys, Ca. 91401, USA). Six issues per annum. Excellent content and production.
Gourmet (7777 Third Avenue, New York, N.Y. 10017, USA). The American establishment travel, food and wine journal.
Food and Wine International (750 Third Avenue, New York, N.Y. 10017, USA).
Wine (2302 Perkins Place, Silver Spring, Maryland 10910, USA). The Journal of the *Les Amis du Vin* organization of America.
Which? Wine Guide (14 Buckingham Street, London WC2). Monthly notes and recommendations for consumers.
Vintage (P.O. Box 2224, Grand Central Station, New York, N.Y. 10017, USA). An American journal owned/edited by the somewhat controversial Philip Seldon.
The International Review of Food and Wine (750 Third Avenue, New York, N.Y. 10017, USA).
Wine Tidings (Suite 414, 5165 Sherbrooke St. West, Montreal, Quebec H4A 1T6, Canada).
La Revue du Vin de France (65 Montmartre, 75002 Paris, France). Five issues per annum. Old-established, high-grade, with French and English editions.
Le Nouveau Guide Gault-Millau (210 Faubourg St-Antoine, 75012, Paris, France). Stimulating, often provocative, always lively *critique* of food, wine and restaurants.
Cuisine & Vins de France (11, avenue de l'Opera, 75001 Paris, France).
Wine & Spirit Buying Guide (P.O. Box 113, Lane Cove, 2066 Australia).
Winestate (80 Pirie Street, Adelaide, South Australia 5000). Authoritative monthly. Articles on wine, areas, personalities. Full coverage new releases.
Wineglass (Wineglass Publishing Ltd., P.O. Box 9527, Newmarket, Auckland, New Zealand).
Vinum (Klosbachstrasse 83, Postfach 8030 Zürich, Switzerland).
Wijn & Spijs (Kleiweg 13, 1396 HV Baambrugge, (Abcoude), Netherlands).
Falstaff Magazin (Opernringhof, Opernring 1, Stiege E, 1. Stock, A-1010 Vienna, Austria).
Vini (Via Sudorno 44, 24100 Bergamo Alta, Italy). A glossy and lively wine and food monthly.
Arnes Journal (Arne Krüger GmbH, K.G., Wintergasse 4, 6203 Hochheim, West Germany). Germany's leading wine and food monthly.

Wine newsletters

Robert Finigan's Private Guide (Walnuts & Wine Inc., 724 Pine Street, San Francisco, Ca. 94108, USA). Frank, outspo-

ken tasting notes and comments. Monthly.
The Wine Advocate (1002 Hillside View, Parkton, Maryland
21120, USA). Robert Parker Jr's highly confident and
competent bi-monthly tasting notes.

Wine trade journals

There are literally dozens of trade journals, varying from
tabloid dailies (*The Morning Advertiser*) and weeklies (such
as the *Off-Licence News*) to esoteric quarterlies. Most are of
limited or local interest; many are vehicles for trade brand
advertising, fine wines rarely being featured. Those of high
quality and/or broader appeal are listed below:
Harper's Wine and Spirit Trade Gazette (Harling House, 47
51 Great Suffolk Street, London, SE1). A widely distributed,
old-established weekly, with up-to-date trade and market
news, recent wine auction prices, etc.
Wine and Spirit (38–42 Hampton Road, Teddington, Mid-
dlesex, TW11 0JE, England). The leading British trade
monthly. Vintage notes, world market notes and reports,
summarized auction prices, etc. Recommended.
La Journée Vinicole (7 Rue Dom-Vaissette, 34 Montpellier,
France). French monthly, with English-language 'export'
issues.
Wines and Vines (703 Market Street, San Francisco, California, 94103, USA.). Monthly: trade news; emphasis on
California wine production and market.
Wynboer (P.O. Box 528, Suider-Paarl, 7624 South Africa).
Monthly, bi-lingual, English and Afrikaans, attractively pro-
duced.
Christie's Price Index of Vintage Wine (8 King Street, London
SW1Y 6QT). The only comprehensive annual record of wine
auction prices, with American, Dutch and Swiss wine price
supplements. Essential for trade and private collectors.

Wine courses/Academies

Books came first, steadily then in profusion. No words can
effectively take the place of the wine itself, so organized
tasting schools, seminars, courses, etc., were bound to follow.
Vini-viticultural schools, sometimes departments of universities, have for many years existed in major wine producing
countries: Geisenheim in Germany, Roseworthy in Australia,
Montpellier in France, at the University of California, Davis
and at the University of Bordeaux, to mention just a few.
  The following establishments run regular structured courses
open to all; they are followed by some of the firms and
organizations which specialize in one-off tutored tastings.
Their effectiveness depends partly on the class of wine and
quality of individual tutors. Naturally these vary, but I
venture to suggest that the overall level is surprisingly high
and keen amateurs as well as beginners will certainly gain a
lot from them.
Christie's Wine Course in association with L'Académie du Vin
(63 Old Brompton Road, London SW7 3JS Tel: 01–581–
3933). Evening courses from introductory, through advanced
to master classes.
L'Académie du Vin, Paris (25 Rue Royale, Cité Berryer,
75008 Paris, France Tel: 265–09–82/265–92–40). Steven Spurrier's original wine school. French wine mainly.
L'Académie du Vin, New York (23 West 39th Street, New
York, N.Y. 10018, USA Tel: (212) 921–1326).
Wine & Spirit Education Trust Ltd., London (Five Kings

House, Kennet Wharf Lane, Upper Thames Street, London EC4V 3AJ Tel: 01–236 3551). Day and evening courses for the trade but open to all. Three levels: elementary, intermediate and advanced (for Diploma).

Wine & Spirit Education Centers of America Inc., Atlanta (Frank H. Stone, P.O. Box 20450, Atlanta, Georgia 30325, USA Tel: (404) 427–4499). Operates with franchises of Wine & Spirit Education Trust (UK).

Windows On The World Wine School, New York (Windows On The World Restaurant, One World Trade Center, 107th Floor, New York, N.Y. 10048, USA Tel: (212) 938–1111). Quite long-established and highly regarded.

International Wine Center, New York (144 West 55 Street, New York, N.Y. 10019, USA Tel: (212) 757–0518). Regular classes. Wine bar below lecture/tasting rooms.

Ecole du Vin, Bordeaux (Château Loudenne, Saint-Yzans du Médoc, 33340 Lesparre, France). Fairly expensive residential courses.

Wijnacademie, Rijswijk (Postbus 1840, 2280 D.V. Rijswijk, Netherlands Tel: 070–908388).

German Wine Acadamy, at Kloster Eberbach (Details from the German Wine Information Centre, 121 Gloucester Place, London W1H 3PJ Tel: 01–935 8164). There are six 5-day courses a year on German wines only.

Flemming Hvelplund's Wine School, Denmark (Magstrade 7, 1207 Copenhagen, Denmark). Effective wine school open to all.

Centre d'Information, de Documentation et de Dégustation, Paris (45, rue Liancourt, 75104 Paris, France Tel: 327–67–21). Evening courses.

KWV Wine Courses, South Africa (Laborie Wine Centre, P.O. Box 528, Suider Paarl 7624 Tel: (02211) 2–2011).

'Wine Captain's Seminar', New York (The Sommelier Society of America, 435 Fifth Avenue, New York, N.Y. 10016 Tel: (212) 686–7435).

Independent Wine Education Guild, Canada (A.C. Hirons, P.O. Box 883, Station Q, Toronto, Ontario, Canada, M4T 2N7 Tel: (416) 485–7500).

Les Amis du Vin Wine Workshops, London (51 Chiltern Street, London W1M 1HQ Tel: 01–487–3419. Individual lecture/tastings organized by a very enterprising wine retailer.

Sotheby's (34 New Bond Street, London W1). Occasional lecture/tastings similar to Les Amis du Vin.

PERSONAL INDEX

The following ruled pages are for your personal tasting notes index.

Name of wine	Page

Name of wine	Page

Name of wine	Page

Name of wine	Page

PERSONAL INDEX

Name of wine	Page

Name of wine	Page

Name of wine	Page

INDEX

A

Acacia 238
Acidity 22, 34, 48, 72, 114, 146
Adelaide 80
Adgestone 81
Aerating wine 191–2
Aftertaste 21, 35, 114
Age, effect of 33, 47–8
Aligoté 39
All Saints 81
Aloxe-Corton 68
Alsace 41, 71, 238, 240–1
Alto Adige 240
Alvarinho 39
Amontillado 56, 78
Angludet, Ch d' 236
Anheuser 238
Anjou 241
Antinori 240
Appearance 26–31, 88, 90–1,
    112, 141–4; see also colour
    and deduction
Aramon 39
Arlay, Ch d' 72
Aroma 33, 88, 114
Assessment 87
Aszu 75
Auctions 246–7
Auslese 73
Ausone, Ch 235
Australia 41, 80, 238, 241;
    colour – muscat 61, red 63;
    wine competitions 87, 141
Austria 41, 74

B

Baden 74
Bailey's Bundarra 81
Balance 35, 147
Bandol 72
Barbaresco 41
Barolo 41, 76, 237
Barossa 63, 80
Barsac 38, 43, 67
Bassermann-Jordan 238
Batailley, Ch 236
Bâtard-Montrachet 68, 197
Beads 91, 144
Beaujolais 40, 69; colour 54;
    temperature 196
Beaulieu Vineyard 238
Beaumes de Venise 72
Beaune 68
Beauséjour-Bécot, Ch 236
Beerenauslese 73
Beychevelle 235

Bibliography 250–8
Bischofliches Konvikt 238
Blanc-fumé see Fumé-blanc
Blass, Wolf 80
Blaye 66, 240
Blind tasting 82–5
Body 34, 146
Bollinger 71
Bonnézeaux 71
Bordeaux red 35, 41, 42, 65–6,
    235–6, 240; colour 50–1;
    temperature 196; vintages
    66
Bordeaux white 41, 66–7
Bottle age 33, 115
Bouchard Père 237
Bouchet see Cabernet-franc
Bouquet 21, 32–4, 88, 91, 112,
    116, 145
Bourg 66, 240
Bourgueil 71
'Bracketing' technique 89–90
Branaire-Ducru, Ch 236
Brand's Laira Winery 80
Breathing time see aerating
    wine
Brédif 238
Brown Sherry 78; finest old,
    colour 57
Browns (Milawa) 81
Brunello 75, 237
Bual 39, 77
Buhl, von 43, 238
Burgundy red 42, 67–8, 236–7,
    239; colour 54–5;
    temperature 196; vintages
    68
Burgundy white 40, 68–9, 238;
    overmature 61;
    temperature 197; vintages
    69
Bürklin-Wolf 43, 238

C

Cabernet franc 39
Cabernet Sauvignon: aroma
    33, 65; grape 39–40; wine –
    Australia 80, 81;
    California 62, 79, 237–8;
    South Africa 81
Cahors 72
California 41, 79, 237–8;
    colour 62
Calon-Ségur, Ch 236
Canon, Ch 236
Capsules 100
Cardonne, Ch La 236

Carema 240
Carignan 40
Cash and carry 246
Cellar book 200–1
Cellar-door sales 241–2
Cellars 187–9; bringing wine
  from 189
Chablis 40, 68
Chalone 40, 238
Chalonnaise, Côte 69
Chamber's Rosewood 81
Chambertin 68
Chambolle-Musigny 67
Chambré-ing 21
Champagne 40, 42, 71; old 31;
  pink 28; temperature 197;
  vintages 72
Champigny 71
Chardonnay: grape 40; wine –
  Australia 80; California 79;
  New York State 80
Chassagne-Montrachet 69
Chasselas 40, 75
Château-Chalon 72
Chateau Clare 80
Château Grillet 44, 70
Chateau Montelena 40
Châteauneuf-du-Pape 44; red
  63, 70, 90–1; white 70
Chateau Reynella 80
Chateau Tahbilk 81
Chenin-blanc 40
Cheval-Blanc, Ch 235
Chevalier, Domaine de 236
Chevalier-Montrachet 69
Chianti 43, 44, 75, 237, 240
Chile 34, 240
Chinon 71
Christie's 246–7
Cinsault 40
Cissac, Ch 236, 240
Clare/Watervale 80
Claret see Bordeaux
Clarity 29–30, 144
Climate 45–6
Climens, Ch 238
Clos du Val 238
Cloudiness 29, 142, 195
Cockburn 237
Colares 76
Colour 20, 26–9, 49–64, 88,
  141–4
Concha y Toro 240
Condrieu 44, 50
Conseillante, Ch La 236
Coonawarra 80, 238
Corked 30, 115
Corks 100; failure 30–1; when
  to draw 189; see also
  aerating wine, corkscrews
Corky 116

Corkscrews 189–90
Corton, Le 68, 237
Corton-Charlemagne 40, 48,
  69
Cos d'Estournel, Ch 235
Coteaux du Layon 71, 238
Côte de Beaune 40, 68–9, 237
Côte de Nuits 42, 67–8, 237
Côte Rôtie 70
Coufran, Ch 236, 240
Coutet, Ch 238
Cream sherry 78
Croft 237
Crozer, Brian 40

D

Dão 76, 240
Daü 42
Decanting 191, 193; equipment
  193–4; procedure 194–5
Deduction, process of 84–5,
  87–92
Deinhard 238
Delaforce 237
Dinner party tastings 83–4,
  107–8
Dow 237
Drouhin, J. 42, 237
Drouhin-Laroze 237
Dryness 34, 146, 248–9
Ducru-Beaucaillou, Ch 235

E

Echézeaux 67
Elimination, deduction by 84,
  88–9
Eltville 73
Emerald Riesling 79
English wine 41, 43, 81
Essence (Tokay) 75
Etoile 72
L'Evangile, Ch 236

F

Faiveley 42
Felstar 81
Fendant 40
Fermentation 38, 46, 47
Figeac, Ch 235
Finish 35, 118
Fino 41, 78
Fitou 72
Flavour 20, 35, 147
Fleur-Pétrus, Ch La 236
Folle blanche 40
Fonseca 237
Food and wine 19, 101
Foreau, A. 238

Franconia 74
Frank, Dr Konstantin 80
Freemark Abbey 40, 238
French wine districts 65–72
Fronsac 66, 240
Fruit 33
Fumé-blanc: grape 40; wine 79
Fürmint 40, 74

G

Gamay 40, 69
Gastric stimulation 23
Gazin, Ch 236
German wines 35, 42–3, 72–4;
    definitions 73; serving
    temperature for white 197
Gevrey-Chambertin 67
Gewürztraminer: grape 41;
    wine – Alsace 71;
    California 79
Gigondas 70
Giscours, Ch 236
Glasses 24, 99–100, 195–6,
    198; ideal 25; washing 30
Gloria, Ch 236
Glossary 114–27; French 128–
    31; German 131–3; Italian
    133–4
Gouges, Henri 68, 237
Gould Campbell 237
Graham 237
Gran Coronas 240
Grand-Puy-Lacoste 236
Grape varieties 33, 38–44
Graves red 66
Graves white 43, 66–7, 238;
    colour 52
Grenache 41
Grocers' licensed sales 245–6
Groenesteyn 238
Gros plant 41
Gruaud-Larose, Ch 235
Grüner veltliner 41, 74
Guiraud, Ch 238
Guntrum, L 238

H

Hardy's 80
Haut-Bailly, Ch 236
Haut-Batailley, Ch 236
Haut-Brion, Ch: red 235,
    white 238
Heitz 238
Herf 238
Hermitage: red 38, 44, 70;
    white 70
Hochheim 73
Hugel 41, 43, 238, 241
Hungary 41, 74–5

Hunter Valley 80

I

Importer see Shipper
Italy 75–6, 237, 240

J

Jaboulet Aîné, Paul 44,
    240
Jadot, Louis 42, 237
Johannisberg Riesling 79, 80
Jordan 238
Jura 72

K

Kabinett 73
Kadarka 41
Kaiserstuhl 80
Kay's Amery 80
Krug 71

L

Lafite, Ch 65, 235
Lagune, Ch La 235
Lake, Max 40, 80
Lamberhurst Priory 81
Language of tasting 106–13;
    see also Glossary
Large-size bottles 238–9
Latour, Ch 65, 236
Latour, Louis 40, 42, 237
Latour-Pomerol, Ch 236
Laville Haut-Brion, Ch 238
Lecturing 107
Leflaive, Domaine 40, 68
'Legs' 30, 91, 144
Léoville-Barton, Ch 236
Léoville-Las-Cases, Ch 236
Léoville-Poyferré, Ch 236
Licensing laws 102–3
Lighting 24–6, 98, 110
Lindeman's 80
Lirac 70
Listrac 66
Loire 41, 70–1, 238;
    temperature – red 196,
    white 197; vintages 71
Lunel 72
Lynch-Bages, Ch 40, 236

M

McWilliams 80
Mâcon 69
Madeira 77–8; colour 64; old
    vintage 64, 78;
    temperatures 197
Maderisation 29

Maderised 28, 33, 118
Madura 76
Magdelaine, Ch 236
Malescot-Margaux, Ch 40
Malmsey: grape 41; wine 77
Manzanilla 78; colour 56
Margaux, Ch 65, 236
Marsala 76
Marsanne 81
Martha's Vineyard 238
Martinez 237
Martini, Louis 238
Maturity 33, 84
Maturity span: Claret 66;
    White Bordeaux 67; Red
    Burgundy 68; Port 77
Matuschka-Greiffenclau 43
Mayacamas 238
Médoc 65–6, 240; colour at
    one year 50
Mercurey 69
Merlot 39, 41, 66, 75
Meursault 27, 40, 69
Microclimate 46
Midi 41, 72
Minho 76
Mission Haut-Brion, Ch La 236
Mondavi, Robert 79, 238
Montagny 69
Montrachet Le 48, 68
Montrose 236
Morey-St-Denis 67
Morris 81
Mosel 27, 29, 43, 44, 73–4, 238
Moulis 66
Mouton Baronne Philippe, Ch
    236
Mouton-Rothschild, Ch 40, 65,
    236
Müller-Thurgau 41, 75, 81
Muscadelle 41
Muscadet: grape 41; wine 71,
    197
Muscat: grape 41; wine 61, 81
Muscat d'Alsace: grape 41;
    wine 71
Muscat de Frontignan 72

N

Nahe 73, 238
Napa Valley 45, 79, 237–8
    vintages 79; wine colour 62
Nebbiolo 41
Nederburg 81
Negociant 242
New York State 80
Noble grapes 39
Noble rot 67
Nose 32–4, 88–9, 91, 145
Noval 77, 237

Nuits-St-Georges 68

O

Oenology 13, 47, 72
Offley 237
Off licence 245
Oloroso 78; colour 57
Orlando 80
Orvieto 44
Osborne, D'Arenberg 80
Ott, Domaine 72

P

Palate 12, 22, 34, 89, 91, 112,
    145–7
Palatinate 41, 43, 44, 73, 238
Palmer, Ch 236
Palo Cortado 78
Palomino 41
Pape-Clément, Ch 236
Pauillac 65
Pavie, Ch 236
Pedro Ximenez: grape 41–2;
    sherry 78
Penedes 78
Periquita 240
Petit Verdot 42
Pétrus, Ch 41, 236
Pfalz see Palatinate
Phelps 238
Pichon Baron, Ch 236
Pichon Lalande, Ch 236
Pilton Manor 81
Pinot: grape 33, 42, 67, 75;
    wine – Alsace 71;
    California 79, 238
Pinotage 42
Pinot blanc 42
Pinot grigio 42
Pinot gris 42; see also Tokay
Plettenberg, von 238
Pointe, Ch La 236
Pomerol, 41, 66, 240
Pommard 68
Port 30, 44, 76–7, 237; colour
    58–9; temperature 197
Portugal 76–7, 240
Pouilly-Fuissé 69
Pouilly-Fumé 70
Prémeaux 68
Price 36–7
Priesterseminar 238
Prieuré-Lichine, Ch 236
Professional tasting panels
    136–7
Provence 72
Prüm, J.J. 238
Pulham 81
Puligny-Montrachet 40, 68

Q

Qualitätswein-mit-Prädikat 73
Quality 34, 35, 48, 87, 147;
    vintage wine defined 48
Quarts-de-Chaume 71
Quelltaler 80

R

Rauenthal 73, 87
Rebello Valente 237
Redman's 80
Red wines 26–7, 28–9, 48, 65–
    81 *passim*, 235–8, 240; soil
    44–5; temperature 196; *see
    also* appearance, colour
Retailers 243; English
    traditional 243–4;
    European 244; North
    American 244, 245
Rheingau 43, 60, 73, 238
Rheingau State Domain 238
Rheinhessen 41, 43, 73, 238
Rhine wine 43, 238; colour 60
Rhône red 41, 44, 69–70, 240;
    temperature 196
Rhône white 44, 70
Ridge 238
Riesling: grape 33, 42–3, 73,
    75; wine – Alsace 71;
    Australia 80; California 79;
    South Africa 81; wine
    colour 60
Rieussec, Ch 238
Rioja 78, 240
Riscal 240
Romanée-Conti 237
Rosé wines 28, 70;
    temperature 197
Rothbury 80
Rousseau 42, 237
Ruby port 76–7; fine, colour 58
Rulander 43
Rully 69
Rutherglen 81

S

Saar-Ruwer 73–4
St-Emilion 44, 66, 240
St-Estèphe 65
St-Julien 65
St-Laurent 66
de Sales, Ch 236
Saltrams 80
Sancerre 43, 70; temperature 197
Sandeman 237
Sangiovese 43
Santenay 68
Saumur 71

Sauternes 29, 43, 67, 238; colour
    52–3; temperature 197
Sauvignon-blanc 43, 70;
    temperature 197
Savennières 71, 241
Scent 101
Scheurebe 43
Schloss Rheinhartshausen 238
Schloss Vollrads 238
Schmitt, Franz Karl 238
Schmitt, G. H. 238
Schönborn, von 238
Schubert, von 238
Scoring 36, 137–40
Seaview 80
Semillon: grape 43, 66; wine
    80, 81
Senfter 238
Seppeltsfield 80
Sercial: grape 43; Madeira 64, 77
Setubal 76
Sevenhills 80
Seyval blanc 43
Seyve-Villard 81
Sherry 41–2, 78; colour 26, 28,
    56–7; temperature 197
Shipper 242
Shiraz: grape 43; wine –
    Australia 80, 81; South
    Africa 81
Siegerrebe 43
Sight, sense of 20; *see also*
    appearance
Simmern, von 43, 238
Siran, Ch 236
Smell, sense of 20–2
Smoking 16–17, 101
Soave 44, 76
Soil 44–5
Sotheby's 247
Soussans 66
South Africa 42, 43, 81
Southern Vales (Australia) 80
Spain 78, 240
Spätlese 73
Spitting 18
Spittoons 97, 98, 99
Stag's Leap Wine Cellars 238
Stanley Leasingham 80
Steen 40, 43, 81
Steinwein 44, 74
Stonyhill 40
Storage 186, 187–9
Stores' wine departments 245
Stumpf-Fitz 238
Sud Tirol *see* Alto Adige
Suduiraut 238
Sulphur dioxide 22, 23, 32, 125
Supermarkets 246
Sweetness 34, 146, 248–9
Switzerland 40, 75

Sylvaner: grape 44, 74; wine 71
Syrah 44
Szamorodni 74

T

Tâche, La 42
Taittinger 71
Talbot, Ch 236
Tannin 34, 48, 125, 146
Tartaric acid 30, 126
Taste: ability to 11; elements
   of 34–5; how to 145–7;
   sense of 22
Tastevin 29
Tasting: basic approach 11–12;
   context 15, 35–6;
   experience 82, 89; expertise
   82–5; memory, value of 12;
   notes 36, 135–6, 147–8;
   reasons for 13–15;
   sequence 24; subjective 65
Tastings: aim of 93–4; AOC
   14; blind 82–5; charts 140,
   142–3; check list 104–5; at
   dinner parties 83–4, 107–8;
   duration 95; horizontal and
   vertical 94; lighting for 24–
   6, 98; organization 93–103;
   tables for 96, 97, 98; table
   covering 98; timing 16, 95;
   trade 15, 16, 94, 95, 99
Tasting terms 36, 106, 108–13;
   see also glossary
Tavel rosé 70
Tawny port 77; finest old,
   colour 59
Taylor 77, 237
'Tears' 30, 114
Temperature: for serving 196–
   8; for storage 187–8; for
   tastings 18, 26
Thanisch 238
Tignanello 240
Tokay (Hungary) 40, 74–5
Tokay (pinot gris): grape 44;
   wine 71
Toltarni 238
Torres 78, 240
Touch, sense of 22–3
Tour-Blanche, Ch La 238
Tour-de-Mons, Ch La 236
Traminer see Gewürztraminer
Transport problems 186–7
Trebbiano 44
Trefethen 238
Trimbach 43, 241
Trockenbeerenauslese 73
Tutored tasting 94, 97–8
Tyrrell 40, 80

U

United States 79–80, 241; see
   also California, New York
   State

V

Valpolicella 76
Vaporisation 21, 32
Varieties, grape 33, 38–44
Ventoux 70
Verdelho 77
Victoria, N.E. 81
Vignelaure 72
Vin de garde 48
Vin doux naturel 72
Vine age 39
Vin gris 28
Vinho verde 39, 76
Vin jaune 72
Vintage charts 46–7
Vintage port 77, 237; colour –
   immature 58, mature 59;
   cracking 190–1; decanting
   195
Vintages: Alsace 71; Barolo
   76; Beaujolais 69;
   Burgundy red 68, white 69;
   Champagne 72; Chianti 75;
   Claret 66; German 74;
   Loire 71; Madeira 78; Napa
   79; Port 77; Rhône 70;
   Tokay Essence 75; White
   Bordeaux 67
Vintages, deduction of 89–90
Viognier 44
Viscosity 42, 144
Vogüé, Comte Georges de 42,
   237
Volnay 68
Vosne-Romanée 67
Vougeot 67
Vouvray 48, 70, 238, 241

W

Warre 237
Weil, Dr R. 43, 238
White port 77
White wine 27–8, 29, 48, 65–
   81 passim, 238, 240–1;
   temperature 196–7, 198
Wholesalers 243
Wine bore 109; snob 18, 36,
   109
Wine card 84
Wine clubs and societies 15
Wine competitions 86–7;
   awards 140–1; descriptive
   ratings 140; numerical